Elusive Pirates, Pervasive Smugglers

ELUSIVE PIRATES, PERVASIVE SMUGGLERS

Violence and Clandestine Trade
in the Greater China Seas

Edited by Robert J. Antony

香港大學出版社
HONG KONG UNIVERSITY PRESS

Hong Kong University Press
14/F Hing Wai Centre
7 Tin Wan Praya Road
Aberdeen
Hong Kong

© Hong Kong University Press 2010

ISBN 978-988-8028-11-5

All rights reserved. No portion of this publication may be reproduced or transmitted in any form or by any means, electronic or mechanical, including photocopy, recording, or any information storage or retrieval system, without permission in writing from the publisher.

Secure On-line Ordering
http://www.hkupress.org

British Library Cataloguing-in-Publication Data
A catalogue record for this book is available from the British Library.

Printed and bound by Kings Time Printing Press Ltd., Hong Kong, China.

For Lanshin

Contents

Acknowledgements		ix
List of Contributors		xi
List of Illustrations		xv
1.	Introduction: The Shadowy World of the Greater China Seas *Robert J. Antony*	1
2.	Violence at Sea: Unpacking "Piracy" in the Claims of States over Asian Seas *Anthony Reid*	15
3.	From Sea Bandits to Sea Lords: Nonstate Violence and Pirate Identities in Fifteenth- and Sixteenth-Century Japan *Peter D. Shapinsky*	27
4.	Merchants, Smugglers, and Pirates: Multinational Clandestine Trade on the South China Coast, 1520–50 *James K. Chin*	43
5.	Pirates, Gunpowder, and Christianity in Late Sixteenth-Century Japan *Maria Grazia Petrucci*	59
6.	At the Crossroads: Limahon and Wakō in Sixteenth-Century Philippines *Igawa Kenji*	73

7.	Piracy and Coastal Security in Southeastern China, 1600–1780 *Paola Calanca*	85
8.	Piracy and the Shadow Economy in the South China Sea, 1780–1810 *Robert J. Antony*	99
9.	Poor but Not Pirates: The Tsushima Domain and Foreign Relations in Early Modern Japan *Robert Hellyer*	115
10.	The Business of Violence: Piracy around Riau, Lingga, and Singapore, 1820–40 *Ota Atsushi*	127
11.	Smuggling in the South China Sea: Alternate Histories of a Nonstate Space in the Late Nineteenth and Late Twentieth Centuries *Eric Tagliacozzo*	143

Notes	155
Glossary	175
Bibliography	179
Index	195

Acknowledgements

The idea for doing this book began several years ago at a workshop on the history of the South China Sea organized by Charles Wheeler, then at the University of California, Irvine. A few years later, at a conference in Shanghai on Asian piracy, I found a number of colleagues and friends interested in participating in another conference on this inexhaustible topic. Things were coming together but we still needed funding and a venue. In 2006, when the National Institute for South China Seas Studies, located on beautiful Hainan Island, invited me to give a talk, I suggested to Dr. Wu Shichun, president of the institute, that Hainan would be the perfect place to hold a conference on Asian piracy. He agreed, and in March 2008, his institute generously funded and organized an international conference on "Piracy and Maritime Security in the South China Sea," held in the resort city of Sanya at the southern tip of Hainan. The more than twenty papers presented at the conference covered a wide range of historical and contemporary issues concerning piracy, smuggling, and maritime security. Participants came from all over the globe — from China, Hong Kong, Macau, Singapore, Canada, the United States, Japan, Australia, and Europe. Unfortunately, we could not include all the excellent papers in this book.

Besides expressing my gratitude to Dr. Wu, I wish to thank other researchers and staff at the institute who made the conference so fruitful and memorable. Special thanks go to Dr. Zhu Huayou, the institute's vice-president, and to Ren Huaifeng, Xu Fang, Deng Yingying, and Chen Pingping for translations and local arrangements. I also appreciate the mayor of Sanya taking time out of his busy schedule to give the opening talk at the conference and Professors Anthony Reid and Zou Keyuan for giving keynote speeches. I wish to thank all the participants for the many lively and informative discussions we had during the presentations, at meals, and on the beach. Everyone benefited from such a diverse group of international scholars from many disciplines. In particular, I am grateful to Li Jinming, Charles Wheeler, Manel Ollé, Patrizia Carioti, Henry Xu, and Lúcio de Sousa for bringing their expertise and camaraderie to the conference. In editing this book, I appreciate the help given by friends and colleagues, especially Michael Pearson, Paul Van Dyke, Bill Guthrie, Vincent Ho, and Lanshin Chang.

Finally, I wish to thank the Yamaguchi Prefectural Archives and the Goyoda City Provincial Museum, both in Japan, for permissions to use illustrations for this book.

Zhuo Jia Cun, Taipa, Macau
December 14, 2009

Contributors

Robert J. Antony, who earned his doctorate in history at the University of Hawai'i, is a professor of Chinese and comparative history at the University of Macau. His research focuses on Asian and world maritime history, and his recent publications include *Like Froth Floating on the Sea: The World of Pirates and Seafarers in Late Imperial South China* (2003) and *Pirates in the Age of Sail* (2007). He is currently working on a book on the evolution of modern piracy in South China from 1837 to 1937.

Paola Calanca is an associate professor of history at the École Française d'Extrême-Orient. Most of her current work, based on extensive archival research in Beijing and Taiwan, examines the theoretical organization and actual performance of the Ming and Qing navies. Over the past few years, she has been conducting fieldwork in China's coastal provinces, studying coastal defense works and collecting local materials, in particular inscriptions relating to social and economic life. Her most recent book is *Piraterie et contrebande au Fujian du XVème au début du XIXème siècle* (2008).

James K. Chin is a research fellow at the Centre of Asian Studies, the University of Hong Kong. His research interests include the history of maritime Asia, Chinese international migration and diaspora, and China-Southeast Asian relations. He has published more than sixty journal articles and book chapters, and is currently working on a book on the Chinese commercial diaspora in maritime Asia before 1800.

Robert Hellyer, who received his doctorate at Stanford University, is an assistant professor of history at Wake Forest University. He specializes in early modern and modern Japanese history. His most recent publication is *Defining Engagement: Japan and Global Contexts, 1640–1868* (2010). He is currently working on a book about Japan's tea export trade in the late nineteenth and early twentieth centuries.

Igawa Kenji obtained his Ph.D. from the University of Tokyo, and is currently an associate professor in the Graduate School of Letters at Osaka University. He specializes in the history of international relations in fifteenth- and sixteenth-century Asia. In 2001, the Society of Japanese History awarded him its prize for his studies. His current research concerns Europe–Southeast Asia–Japan relations. In 2007, he published *Daikōkai Jidai no Higashi Ajia* [East Asia in the fifteenth and sixteenth centuries].

Ota Atsushi obtained his Ph.D. from Leiden University and is an assistant research fellow at the Center for Asia-Pacific Area Studies, Research Center for Humanities and Social Sciences, Academia Sinica, Taipei. He specializes in the maritime history of Southeast Asia. His recent publications include *Changes of Regime and Social Dynamics in West Java: Society, State, and the Outer World of Banten, 1750–1830* (2006) and "Eighteenth-Century Southeast Asia and World Economy," in Momoki Shiro (ed.), *Kaiiki Ajia-shi nyūmon* [Introduction to history of maritime Asia] (2008). He is currently researching maritime violence and the changing trade order around the Malacca Strait from the 1780s to the 1840s.

Maria Grazia Petrucci is a doctoral student in the University of British Columbia, specializing in Japanese history. Her research focuses on sixteenth-century Japanese piracy, Christianity, and mercantile associations. She is also interested in comparisons between Japanese piracy and Mediterranean piracy in the sixteenth century. Her contribution to this volume is part of her dissertation.

Anthony Reid is professor emeritus in the Department of Pacific and Asian History, Australian National University. His books include *Southeast Asia in the Age of Commerce, 1450–1680*, 2 vols. (1988–93); *Charting the Shape of Early Modern Southeast Asia* (1999); *An Indonesian Frontier: Acehnese and Other Histories of Sumatra* (2004); and *Imperial Alchemy: Nationalism and Political Identity in Southeast Asia* (forthcoming).

Peter D. Shapinsky is an assistant professor at the University of Illinois at Springfield, where he teaches East Asian history. He is completing a book, *Lords of the Sea: Pirates, Violence, and Exchange in Medieval Japan*, which interprets late medieval Japanese history (c.1300–1600) from the perspective of the sea by exploring the roles of seafarers labeled as pirates in the maritime networks linking Japan and Eurasia.

Eric Tagliacozzo is an associate professor of history at Cornell University, where he teaches Southeast Asian history and Asian studies. He is the author of *Secret Trades, Porous Borders: Smuggling and States along a Southeast Asian Frontier,*

1865–1915 (2005), which won the Harry J. Benda Prize from the Association for Asian Studies in 2007. He is also the editor or co-editor of three books: *Southeast Asia and the Middle East: Islam, Movement, and the Longue Durée* (2009); *Clio/Anthropos: Exploring the Boundaries between History and Anthropology* (2009); and *The Indonesia Reader: History, Culture, Politics* (2009). His next monograph will be *The Longest Journey: Southeast Asians and the Pilgrimage to Mecca*.

Illustrations

Map 1.1	The Greater China Seas Region	4
Map 1.2	Sailing Routes in the Greater China Seas, c. 1600–1800	6
Map 3.1	The Seto Inland Sea in the Fifteenth and Sixteenth Centuries	29
Map 4.1	Shuangyu Island and the Zhejiang Coast, c. 1550	45
Map 5.1	Southwestern Japan in the Late Sixteenth Century	61
Map 6.1	The Philippines and Southeast Asia in the Sixteenth Century	75
Map 6.2	Areas of Lin Feng's Activities, 1571–89	81
Map 7.1	The Southeast Coast of China in the Eighteenth Century	86
Map 8.1	The Guangdong Coast, c. 1800	101
Map 8.2	The Pearl River Delta, c. 1800	104
Map 9.1	Japan in the Early Nineteenth Century	117
Map 10.1	Riau, Lingga, Singapore, and the Malacca Strait, c. 1840	128
Figure 2.1	European Representation of a Dayak Warrior	23
Figure 3.1	Noshima Murakami Flag-Pass	36
Figure 4.1	Ming Dynasty War Junk	48
Figure 5.1	Samurai Drilling with Firearms	63
Figure 7.1	Famine Victims Selling Their Children	90
Figure 7.2	Qing Era License for Fishing Boats	96
Figure 8.1	Clandestine and Legal Trade Routes	105
Figure 8.2	The Unsanctioned Port of Giang Binh	106
Figure 10.1	Bugis Warriors	130
Figure 10.2	Sumatran Weapons	134
Table 8.1	Sanctioned Ports, Unsanctioned Ports, and Pirate Lairs in Guangdong, 1780–1810	102
Table 8.2	Amounts of Ransoms Paid to Pirates, 1796–1809	110

1

Introduction:
The Shadowy World of the Greater China Seas

Robert J. Antony

Many problems of the past still haunt us today — piracy and smuggling among them. Although maritime marauding reached a peak in the late seventeenth and early eighteenth centuries — the so-called "golden age of piracy" — it has never completely vanished from around the globe. Today, piracy appears in many of the same areas where it thrived two or three hundred years ago. Although a worldwide presence, the largest number of pirates and the highest total of incidents of piracy today, as in the past, take place in Asian waters. Alongside piracy, smuggling always has posed a problem, and comprised a way of life in this area of the world. In fact, piracy and smuggling usually went hand-in-hand and have continually occurred for many of the same reasons. As recurring cyclical phenomena, the piracy and smuggling of today are inescapably bound to the piracy and smuggling of the past. Viewed from this vantage point, we should regard them as malleable concepts with multiple layers of meanings relative to time, place, and culture. Both piracy and smuggling involve complex, still-evolving historical processes. Although often dismissed as historically unimportant, in reality, pirates and smugglers have played key roles in the development of modern society.

We like to read about pirates and smugglers because their stories are captivating. Just to mention the word pirates evokes colorful and fanciful images of rogues like Blackbeard and Long John Silver. We can appreciate them as treacherous and bloodthirsty villains, yet at the same time, we might look upon them as romantic, swashbuckling heroes. Our appetite for stories about piracy and the sea seems unquenchable; there are hundreds of books, cartoons, songs, television dramas, and movies produced on these subjects each year. However, we should look at pirates and smugglers not only because of their intrigue but also because of their importance. Piracy and smuggling always have been closely linked to issues of maritime security and national sovereignty. Today, as in past ages, they have cost honest, legitimate commerce and business millions of dollars every year, not to mention the toll in human lives and destroyed property. Conversely, piracy and smuggling also have stimulated and fostered an extensive shadow or informal economy and a vibrant subculture.

Pirates and smugglers were elusive, but pervasive, creatures with different but interrelated activities. Though both may also have had political and social overtones, economic factors fundamentally motivated them. Most people engaged in piracy and smuggling to earn money, but they may also have used these activities to gain social status or as forms of protest, for example, against colonialism. Unlike smugglers, pirates traded in stolen goods obtained through violence. Still, like smugglers, pirates disposed their loot in the same black markets and trading networks. Pirates and smugglers contrasted the most, it seems, in the methods used to procure the goods that they traded; in disposing of them, however, they were functionally the same. Also, because smuggling was illegal, sometimes smugglers had to use violence to protect their interests or to defend themselves against repressive authorities, thereby becoming little different from pirates.

Furthermore, some people who became pirates and smugglers did not consider themselves outlaws or their activities illicit. As Anthony Reid reminds us in his chapter, what we label as piracy is a Western construct, and may have had little to do with native Asian perceptions. From the perspective of most governments and victims, pirates and smugglers appeared as merely criminals, but in the eyes of their supporters and their own self-image, they believed their enterprises justified and proper. It was not uncommon for pirates to become folk heroes; Asian societies also have their equivalents of Francis Drake and Henry Morgan. Likewise, many smugglers considered themselves as authorized because local practices and official connivances safeguarded such activities and thereby gave them a sense of validity. In some cases, such informal trade appeared safer and better protected than the legitimate trade. Since the illicit trade supported the licit trade, and the two were interconnected, smuggling proved difficult to eradicate and, in fact, some officials even tolerated it.[1]

Because of the nature of their work, pirates and smugglers left few records, which would, indeed, have been risky to keep. They did not want to draw attention to themselves from officials. Sometimes, pirate gangs went to extraordinary lengths to remain anonymous, even murdering entire crews of ships that they attacked in order to eliminate any witnesses. Hence, the famous pirate adage: "Dead men tell no lies." What we know about pirates and smugglers, therefore, comes chiefly from their enemies and victims. As the documents are biased, obscure, and fragmentary, we need to use a broad range of sources in many different languages. The studies in this volume do exactly that.

This book examines the extent, diffusion, and characteristics of piracy and smuggling in the greater China Seas region over the past six centuries. At the fringe of the Pacific Ocean, the China Seas encompass over four million square kilometers from Indonesia and Borneo in the south to China, Korea, and Japan in the north. The

Philippine Islands and Taiwan border the east, with the Malay Peninsula, Thailand, Cambodia, and Vietnam on the west (see Map 1.1). Following the five oceans, this region constitutes the next greatest body of water. Even before the appearance of European explorers and adventurers in the sixteenth century, it was and has since remained one of the busiest shipping zones in the world. Today, in terms of world annual merchant fleet tonnage, over fifty percent passes through the Malacca, Sunda, and Lombok Straits. This vast expanse of water, with its countless islands and harbors, has provided not only seamen and merchants but also pirates and smugglers with jobs and livelihoods for centuries. In fact, as the authors in this book demonstrate, piracy and smuggling played integral, even essential, roles in shaping East and Southeast Asian history.

The Greater China Seas Region

Most histories of Asia stop at the water's edge, treating the littoral and the seas beyond as peripheral and, therefore, less important. According to conventional wisdom, major events and ideas emanated from the land and not from the sea.[2] In this book, however, we depart radically from the standard terra-centered histories to place the seas at the center rather than at the margins of our inquiries. Ocean and sea basins encompass, as Jerry Bentley explains, important "units of analysis to the extent that human societies engage in interaction across bodies of water."[3] The seas acted as buffers between land-based polities, contested "zones of transition" that were "crucial both for the conduct of commerce and for the exercise of power."[4] Making the seas the focus of our analysis allows us to more easily transcend geopolitical boundaries to examine the interconnectedness of the entire region encompassing East and Southeast Asia. Focusing on the water, rather than on the land, better enables us to stitch together the diverse histories of Japan, China, and Southeast Asia. The greater China Seas region is best viewed as the sum of its multiple parts and pasts.

What we call the greater China Seas region does not appear as an autonomous body of water easily delineated by a simple set of boundaries, but rather, a vast water world of "porous borders" and "flows and seepages."[5] Matt Matsuda's description about the Pacific applies equally well to the China Seas: "an Oceanic space of movement, transit, and migration in a *longue durée* of local peoples and broad interactions."[6] Indeed, it consisted of not one sea but a "complex of seas" radiating from the core South China Sea into the East China Sea and Japan's Seto Inland Sea to the north, and into the smaller Sulu, Java, Celebes, and Banda Seas to the south. Open waters and narrow passages — the Malacca, Sunda, and Tsushima Straits — connected the China Seas and its shores to their various component parts and to the world at large.

Map 1.1 The Greater China Seas Region

Paradoxically, the greater China Seas combined both diversity and cohesion. On the one hand, there was the multiplicity of peoples, cultures, languages, and histories of Japan, China, and Southeast Asia; on the other hand, the seas were a unifying conduit for the transmission of goods, peoples, germs, ideas, and religions. Like Braudel's Mediterranean, the China Seas tied an area of heterogeneous civilizations together through commercial and cultural exchange.[7] As Eric Tagliacozzo points out in his chapter, this water world "both connects and fragments at least a dozen countries in Asia, as well as the shipping of other nations whose vessels transect its open waters." This paradox of diversity and cohesion represented a defining characteristic of the region.

The China Seas region blended peoples and cultures from not only Asia but from around the world in a maritime melting pot. It provided an area of transit and a source of income for untold numbers of people. Despite their different languages and ethnic origins, the indigenous groups of "sea peoples" — the *ama* of Japan, the Dan (Tanka) of southern China, and the "sea gypsies" (Orang Laut), Iranun, Balangingi, and Bugis of insular Southeast Asia — shared a common maritime culture and life experiences that distinguished them from their countrymen living on shore.[8] Throughout history, people continuously moved in and out of the region — migrants, sojourners, emigrants, missionaries, traders, sailors, and slaves — first from India, China, and Southeast Asia, and later from Japan, Europe, and Africa. They intermingled, intermarried, and struggled with one another and with native sea peoples. A persistent, systematic, and constant interaction among the diverse groups of people living and working in the region prevailed after the sixteenth century.[9]

Ships and shipping constituted the lifeblood of the region. By the early sixteenth century, as Igawa Kenji informs us, numerous sea lanes crisscrossed the entire China Seas region linking Japan, Korea, and China to the Philippines, Vietnam, Siam (Thailand), Borneo, Sumatra, and Java. Even earlier, for many centuries, Indian and Chinese traders and sojourners had visited the area, followed by Japanese and European merchants and adventurers in the sixteenth century. By the late eighteenth century, the maritime economy of the greater China Seas had become sophisticated and highly integrated while also "brimming with vitality."[10] An intricate patchwork of interconnected markets linked the smaller ports, harbors, and fishing villages to the larger entrepôts of Canton, Chaozhou, Amoy, Nagasaki, Bangkok, Saigon, Malacca, Batavia, and Manila. After its founding in 1819, Singapore was added to this vast maritime network (see Map 1.2). Trade routes connected these larger marts with one another and with the global markets in Europe and the Americas. These earlier commercial patterns continued and expanded during the period of "high imperialism" (1870–1940).[11]

Despite the intrusion of the West, the entire region continued to be dominated by Asians and intra-regional trading networks well into the nineteenth century. Indian, Chinese, and Southeast Asians were all involved in both long-distance and

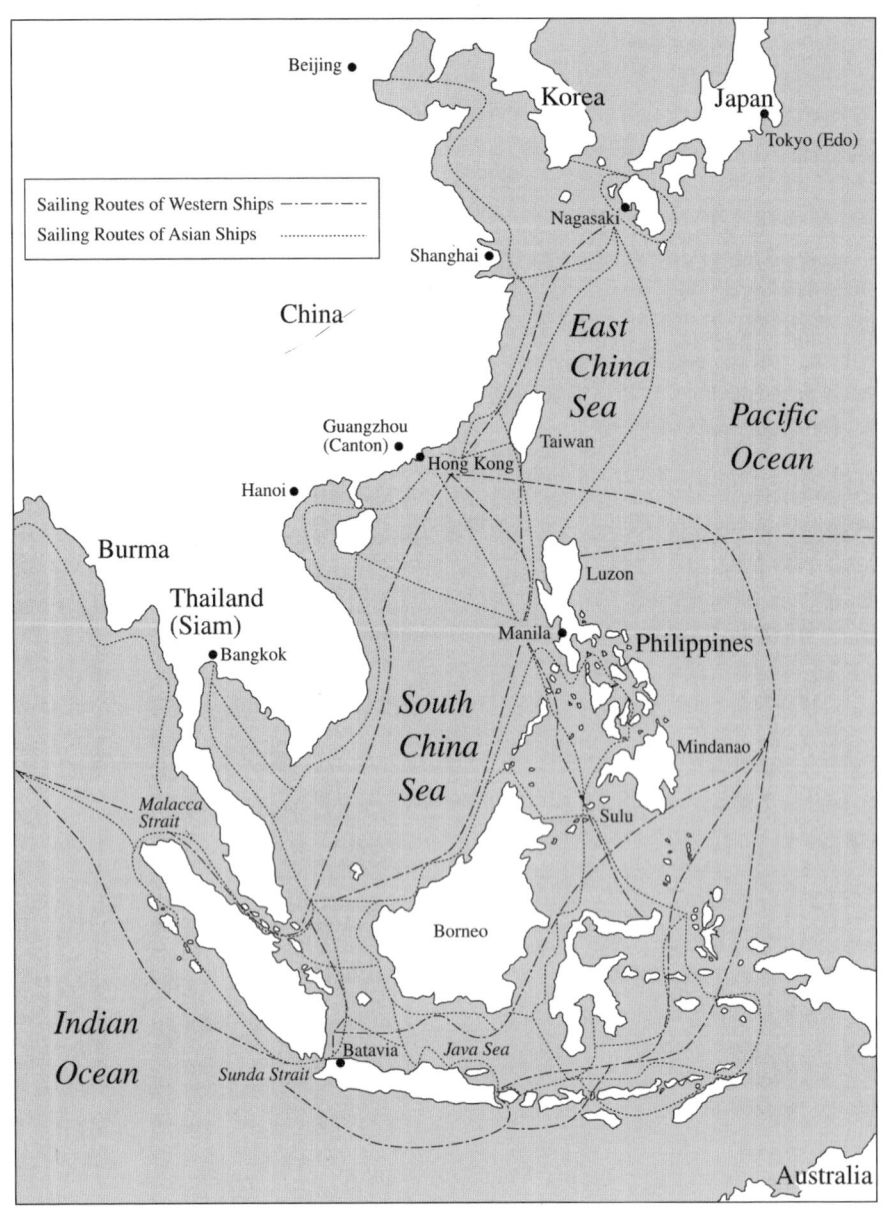

Map 1.2 Sailing Routes in the Greater China Seas, c. 1600–1800

local trading networks long before Western merchants entered the area. In fact, when the Europeans first arrived in the South China Sea, they found Gujerati and Chinese vessels virtually monopolizing commerce there. In the sixteenth and early seventeenth century, despite Ming and Qing bans on overseas trade, a tremendous growth of "private" (illegal) trade with Japan and Southeast Asia took place.[12] Likewise, before the Tokugawa government began to restrict maritime trade in the 1630s, Japan also markedly expanded commerce throughout the greater China Seas region.[13]

China had long been the economic powerhouse in the region. When Europeans established their settlements around the rim of the China Seas, they did so in places along well-established Chinese trunk routes to Southeast Asia. According to Leonard Blussé, Western trading ports, including Batavia, Manila, and Singapore, "were only feasible because of Chinese participation."[14] After the Qing government opened up maritime trade in 1684, the Chinese junk trade proliferated and reached its zenith between 1740 and 1840, during the so-called "China Century." Also, native trade within Southeast Asia greatly increased to accommodate the growing commerce with China as well as other global markets.[15] Throughout this period, the number and tonnage of Chinese junks surpassed those of Western vessels in the region.[16] Although after the 1870s, the number of steamships had risen tremendously, still, even in the early twentieth century, large numbers of Chinese and native sailing ships plied the greater China Seas. As Tagliacozzo explains in his chapter, the region "bustled with a wide variety of ships."

The Shadowy World of the Greater China Seas

In the shadows of legitimate society lurked the elusive pirates and pervasive smugglers. A confusing assortment of clandestine activities and the nomenclature used to describe them proliferated in the greater China Seas region. What Westerners called "pirates" were in China commonly referred to as "sea bandits" (*haidao, haizei, haifei,* or *haikou*); in Japan the most common term was *kaizoku*, which likewise means "sea bandits." Depending on the context, the terms also implied "sea rebels" or "sea traitors."[17] The Chinese and Koreans pejoratively called Japanese maritime raiders and smugglers "dwarf bandits" (Chinese *wokou*, Korean *waegu*); but as Peter Shapinsky explains, Japanese sea people would never have regarded themselves in such a way, though the word *wakō* remains in common use today. In fact, the *wokou* or *wakō* of the sixteenth century were predominantly Chinese, not Japanese. Apparently, before the nineteenth century, Southeast Asia did not even have a local term for "pirate" or "piracy." The people there considered maritime raiding as a form of warfare essential for statecraft. Our modern concepts of piracy only became globalized in the colonial era.[18]

For many people, the seas symbolized lawless space, beyond the pale of civilization. They were, to paraphrase Eliga Gould, a zone where people freely engaged in practices that would have been unacceptable on shore.[19] For land-based elites in China and Japan, pirates represented an exotic and dangerous "other."[20] In labeling pirates as *haifei*, the suffix *fei* in Chinese, an absolute negative, denied individuals their humanity and, consequently, their right to exist. In imperial China, piracy constituted a serious crime linked to treason, and was punishable by beheading, a most dehumanizing form of execution. The Chinese state, like Western colonial powers, viewed its war against piracy, and, to some extent, also against smuggling, as a conflict between civilization and barbarism. In the colonial mindset of nineteenth-century Southeast Asia, the terms "Malay" and "Illanun" (Iranun) practically equated with "pirate." Reid quotes an American poet who likened Acehean pirates to "demons from hell." From the Western perspective, it defined those who operated outside the colonial trading system or who opposed its rule as pirates. The suppression of piracy functioned not only as a crusading and civilizing mission, but it also motivated and justified colonial expansion.[21]

Yet, some areas and some people regarded pirates and smugglers as neither criminals nor shadowy figures. Sometimes local communities and states knew their presence and activities well and even encouraged and approved them. In 1562, Zheng Ruozeng described Japanese pirates in this fashion: "When they return to their [home] islands from plundering ... they say they have come back from trading ... Even the neighbors do not know, or [if they do know] they think it honorable."[22] In Satsuma, during the Tokugawa period, contrabanding became a highly regarded, even legitimate profession after the domain's leaders sanctioned smuggling in order to boost the local economy.[23] Traditionally, much of archipelago Southeast Asia looked upon so-called "piracy" as a respectable occupation supported by local chiefs and regional sultans.[24] The Iranun and Balangingi of the southern Philippines accepted state-sanctioned maritime raiding as a way of life crucial to the region's social, economic, and political structures.[25] In these cases, indigenous peoples would hardly have labeled such activities as illicit, and in fact, often they treated the outlaws as local heroes. In coastal South China, according to Paola Calanca, villagers, who worked with pirates and smugglers as fences, suppliers, and arms dealers, interacted cordially with the outlaws. In Fujian, people considered the pirate-smuggler Zheng Zhilong an upright, benevolent man because he aided the poor and provided many people with jobs.[26] The Chinese of southern Taiwan even eulogized his son, Zheng Chenggong, as a god after his death in 1661.

The reality, of course, is subtle and complicated, and there appear no firm distinctions between legitimate and illegitimate in the actions of what we and others label pirates and smugglers. It is better to think in terms of a continuum, with activities that are completely legal on one end, those that are completely illegal on the other end, and most activities somewhere in between.

Coming from all walks of life, pirates and smugglers included not only rascals and social deviants, but also ordinary sailors and fishermen, as well as merchants, samurai, and *datu* chieftains. Because the seas were, by their very nature, transnational spaces, piracy and smuggling were multi-ethnic and multi-national enterprises. Ota Atsushi describes a gang of local Southeast Asian pirates in the 1830s, led by two Chinese from Riau who professed Islam and wore Malay clothing. In the 1850s, one of the most notorious pirates on the South China coast was an American named Eli Boggs, who was finally apprehended in 1857 by an equally colorful compatriot, Bully Hayes, a well-known opium smuggler. In modern times, Chinese very actively participated in the smuggling trade, as did Malays, Bugis, Europeans, Americans, Muslims, Armenians, Parsees, and nearly every other ethnic group.[27]

Piracy and smuggling were part of the process of commercialization. As licit trade increased, so too did illicit trade, and the two were intimately connected. Although pirates and smugglers engaged in a different sort of business from legitimate merchants, they also contributed importantly to the economic development of the greater China Seas region. During the sixteenth and early seventeenth centuries, because of the repeated banning of maritime trade by successive Chinese governments, it became impossible to distinguish between trader, smuggler, and pirate. In the Ming period, as James Chin explains, piracy and smuggling necessarily evolved into the most common and profitable form of commerce. In Southeast Asia, according to Richard Leirissa, piracy operated as a form of trade based on theft rather than exchange.[28] Ota's chapter clearly employs this approach which depicts early nineteenth-century piracy in the Malacca Strait as a type of commercial competition and network-building among Asian, Dutch, and British traders seeking to obtain goods for the China market. According to Tagliacozzo, smuggling remains just as pervasive and important today as when it thrived a century ago in the South China Sea.

Pirates and smugglers also needed support from people on land as well as in friendly ports where they could outfit their ships, recruit new crews, and sell their goods. Chin and Antony argue that although smuggling and piracy detracted from legitimate trade and profits, nonetheless, they also had important positive economic consequences, and in fact, helped to boost local and regional economies. Both authors suggest that the "shadow economy" became significant since it allowed large numbers of otherwise excluded, poor, and marginalized people to participate in the wider commercial economy. Piracy and smuggling provided jobs, either directly or indirectly, to tens of thousands of people living around the rim of the greater China Seas.

In addition, as several chapters explain, piracy and smuggling also played important parts in the development of new ports created specifically to handle the growing illegal trade.[29] In some cases, such as the island of Shuangyu in the sixteenth century and Giang Binh in the early nineteenth century, when the state could not control such illicit trading hubs, the government sent in the military to destroy them. Sometimes, official trading areas declined and became bases for covert activities, as in the case of Riau after the Dutch War of 1784.[30] Other areas more successfully made the transition from illegitimate to legitimate, such as the islands of Itsukushima and Tsushima in Japan, and the ports of Yuegang and Amoy (Xiamen) in China. In the latter two cases, for example, Yuegang emerged as a prosperous smugglers port in the fifteenth century and an offset to the official port at Quanzhou. After the government recognized Yuegang as an administrative seat in 1567, smugglers and pirates moved elsewhere, in particular, to Amoy. During the late sixteenth and early seventeenth centuries, Chinese and foreign smugglers and pirates used Amoy as their meeting place, and, for much of the seventeenth century, it also served as the major base of operations for the Zheng family's piratical empire. In 1684, with the downfall of the Zhengs, the Qing court designated Amoy as a legitimate port and the clandestine trade moved elsewhere.[31] A majority of the illicit ports, however, were not as successful as Yuegang and Amoy; most were small and remained anonymous and unsanctioned.

As several chapters in this volume explain, the aid that pirates and smugglers received from coastal residents, including fishermen, sailors, merchants, soldiers, and officials, factored significantly in their success. Whenever they lost that patronage, piracy and smuggling declined. As Calanca explains, piracy in southern China diminished greatly in the eighteenth century in large measure because wealthy and powerful coastal families in Fujian decided to back the new Qing government and oppose piracy. A century earlier, in Japan, the new Tokugawa shogunate substantially curbed the power of piratical "sea lords" around the Seto Inland Sea by forcefully relocating them inland away from their bases of support.[32] Hellyer also shows that nineteenth-century Japan had few pirates because financial assistance, first from the Korean government and later from the Japanese government, obviated the need for turning to piracy. Over the latter part of the nineteenth and early twentieth centuries, while never completely disappearing, piracy had greatly decreased. It happened not only because of the appearance of steam warships after the 1830s, and the relentless destruction of pirate strongholds, but also because national and colonial authorities resettled maritime raiders away from the coast where they expected them to engage in farming and other peaceful trades.

Studies in This Volume

This volume arranges the following ten chapters, which cover six hundred years from the fifteenth century to the present, more or less chronologically. After Anthony Reid's chapter, which discusses the perceptions of piracy in China and Southeast Asia over several centuries, the next four chapters look at piracy and smuggling in the fifteenth and sixteenth centuries. In Chapter Seven, Paola Calanca closely analyses the crucial transitional period between 1600 and 1780, providing a bridge between the first and second halves of the book. The remaining four chapters deal with the nineteenth century and afterwards. The three chapters by Shapinsky, Petrucci, and Hellyer focus mainly on Japan and the seas around it; the three chapters by Chin, Calanca, and Antony concentrate chiefly on China and Chinese maritime outlaws; and the chapters by Reid, Igawa, Ota, and Tagliacozzo principally concern the water world of Southeast Asia.

While piracy might have been economically motivated, it also carried intensely political overtones. Modern states view any acts of violence in their territories or possessions not by their own agents as illegal and potentially subversive. In his chapter, Anthony Reid examines "piracy" — a particular type of violence at sea — over the past several centuries. Because the word piracy is specifically English, and comes out of a particular European experience, it does not so easily translate into Asian languages. This chapter seeks to connect our present concern with piracy by studying understandings of the term by the Chinese and Malay, the two Asian experiences that have intersected most with European concepts of piracy. In so doing, Reid utilizes the concept of "organized hypocrisy" in the international system to demonstrate the way both outlaws and states have manipulated piracy over the past several centuries. In hindsight, he concludes, we must recognize the period of "pirate" suppression in the first half of the twentieth century as an exception rather than the norm for our contemporary international order.

Peter Shapinsky discusses further the meanings of piracy in the context of fifteenth- and sixteenth-century Japan. Departing from most Japanese scholars' depiction of pirates as feudal vassals, he describes them as entrepreneurs of violence, as free agents who sold their services in the emerging monetized economy — the embodiment of mercenarism rather than vassalage. Commerce and violence did not contradict each other. His chapter explores the potential for using Janice Thomson's concept of "nonstate violence" as a way to understand the challenges that seafarers labeled pirates posed for land-based polities in contemporary and historical contexts. To do so, Shapinsky considers the trans-border cultures of seafaring in a case study of one of the most traveled sea lanes in premodern Japanese as well as East Asian history — the region known today as the Seto Inland Sea.

The first half of the sixteenth century marked a unique period in the history of maritime Asia, when large numbers of Chinese smugglers and pirates congregated on the South China coast, where they bartered with merchants from different countries. While most historians have viewed the foreign presence along the China coast as an unwelcome intrusion and a manifestation of imperialism, James Chin argues that the foreigners, in truth, positively influenced the Chinese economy by bringing it new life. In fact, this period saw a new maritime economy and regional trade system emerging in southern China with joint ventures and emporia established through close collaborations between Chinese merchant-pirates and multinational smuggler-traders from Japan, Ryukyu, Portugal, and the port polities of Southeast Asia. Chin explains that although the piracy and violence that was closely associated with smuggling had a negative impact on the local social order, nevertheless the booming illegal trade on the South China coast had, in fact, greatly facilitated the development of a new commodity economy in local society which filled a need that the regular economy failed to offer.

Maria Petrucci's chapter, which analyzes the interactions between merchants, Christian missionaries and Japanese converts, *daimyos*, and pirates in the late sixteenth century, expands on themes developed by Shapinsky and Chin. She discusses the roles that Japanese and Chinese pirates played in the clandestine manufacturing and smuggling of gunpowder between Japan, China, and Southeast Asia, as well as their partnerships with regional Japanese hegemons and Portuguese traders and missionaries. She also shows how piratical "sea lords" helped develop castle towns around the Seto Inland Sea. Petrucci critically examines the dynamics of powerful bands of pirates, such as the Shirai clan, that depended for survival on support and recognition from land-based *daimyos* and on the geopolitical forces that shaped southern Japan in the late sixteenth century.

In his chapter, Igawa Kenji shifts the focus away from Japan and China to discuss the important role that the Philippine Islands played in the international relations of sixteenth-century Asia. Significantly, Igawa demonstrates how Chinese and Japanese pirates critically impacted the development of early sea routes throughout the greater China Seas region. The *wakō*, who were multiethnic bands of Japanese, Chinese, and Southeast Asians, pirated the area from the Korean Peninsula to Southeast Asia, mainly in the sixteenth century. From bases in the Japanese archipelago, they conducted raiding and trading expeditions throughout the entire region. Their wide-ranging activities and far-flung commercial networks required relay points, first off the Chinese coast (such as on Shuangyu Island), and then later in the Philippines, at a time when the Spanish were also occupying the islands. In analyzing this complicated history, Igawa focuses on the famous Chinese pirate, Limahon (Lin Feng), and his vast piratical and commercial networks. He provides a rare example of a pirate who appeared not only in Asian but also in European sources, and who furthermore operated in both China and in the Philippine archipelago.

In the next chapter, Paola Calanca examines an important transitional period (1600–1780) in South China's history and in the history of piracy, in particular. Before the watershed year 1684, both the Ming and Qing governments followed rigid closed-door policies that banned maritime trade and labeled private sea merchants outlaws. During the turbulent Ming-Qing dynastic wars from the 1600s to the early 1680s, powerful coastal families, in particular the Zhengs of southern Fujian, took advantage of the anarchy to form a huge maritime empire that dominated the greater China Seas region from bases at Amoy and later on Taiwan. After 1684, once the Qing had conquered Taiwan and had consolidated its power over China, the government reversed earlier policies and began to open China up to overseas trade. With legitimacy came stability and prosperity, and most merchants quickly became strong bulwarks of support for the state and staunch opponents of piracy. Although piracy declined, it never disappeared between the 1680s and 1780s. As Calanca shows, this reduction in piracy resulted from several factors, one of the most important being the government's co-optation of powerful coastal families, with close ties to overseas trade, into the Qing naval apparatus.

In the late eighteenth and early nineteenth centuries, piracy once again had become a huge problem in the South China Sea. Tens of thousands of poor, marginalized fishermen and sailors became involved both directly and indirectly in piracy. Robert Antony's chapter examines the roles that pirates and their networks of accomplices played in promoting the shadow or informal economy. Not only did the growth of legitimate commerce facilitate the development of new ports and markets, but so too did the pirates' illicit trade. Black markets sprang up everywhere along the southern coast to trade with pirates and smugglers and to service their ships and crews. Pirates and their collaborators became economic pioneers who fostered the opening up of new commercial facilities and opportunities in areas not easily reached by the established trading system. By selling their booty at bargain prices, pirates brought many goods within the reach of a wider public while, at the same time, they expanded distribution networks. Because so many people came to depend on piracy for their livelihoods, it developed into a self-sustaining enterprise and a significant and integral feature of South China's maritime world in the early modern period.

Not all poor seafarers became pirates. Robert Hellyer gives us a case study of Japan's Tsushima domain from the sixteenth through the nineteenth centuries. Although during the late medieval period, the island of Tsushima served as a major center for piracy in the waters around Japan and Korea, in the sixteenth century, the island's leaders entered into agreements with the Korean court and with the Japanese central authority that gave them special privileges in Japanese-Korean trade. For nearly a century, the profits from trade mitigated against a return to the piracy of the island's ancestors. When trade declined dramatically in the eighteenth century, Tsushima faced economic hardship, a situation exacerbated by its dearth of agricultural production. Hellyer's chapter considers why at this point, poverty did not lead Tsushima leaders to revive piracy, especially given that the Japanese central authority and the Korean court lacked the naval power to police the waters around it. The author persuasively argues how financial and other awards from the Korean and the Japanese governments stifled piracy. By examining the reasons piracy did not emerge in Japan, Hellyer also offers a comparative perspective from which to study the development of piracy in other parts of Asia in the eighteenth and nineteenth centuries.

Ota Atsushi's chapter re-examines piracy and trade around the Malacca Strait in the early nineteenth century, a period of colonial expansion and so-called increased piratical activities. Piracy was a violent enterprise deeply tied to the region's culture, economy, and society. Ota characterizes the trade in the area of that period as one of competition and network-formation between Asian (mostly Chinese and Bugis), Dutch, and British traders who sought to obtain export commodities for the China market. He sees the intricate role piracy played in local and regional commercial development, especially in the burgeoning China trade. In this chapter, Ota views piracy from the perspective of the victims, characterizing it as economically motivated and as a fundamentally local strategy that both reacted to changing conditions in the region and spurred the formation of colonial states.

In the final chapter, Eric Tagliacozzo takes a long view of smuggling in the South China Sea over the past two centuries. Smuggling has operated as big business in the region for many centuries, and a variety of actors and interested parties have all participated in these activities. This chapter links historical data and ethnographic fieldwork together in reflecting on these processes over what the French historian Fernand Braudel has called the *longue durée*. In his discussion of smuggling and other clandestine activities, Tagliacozzo considers the interplay among European, Chinese, and other Asian actors over the past several centuries.

While much has already been written about pirates and smugglers, still, little rigorous scholarly research exists on these subjects. Amateur historians, who have had little or no training in methodology and research, have written most of the literature on piracy and smuggling. Even serious historical inquiries usually discuss piracy and smuggling within limited national contexts, and fail to examine the issues within a broader context. Individuals with insurance, police, and policymaking backgrounds largely write analyses of current-day piracy that deal rather narrowly with pressing legal, economic, and security issues. The connections between piracy and terrorism, for example, are currently hot topics of research.

With few exceptions, most previous studies lack in-depth historical and comparative perspectives, making this the first book to carefully examine piracy and smuggling from that angle for the whole East and Southeast Asian region, the area that we call the greater China Seas. The approaches the authors take in this book offer important vantage points because in order to more fully understand the problems of piracy and smuggling, we must appreciate the fact that they are deep-rooted, complex, and evolving phenomena. Furthermore, piracy and smuggling did not limit themselves to a single geographical space, but, rather, they traversed the entire region of the greater China Seas. We hope that the studies in this book will stimulate further discussions on piracy and smuggling as subjects worthy of serious research. The history of piracy and smuggling is important.

2

Violence at Sea:
Unpacking "Piracy" in the Claims of States over Asian Seas

Anthony Reid

The contemporary international community is rightly concerned with piracy as a global problem that challenges its system, and needs to be addressed by all. The word "piracy," however, derives specifically from English, and comes out of a particular European experience of interstate rivalry. It translates readily into the major European languages, which used the concept when interacting with each other legally and commercially. Outside of that world, though, the Europeans employed the term to justify military expansion at the expense of Asians. Asian languages use several expressions that modern scholarship has translated as piracy, although no real equivalence of meaning or associations can be assumed.

It must be remembered that the European definition of piracy as illegitimate armed robbery at sea was imposed progressively on the rest of the world within an imperial context. With the advent of the steamship in the mid-nineteenth century, the European powers, acting in concert, extended their authority gradually over the world's seas, destroying or dispersing one "pirate nest" after another that had resisted the hegemony of European shipping. Led by Britain, the imperial states also included the world's great shippers and possessed a direct interest in making the sea lanes safe. That coincidence of interest and might lasted from roughly 1870 to 1940, the only period, in modern times, when piracy in the European sense disappeared from Asian waters. This chapter will seek to connect our present concern about piracy with reference to the two Asian experiences which have intersected most with European ideas of piracy, namely the Chinese and the Malay.[1]

It will be helpful here to utilize the concept of "organized hypocrisy" in the international system, as it passed through different paradigms.[2] The present form, "sovereign equality," manifests itself in the United Nations Charter of 1945, whereby all nations purport to accept the equal sovereignty of all others, extending in a homogeneous way exactly to their border with the next sovereign nation-state. Earlier paradigms of "organized hypocrisy" included the high colonial system in which "civilized [European] states" partitioned the world among themselves, and obeyed an agreed upon set of rules among the members of this club, but extended it through colonialism at the expense of the rest of the world; and the previous Chinese "tribute system," whereby Southeast Asian countries, or those claiming to act for them, at times pretended to play the Chinese game of world hegemony in return for commercial monopolies.[3]

The UN Law of the Sea well reflects the contemporary international understanding of piracy. Like the UN itself, it understands the world as a territory divided into uniform parcels of sovereignty among a large number of states. It narrowly defines piracy as "acts of violence and robbery" in the neutral space falling outside the domain of these equal sovereign states — "on the high seas or in a place outside the jurisdiction of a state." By the same UN edict, sovereign states cannot be piratical, thereby limiting piracy to private acts by private persons and ships.[4]

The real world, of course, has been much less clear-cut. In maritime regions, such as much of Southeast Asia, states depended rather more on their control of the sea than of the land. Forcing or encouraging trade to come to one's port exemplified the essence of statecraft, and the ability to protect such trade from attack by enemies, the proof of accomplishment. The path to statehood often began with violent seizures at sea that established powers resisted as aggressive and illegal. Successful states more effectively channeled the sometimes forceful activities of sea peoples in their favor.

I want to argue here that this modern, restricted definition of piracy derives from a specifically European concept which became globalized in the colonial era. The contemporary imperative that *all* states should join together to combat piracy arises directly from the nineteenth-century European requirement that "civilized states" should so cooperate. But today's world differs greatly from the colonial period, and we should not be surprised at the setbacks in the control of piracy that have happened.

European translations of Chinese texts make it appear that "piracy" occurred everywhere during the Ming and Qing, as indeed it actually does in the chapters of this volume. Similarly, European desires to suppress attacks on their shipping in the treacherous waters of Southeast Asia made "Malay" and "pirate" seem almost synonymous.[5] But in these early periods, only the European gaze could make the Asian phenomena resemble "piracy." Let me elaborate by examining the opposite Chinese and Austronesian ("Malay") worlds, and how each tradition seems to have regarded armed robbery at sea.

Chinese Understandings

At one extreme of the Eurasian experience, China operated as a bureaucratized empire with a low regard for seaborne trade in some periods, but with a clear sense of the distinction between the "civilized" subjects of the empire and the "barbarian" peoples outside it. The distinction made in Chinese records was not so much between robbery in coastal waters or the free oceans as between various kinds of "bandits." Although the Chinese never made such sharp distinctions, in general (and for the sake of argument), two of the most common terms for "bandits," *zei* and *kou*, can be broadly differentiated: the former referring to lawbreakers working within the imperial system and the latter to those working from the outside. Thus, the English term "pirate" has been used to translate a spectrum of Chinese terms, including *haizei* ("sea bandit"), perceived as being Chinese outlaws, and *wokou* ("dwarf bandit"), officially seen as barbarian "others," specifically evoking a hostile Japanese stereotype.[6] As for *wokou*, Chinese authorities in the Ming period viewed them as pirates lurking on the periphery of or outside the imperial system — as a conspiracy between foreign barbarians and dynastic traitors who not only engaged in illegal commerce but also armed robbery at sea and on the coast.[7] Because China, particularly during the Ming and early Qing dynasties (before 1684), took an exceptionally negative view of seaborne trade, except as an aspect of the so-called tribute system, the second type of lawbreaker filled it sources.[8]

As a perceptive Ming official noted, pirates and merchants comprised fundamentally the same group of people. "When trade is permitted, pirates become merchants. When trade is prohibited, merchants convert to pirates."[9] The draconian early Ming ban on trade, and on Chinese traveling overseas on any business except that of the emperor, ensured that it would consider virtually all international commercial activity illegal. Often the smugglers got around officialdom by bribery and collusion with local authorities, who themselves depended on trade, but frequently also needed to resort to arms to defeat or intimidate them. Early in the Qing period, in May 1652, a Dutch official wrote that their principal rival in the Japan-Vietnam trade, Nagasaki's largest Chinese merchant, Wei Zhiyuan (Itchien), could not go home "because he is considered a bandit in China."[10]

This book gives so many examples of these phenomena that I do not need to elaborate. Let me just remind the reader of four rather different cases that English translations of Chinese material have too readily rendered as piracy:

1. Chinese commercial activity in Southeast Asia in the fifteenth century encompassed several important centers, including Palembang, which Zheng He conquered in 1407 by killing five thousand "pirates" and capturing its ruler, "the pirate chief Chen Zui."[11] Patani owed its commercial origins to another group of Chinese settlers in the sixteenth century, also described as "pirates."[12] Since Chinese traders outside China seemed necessarily illegitimate in the eyes of the Ming state, Ming sources characterized them as "sea bandits" or "sea traitors" (*haikou*), translated into English by the early orientalists simply as "pirates."

2. In the sixteenth century, foreign traders anxious to circumvent the Ming trade ban, first, primarily Japanese but later European, needed to work with Chinese traders on the fringes of the imperial system. Officials regarded them as smugglers, while the Chinese, in turn, exaggerated the importance of the foreign element to evade and also intimidate local authorities. Hence, the term "Japanese" or "dwarf bandit" (*wokou*) appeared most commonly in Ming records, and came to be translated as "pirate" in English. The Ming officials tasked to tackle the problem themselves realized full well, however, that most *wokou* they were dealing with were Chinese. According to Censor Du Zhonglü, in a memorial to the Ming throne, dated 1553, barbarian people were ten percent, Ryukyu people twenty percent, and the rest hailed from the Fujian and Ningpo areas in China.[13]
3. In the mid-seventeenth century, the Zheng family organized what we might fairly describe as a pro-Ming and pro-commerce resistance against the Manchu (Qing) conquest of China. Calling the Zheng and their followers "pirates," though, does little to help our understanding. They were rebels, indeed, but also an alternative Chinese polity responsible for most of China's international maritime trade for three decades.[14]
4. In the period 1780–1810, tens of thousands of mariners of the Sino-Vietnamese water world were classified as "pirates," partly because of shifting political fortunes during the Tay Son interregnum in Vietnam.[15]

The "piracy" that found its way into the European literature by translating categories from the Ming sources, in particular, consisted of a maximalist category, potentially including almost all the international maritime commerce of the world's then largest economy, and that of its sons outside China.

Malay World

The states of the Indonesian archipelago or "Malay world" comprised the opposite type, not only embracing international commerce but actually depending upon it. If Ming China legitimated trade only as a handmaid of diplomacy, the Malay states used diplomacy as a handmaid of trade. European traders quickly learned the value of bringing a royal letter and presents for the king, just as Asian traders did from their home ports, "with letters full of praisings and compliments and also with small presents. This is done only to promote trade."[16]

Such states needed to encourage shipping to come to their ports, and frequently used their naval power to attack those who preferred to trade with their rivals or enemies. While Chinese or European sources could consider this piracy, Southeast Asian ones regarded it as warfare or statecraft. John Crawfurd noted in the 1850s,

"There is no name in Malay and Javanese, or indeed in any other native [Southeast Asian] language, for piracy or robbery on the high seas."[17] The verb, *rampok*, means to plunder, in general, but, at least by 1900, a more specific variant, *rompak*, had developed (perhaps precisely to translate the English term), meaning to plunder at sea. R. J. Wilkinson even produced a proverb to prove it: "wherever there are seas there are pirates" (*ada laut, ada-lah perompak*).[18] A more common usage, the ethnonym Illanun (more properly Iranun), referred to one of the southern Philippine groups most given to the practice of raiding from the late eighteenth century, though this usage, too, did not distinguish piracy as a separate type of activity from sea robbery and marauding more broadly.

The key point remains that, as Sultan Husain of Singapore said to Raffles, what the Europeans called piracy "brings no disgrace" to a Malay ruler.[19] Successful port-rulers in the Malacca Strait area needed to attach to their own service the sea people (Orang Laut), who for centuries lived on their boats by foraging and trading or plundering. As Carl Trocki put it: "As long as the Malay political system was operative, the activities of the sea peoples had been violent but perfectly legitimate pursuits ... So long as their chief held a valid title from the Sultan, their 'patrol' activities regarding trade were a legitimate naval operation."[20] A strong and successful ruler used them to encourage shipping to call at his port and avoid those of his rivals or those he considered his vassals. When no effective ruler regarded as legitimate by the Orang Laut reigned, as occurred in the Straits during the late eighteenth century, they could resemble the stereotype of the "Malay pirate" of European imagining. Even if Europeans looked upon large communities of sea peoples as permanent or temporary pirates, no indication exists that this category was clear to Southeast Asians.

European usage has differed since the Renaissance, in specifying piracy as robbery at sea unsanctioned by one of the competitive nation-states then beginning to dominate the European scene. The first usage in English dates back to 1555, and the 1944 *Oxford English Dictionary* (third edition, reprinted with corrections through the 1970s) still gave a definition of it which seems very evocative of the nineteenth century: "Piracy: Robbery and depredation on the sea or navigable rivers, or by descent from the sea upon the coast, by persons not holding a commission from a *civilized* state" [my emphasis]. This last point is very telling, since it reflects the nineteenth-century European system of extending its rules to the whole world but reserving their benefits for Europeans, the domain of so-called "civilized states." On the one hand, since they did not authorize the maritime conflicts of Asians, they could regard all of them as piracy and suppress them as such. On the other hand, the European states could and did license private shipowners to raid the shipping of those considered enemies during times of war, which they deemed legitimate privateering.

Privateering

Privateering deserves more discussion, since the legal distinction Europeans made between privateering and piracy could not have been clear to most Asians. Roman law already acknowledged a right of reprisal for private ships to recover by force losses sustained by attack by another. This pattern evolved in sixteenth-century Britain, Holland, and France into one that contracted private traders or ships-of-war to assault ships of a rival country, and to bring the prize taken back to their home country where they could legally adjudicate the cargo, most of it falling to the captors. The celebrated "Sea Beggars," who began the revolt of the Netherlands against Spain in 1568, offered a notable example of privateers, as did the plethora of British heroes such as Francis Drake and William Dampier, who raided Spanish shipping, and incidentally circumnavigated the globe. The Caribbean provided a prime site for all comers to prey upon the Spanish ships returning from Mexico. In all the revolutions of the New World, starting with the United States in 1776, privateers played an important role in attacking the shipping of the metropolitan power.[21] In Asian waters, the raids of Portuguese and Spanish vessels on Muslim ships in the Indian Ocean could also fall under this category, while the eighteenth-century Anglo-French Wars gave rise to a further burst of privateering there.

Although privateering appeared as a "legal" form of piracy which arose from the peculiar European system of competitive nation-states, nonetheless, most Asian polities would have been familiar with the concept of government-sponsored maritime raiding, which lay at the heart of privateering. For instance, in the late eighteenth century, the Tay Son regime in Vietnam employed Chinese seafarers to plunder shipping on the Chinese and Vietnamese coasts (see Antony's chapter). As a common practice, both large and small polities in archipelago Southeast Asia supported sea raiding on the vessels and settlements of their enemies, using such raiding as an important part of warfare and statecraft.

The Imperial High Tide

Whereas privateering divided the European states, their usage understood piracy as an agreed-upon evil which all should cooperate to eradicate. Only after 1816, however, when the European wars in Asia had largely ended, did European powers begin to use this doctrine to unite against independent maritime forces in Asian waters. The nineteenth century uniquely marked a turning point when the world's dominant shipping interests obtained state support to suppress piracy virtually everywhere on the planet.

The establishment of an expanded Kingdom of the Netherlands (including today's Belgium) following the French Revolutionary upheavals, and the decision to restore its Indonesian territories despite Raffles' objections, already signified that Dutch colonial influence would operate beneath the protective umbrella of British naval hegemony. In entering into post-war negotiations with the Dutch about Southeast Asia in 1819, Britain had only two fundamental aims: to retain control of the Malacca Strait route to China (through the Straits Settlements), and to safeguard the freedom of British commerce throughout Southeast Asia, except in those few areas ruled directly by the Dutch, in Java and Maluku.[22] In fact, the Dutch sought territorial demarcation, so that their prior boundary demands would be recognized even without the military and commercial power to give them substance. The London Treaty of 1824 labeled the Indonesian Archipelago as an area where the British would construct no establishments. In the new developing world where "civilized states" were asserting responsibility for every corner of the planet, this, therefore, became potential Dutch possessions. Article V of the 1824 Treaty particularly stressed the obligation of both British and Dutch parties "to concur effectually in suppressing piracy." Although Britain had the larger interest in security for its then-dominant shipping, the Dutch knew that their claims to particular areas would be challenged if piracy occurred without appropriate retaliation from them. Throughout the rest of the nineteenth century, treaties involving the British, Dutch, French, Spanish, Portuguese, Siamese, and, eventually, Chinese governments parceled out the whole of Southeast Asia into a system of "civilized states."[23]

The suppression of "piracy" both motivated and justified this expansion — in a sense providing *the* major justification. On the one hand, the Dutch and British capture of the most lucrative arms of Asian trade in the seventeenth century had removed any chance that any of the trade-dependent port-states of the Archipelago could progress into a strong enough polity to cross the threshold to "civilized statedom." Rather, a widespread assumption of the "decline" of Asian states emerged.[24] On the other hand, it elevated piracy in the nineteenth century to "a great and blighting curse"[25] that "civilized states" should combine to suppress, and would define it as any act of robbery at sea not authorized by such civilized states. Hence, European shippers and shipping interests possessed the perfect weapon to push their respective states into ever further expansion to eliminate whatever remained in the Malay world by way of independent military capacity by sea. In truth, the early nineteenth century witnessed a period of unusual anarchy in Southeast Asian waters (see below, as well as the discussion in Ota Atsushi's chapter), while the argument that piracy represented the greatest scourge to increased trade contained much plausibility.

Whereas in the eighteenth century and earlier, European (and Indian, Arab, and Chinese) ships armed themselves to exact their own view of justice, in the nineteenth century, appeals to the fleets of the European/American governments concerned most often punished offences against shipping. The Straits Settlements and Hong Kong became the favored bases for Chinese, Indian, and Arab shipping in

Southeast Asia partly for this reason — that they, too, could claim British protection, if attacked. Aceh operated the freest trade zone anywhere in the archipelago as the only state left formally independent by the 1824 carve-up. Both the Americans (1826, 1832, and 1838) and the French (1839) sent naval ships to "avenge" assaults on their pepper-ships by destroying the coastal port-villages where they deemed the piratical crimes to have occurred.

I might quote some words from a poem celebrating the bloody deeds of one of the American warships concerned, because its horrific tone to modern ears does illustrate some of the flavor of a particular period of so-called "civilized states" combating so-called "piracy":

> To revenge the sad wrongs which our friends and our nation,
> So oft have sustained from these demons from hell;
> Our work we commenced, and the bright conflagration,
> Left but few of our foes that sad story to tell.[26]

Of course, the case of James Brooke illustrated the most successful alliance between the private adventurer and the European navies commissioned to suppress piracy. His successful portrayal of his Malay and Dayak enemies in Sarawak as "pirates" and "slave-traders" convinced Captain Henry Keppel, who commanded a small steamer of the Singapore squadron, and his superior, Admiral Cochrane, to join him in destroying them (1843 and 1846). Figure 2.1 shows a nineteenth-century European representation of a Dayak warrior. Because the British did not yet demonstrate any interest in direct authority over Archipelago societies, Brooke ended in a curious position as a private ruler with British support, founding his own "white raja" dynasty.

The middle decades of the nineteenth century marked something of a turning point, as steamships, better firearms, the telegraph, and a regular system of scheduled shipping services conspired to turn the tables on the "pirates." All the major maritime powers developed permanent standing navies which would come to the aid of shippers against alleged pirates, eventually eliminating the role of privateers. After many appeals from Chinese and Bugis shippers servicing Singapore, as well as the British shipping interests, Britain sent out six warships and gunboats to Singapore specifically to suppress piracy. The first armed steamship arrived in 1836, which greatly helped in pursuing the fast galleys of raiders such as the Iranun. The expansion of telegraphic services around the world in the 1850s and 1860s provided another powerful incentive for cooperation between the European states in ensuring the safety of telegraph routes through hitherto unstable territory. Telegraph interests were among the strongest lobby for British advance on the Malay Peninsula. While the most advanced country, England, inclined toward going it alone, an International Telegraphic Union was established in Paris in 1865, as the first of the potentially global organizations designed to unify the world's communications. A comparable

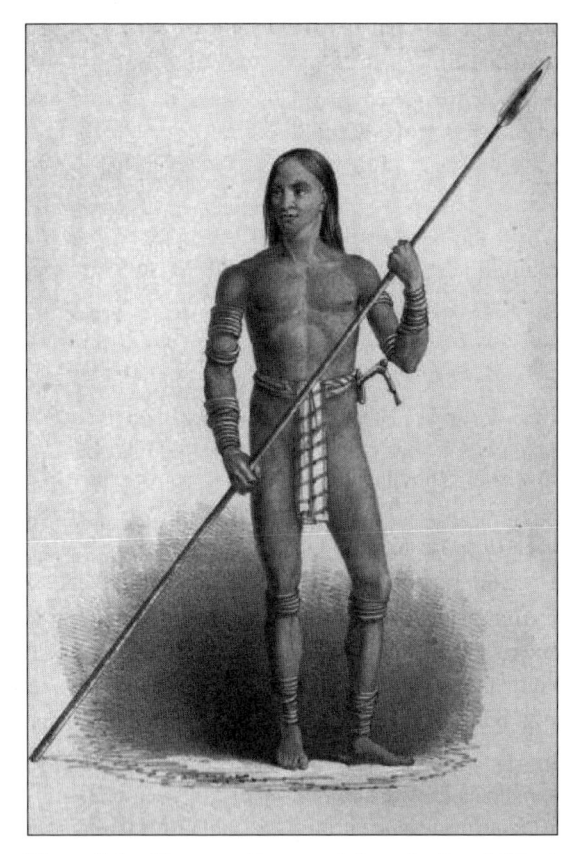

Figure 2.1 European Representation of a Dayak Warrior
(Source: Frank S. Marryat, *Borneo and the Indian Archipelago*, London, 1848)

association of shippers came about more slowly, partly because of the dominance of British interests — the International Maritime Organization did not actually form until 1948, under UN auspices.

A fleet headquartered in Singapore combined with a small Dutch naval force in Tanjung Pinang (capital of the Riau Archipelago, to the south) to destroy one base after another of the Orang Laut, and reduce them first to a client people living on boats in the Singapore River, and then, finally, to land-based peoples of varying degrees of misery. "By the 1870s piracy in peninsula waters had effectively been eradicated."[27] As Trocki notes, the loss of the Orang Laut deprived Malay rulers of the Straits area of their subject class for all practical purposes. The most successful of them, like the Temenggong of Johor, survived by switching in the mid-nineteenth century to an alliance with Chinese entrepreneurs, who then, for the first time began to tame the forests of the Peninsula and Riau.[28]

Northern Sumatra and the southern Philippines held the last two concentrations of maritime power in the Archipelago outside European naval control, each positioned at vital maritime crossroads. They traded with British ports and ships more than with the colonial power that felt "entitled" to this sphere of influence. In the two cases, this hinge location between different commercial orbits, a strength in earlier times, now endangered them. The British in the last third of the century abandoned its policy of keeping such ports open to trade, in favor of holding "piracy" in check, and maintaining smooth relations with European allies. Both the Spanish and the Dutch feared that if they could not suppress "piracy" by expanding efficiently into these areas, some other power (Britain or Holland in Sulu, and France or the United States in Aceh) would do so under the pretext of protecting its shipping. Nevertheless, the brutal methods that proved necessary to subjugate these two centers caused problems for the later heirs to power in Manila and Jakarta.

James Warren has ably described how the Spanish effectively ended the century of Sulu power through conquest and an "Act of Incorporation" into the Spanish monarchy in 1851.[29] Armed with the new steamships and firearms, and the powerful motive of British flirtation with the Sultan of Sulu, they insisted on removing "piracy" from this zone, and they attacked the chief Balagnini Samal raiding center in the Sulu Archipelago in 1848. In early 1851, a force of nearly four thousand troops stormed the capital of the Sultan of Sulu at Jolo, and destroyed the town which served as the principal metropolis of Sulu's commercial heyday. In the aftermath of this success, the Spanish intimidated all the Muslim rulers of the south — Sulu itself, Magindanao, and Buayan — into accepting their position as "an integral part of the Philippine Archipelago." Of course, this proved insufficient to control the south, and, in 1876, Spain sent a massive force of thirty-two ships and nine thousand men to complete the conquest of the "pirate's nest" of Sulu. The Sultan appealed to his British trading partners for aid, but as they did in Aceh, the British had then switched their policy to supporting rival colonial powers in the name of a united front against "piracy."[30] Sulu remained a hotbed of resistance, and, therefore, of occasional attacks labeled piracy, and it was only a full-scale American war of pacification in the first decade of the twentieth century that brought a comparable colonial order to the southern Philippines as in the rest of Southeast Asia.

Aceh was also accused of being a nest of piracy, but much less persuasively. It had no Orang Laut population that lived by raiding and foraging, but instead, a very long coastline with scores of tiny river-ports, each with its own raja or *uleebalang*. Disputes with the Europeans throughout the nineteenth century had centered on the merchants' wish for untrammeled access to each of these ports, in conflict with the sultan's desire to oblige trade to concentrate at his capital and pay him the requisite duties. When the Dutch were looking for an excuse to intervene after the 1871 Treaty with Britain allowed this, they of course found it in what they claimed was "piracy." Among the pepper-rich rajas of eastern Aceh, the more influential and reformist supported the sultan's party, while the raja at Idi was using appeals to the Dutch and British to ensure his ability to trade freely. The Dutch sent a warship to Idi on the grounds that the partisans of the Sultan were blockading him and keeping out vessels including some with Dutch flags.[31] The story is well known of how another disastrous colonial war was fought from 1873 to 1913, largely on the presumption that ensuring the absolute safety of European (and incidentally, among others, Chinese, Indian, and Arab) vessels throughout the seas had now become the responsibility of a colonial power.

Conclusion

This background of the modern world system needs to be understood. The world was made secure for European shipping, and, as a by-product, that of others, because the dominant shippers in the nineteenth century had the total support of their governments in suppressing piracy militarily. Those governments expanded their territory throughout Southeast Asia and much of the rest of the world precisely in order to make that shipping and other forms of commerce safe. That period ended in 1942 with the Japanese conquest of Southeast Asia. Piracy and smuggling revived under the Japanese, who unwittingly encouraged them by attempting to install a draconian system of self-reliance in each *syu* (province) of occupied Southeast Asia.

During the tumultuous revolutionary period that followed the Japanese surrender, piracy and smuggling became patriotic in the struggle against the returning Europeans. Twang Pek Yang has well described how whole new classes of small entrepreneurs with little to lose began as merchants in independent Indonesia by sending small boats across the Malacca Strait.[32] Like the Malay "pirates" of an earlier period, they took their chances in a violent age, and some of them survived to become great traders in more stable times.

In the almost equally turbulent 1950s, the local authorities in Sumatra and Sulawesi saw no reason to give up their lucrative direct commerce with Singapore and Malaysia, even when the government in Jakarta declared it "smuggling."[33] Muslim small traders in the southern Philippines resumed their personal trade with Sabah, and even Saigon and Singapore. At each of the other unstable periods that followed, piracy revived. Most recently, the opening of China combined with the sharp decline of order in Indonesia accounted for the peak of piratical activity in the Malacca Strait area in the late 1990s — as James Warren and others have so ably explained.[34]

In hindsight, one must recognize the period when "piracy" was suppressed, from about 1880 to 1940, as an exception rather than a norm for our international order. The powerful ship-owning states were then precisely the entities that thought it their primary mission to eliminate piracy. Through the colonial system, and the fiction of an alliance of "civilized states," they had or acquired the authority on the ground to achieve it. In contrast, the prosperous era of global shipping expansion since 1960 has been one in which shippers registered their vessels under flags of convenience, of countries that have absolutely no capacity or desire to counteract piracy. As of 2000, half the world's shipping corporations registered their flags of convenience to evade taxes and labor regulations. Panama nominally has the biggest fleet in the world; and Liberia's vast nominal fleet is coordinated by nobody in that country, but by a company in Virginia. On the other hand, desperately poor countries, as for example, Indonesia and Somalia have neither the resources nor the motivation to patrol their vast coastlines, which offer shelter to piratical actors. The age-old collusion between legitimate traders and violent ones continues.

The world of shipowners and related interests can afford, more readily than ever before, to end the irritation of piracy. But it needs a new system to do so, more equitable than the colonial system but just as efficient.

3

From Sea Bandits to Sea Lords:
Nonstate Violence and Pirate Identities in Fifteenth- and Sixteenth-Century Japan[1]

Peter D. Shapinsky

Despite the significant presence of pirates in both popular and scholarly media, all too often in history, the subjectivities of seafarers labeled pirates remain elusive. The term pirate does not constitute a stable, objective category that a simple legal definition can make comprehensible. In most cases, the meaning of "pirate" depends on its representations in various historical and cultural contexts.[2] Although seafarers seldom classified themselves as pirates, nonetheless, some were aware of how land-based authorities depicted them as pirates and engaged with those depictions in order to craft identities. In this chapter, I propose that piracy in fifteenth- and sixteenth-century Japan constitutes such a case.

For most of premodern Japanese history, the term for "pirate" (*kaizoku*)[3] reflected the land-based state's perspective, and signified a "sea bandit" who engaged in what it considered illegitimate violence. By the fifteenth and sixteenth centuries, however, Japanese authorities lacked the capability to enforce their will at sea without employing nonstate actors, such as "pirates." As in other parts of the world, land-based elites in Japan called on pirates to perform various types of violent and peaceful services: fighting sea battles, purveying goods and people, protecting ships, and managing littoral holdings. As a result of this sponsorship, the term *kaizoku* took on the additional meaning of licit as well as illicit behavior. In particular, sources from this period detailing negotiations between state-level patrons and nonstate seafarers over the performance of various services are particularly revealing. They show that some "pirates" took advantage of the access the negotiations provided to land-based forms of representation and lordship and capitalized on the dependence of land-based elites upon their services to describe themselves as sea lords.

Although not a historical term, I use the expression "sea lord" to refer to the leaders of seafaring bands who sought to gain dominion over maritime networks of people, routes, and resources. In fact, methods of self-representation constituted a major tool of sea-lordship. Sea lords considered continued external recognition and validation of their authority by the land-based dignitaries, such as shoguns and *daimyo* who supported them, integral to their success as both authorities and mercenaries.[4] Sea lords recognized and manipulated how land-based elites perceived their actions; situated themselves between the political, geographical, and cultural borders of potential sponsors of nonstate violence; and, in so doing, created their own autonomous domains. Although we might assume that patronage should have enabled land-based states to exercise some influence over nonstate violence, the case of Japanese sea lords suggests the opposite. Border-straddling allowed seafaring bands labeled as pirates to establish independent realms by depicting themselves in forms familiar to land-based elites and, then, to take advantage of those authorities' desperation for their nautical services to preserve that sea-based autonomy.

This chapter will explore how seafarers embraced an identity of trans-border "betweenness," established themselves as sea lords, and, in this way, caused a semantic shift in the meaning of *kaizoku* in fifteenth- and sixteenth-century Japan. To do so, I investigate how Japan's littoral in this period provided an environment conducive to sea-lordship and nonstate violence. Here I examine three ways in which Japanese seafarers employed nonstate violence to become sea lords. First, sea lords situated their bands and domains between land-based cultural and political realms by maintaining distinctly maritime power bases, and by representing themselves in ways that manipulated land-based expectations regarding the sea and seafarers. Second, sea lords exploited the multivalent nature of the perceptions of maritime chokepoints and toll barriers in Japan in this period in order to create domains within those narrow channels and to develop lucrative protection businesses. Third, sea lords engaged in maritime mercenarism. They played land-based patrons against each other and sold types of nonstate violence that symbolized both the ambitions of patrons and the autonomy and maritime culture of sea lords.

Nonstate Violence in Fifteenth- and Sixteenth-Century Japan

I focus on those bands (*shū*) who, though often labeled as *kaizoku*, came to dominate premodern Japan's aortic sea route, the Seto Inland Sea (see Map 3.1). This important body of water sutured the main islands of the archipelago together and tied the capital, Kyoto, to the rest of the world. Bands tended to establish themselves in a particular locale; to follow the hereditary leadership of a single family; and to take their name from both the place and ruling family. The Noshima Murakami, the Tagaya, and the Shirai (discussed in Petrucci's chapter), among other bands, found the Inland Sea region ideally suited for developing businesses, identities, and dominion through practices of nonstate violence during this period due to its combination of political decentralization and dynamic commercialization.

Politically, many of the powers of traditional state institutions headed by shoguns and emperors were devolving at that time to *daimyo*. However, no part of

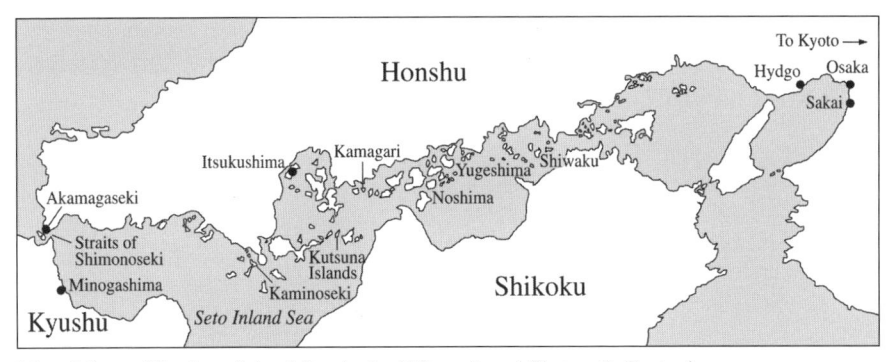

Map 3.1   The Seto Inland Sea in the Fifteenth and Sixteenth Centuries

this complex array of state institutions possessed a navy; all naval projects — whether the defense of trade ships, the protection and management of littoral holdings, or the fighting of sea battles — required the assistance of *kaizoku* mercenaries. Maritime "mercenarism" became possible because of a marketized service economy that emerged as part of Japan's increasing commercialization.[5] This upsurge in patronage relations also permitted the creation and subsequent survival of a significant corpus of documents detailing their transactions and structure. These sources permit us to explore the effects and perceptions of nonstate violence among sea lord purveyors as well as patrons and suggest new interpretations of patron-pirate relationships.

Older scholarship on pirates in fifteenth- and sixteenth-century Japan tended to follow the patron-centered grain of the documents and portrayed *kaizoku* service relations as forms of feudal vassalage.[6] However, such representations — like the term pirate — most often reflect the interests of the sponsors, not the identities of the seafarers. In contrast, more recent scholarship has begun to explore characteristics of trans-border "betweenness" as a way of understanding pirate identities in Japan. The historian Murai Shōsuke has argued that we should consider the multiethnic pirates who sailed between Korea and Japan, what historians call *wakō*, as marginal figures who "lived in spaces which two [political] centers considered peripheries … but who could mediate with either."[7]

Such betweenness tied to pirates and maritime mercenaries occurred at many times in different parts of the world. Across the globe in this period nonstate actors supplied violence as a salable service no different from the luxury and subsistence commodities already purveyed by seafarers in commercial systems. They and their sponsors perceived commerce and violence as parts of seafaring identities and livelihoods, not as contradictory phenomena. Janice Thomson defines such practices performed by nonstate agents as forms of "extraterritorial violence" — violence that European states recognized as acceptable when performed on their behalf outside home borders. She argues that during medieval and early-modern Euro-America, states did not monopolize legitimate violence, but instead state and nonstate organizations alike, "democratized, marketized, and internationalized" it.[8] Although Thomson's primary interest centers upon how European sovereignty changed as a result of nonstate violence, her concept can equally apply to addressing seafarers' perspectives and identities in fifteenth- and sixteenth-century Japan. She traces a pattern in which trans-border, nonstate actors who dealt in violence — such as privateers, mercenary bands, and the various East India companies — acquired state sponsorship, thus enabling them to develop a significant degree of autonomy, what she calls an "unintended consequence" of patronage.[9]

The shoguns and other elites of fifteenth- and sixteenth-century Japan may have perceived the growing autonomy of sea lords as a mixed blessing. Although these patrons considered pirate mercenaries integral to the functioning of military, political, and economic systems, and the provision of rewards may have given sponsors "symbolic capital,"[10] the nonstate violence of Inland Sea pirates also destabilized the hegemonic projects of land-based *daimyo*, in as much as the interests and ambitions of sea lords differed from those of land-based authorities. That said, embracing the side of their identity that employed signs and symbols of land-based lordship ironically allowed houses like the Noshima Murakami to survive the establishment of a unified, early modern Japanese state.

Establishing a Trans-Border Identity

For the Noshima Murakami and other sea lords, establishing autonomy and a trans-border identity rooted in nonstate violence and other practices meant navigating cultural boundaries as much as political and geographical ones. To understand how they did so, it is useful to think of sea lord practices and livelihoods as including sea-based "cultures of work."[11] Given the land-centeredness and institutional nature of both the content and the form, however, the historical records do not transparently reflect seafarers' work-cultures and other sources of *kaizoku* identity. Scholars should understand them as a fusion of land-based writing and representations of maritime action.[12] Particularly after the fifteenth century, when sea lords gained significant access to the new methods of discourse, they accepted its land-centered forms to make themselves familiar and attractive to potential sponsors, while at the same time emphasizing a distinctive maritime, work-based identity.[13]

Writing in premodern Japan tended toward the terra-centric because it served the elite, land-based institutions that developed its various forms. By the fifteenth century, these sources reveal that land-based authorities in Japan had developed ambivalent, protean attitudes towards the sea and seafarers. These evolving attitudes determined the meaning of "pirate" (*kaizoku*) in Japan. On the one hand, these elites saw the sea as a productive space to incorporate. Beginning in the seventh century, they implemented the Ritsuryō reforms, building legal and institutional structures on Chinese models in order to forge a centralized, bureaucratic imperium based on grain agriculture. This regime established enduring institutional precedents that represented the productive capacity of the archipelago in standardized measures of rice production and incorporated both land and sea within the institutional apparatus of provinces and circuits.[14] Economically, central authorities also founded various iterations of estate systems with boundaries that extended out into the ocean, dedicated to the production of maritime as well as terrestrial foodstuffs and handicrafts.[15] For the ruling authorities in Kyoto, including the Ashikaga shoguns (c.1336–1573), these precedents continued to have real meaning even into the fifteenth and sixteenth centuries.[16]

On the other hand, the sea also represented an "other-space," uncontrollable and dangerous for land-based elites. During most of the premodern period, they exercised little direct control over the sea and relied on intermediaries for the management of littoral holdings, shipping, and naval warfare. For Kyoto aristocrats, sea lanes connected the pure imperial center with impure foreign lands, and thus carried foreign contagion.[17] Land-based elites found sea travel terrifying. The author of the tenth-century *Tosa Diary* (*Tosa nikki*) related the degree to which on an ocean voyage, he and his fellow shipmates relied entirely on the captain and crew. This sense of helplessness paralyzed the travelers with fear:

> As for the weather, all we could do was depend on the captain and crew. For men unused to these journeys, it was a great source of worry. Women lay their heads on the deck of the ship and cried.[18]

To assuage such dread and to arrive safely often required divine intervention from Shintō and Buddhist deities.[19]

Authorities on land categorized the inhabitants and workers of both controlled and uncontrolled sea spaces as "sea people" (*ama*). This ambiguous term held meaning only for land-based writers, who used the term to strengthen the perception of land-based lives and livelihoods as normative.[20] These writers used their perception of an experiential gap between land and sea dwellers as an excuse to treat sea people as "other." As the following excerpt from a 1481 travelogue demonstrates, the author could only goggle in stupefaction at the ability of sea people to manage boats and the maritime environment:

> … as our ship left, the winds grew fierce. Everyone moaned to each other in fear. Seeing how the sea people in their little fishing smacks acclimated to the pitching waves was amazing.[21]

Land-based authors divided these "sea people" into populations along the same controllable/uncontrollable continuum that they used to understand the sea. Fisher folk, potential naval vassals, prostitutes, and entertainers lived in the incorporated spaces, obeyed laws, and owed services to land-based lords.[22] Pirates were inextricably linked to maritime violence and traditionally embodied the dangerous aspects of the sea. Some writers on land even depicted piratical ferocity as natural — as unpredictable as tempests unleashed by the sea. One 1313 missive by an estate proprietor lists "capsizing and pirates" as "unexpected [natural] disasters."[23] By the fifteenth century, land-based authorities could draw on a number of legal precedents to characterize piratical violence as anathema to the proper functioning of the state. The ancient Ritsuryō codes outlawed pirates as rebels and ruffians who harassed travelers at sea just as bandits did on land.[24] After the thirteenth century, warrior law tended to tie pirates to their maritime environment by pairing them with mountain bandits (*sanzoku*), identifying seas and mountains as geographies rife with the potential for illicit violence.[25]

By the fourteenth century, however, officials also called on figures they knew as *kaizoku* to fight battles and to defend littoral estates. Documents commonly employed the term "protection" (*keigo*) to euphemistically describe sponsored piratical violence. An account statement detailing the amounts paid to them in exchange for giving protection to residents of the island-estate of Yugeshima provides the first extant mention of the Noshima Murakami sea lord band (from 1349).[26] By the fifteenth century, even the division between illicit (*kaizoku*) and licit (*keigo*) had disappeared. Examples of *kaizoku* signifying licit violence[27] and *keigo* illicit[28] began to appear in records, as civil war spread, state patronage of "pirates" increased, and local magnates on land and sea sought to extend their dominion.

Sea lords contributed to and took advantage of this confusion by playing patrons against one another, seeking ever greater license in running sea-based protection businesses, and increasing legitimacy for enhancing their authority over additional ports, toll barriers, and littoral villages. To legitimize this dominion, they contracted with competing *daimyo* to engage in various forms of nonstate violence such as fighting sea battles, administering littoral holdings, escorting ships, and transporting goods.[29] Between 1540 and 1582, the Noshima Murakami proffered services to seven different land-based *daimyo* as they expanded their domain from a few small islands to networks of tiny island fortresses, ports, and maritime production centers across the length of much of the Inland Sea.[30]

The negotiations between sea lords and patrons consisted of a dialogue between the work-based cultural forms of the former and the dominant, land-based written discourse of the latter. Sea lords used the land-based writings to depict themselves in ways patrons would find familiar — they employed literary forms that rendered them indistinguishable from land-based lords. By the mid-sixteenth century, for example, although the Noshima Murakami family possessed a strong reputation as fearsome pirates whom patrons also often hired to perform naval services, in correspondence with them, the leader of the Noshima band, Murakami Takeyoshi (d.1604), used honorary titles like Governor of Yamato Province and the imperial clan-name Minamoto, wording that signified lordship within Japanese society in that period.[31] To describe the hierarchy of their group, sea lords, including the Tagaya and the Shirai, employed the institutional language of warrior bands, for instance, the terms "follower" (*rōjū*) and "servant" (*bokujū*) to describe "sailors" (*kako*) and others who crewed ships.[32] The use of land-based written documentary forms of lordship previously reserved for land-based officials, such as "orders" (*gechijō*),[33] "regulations" (*sadamegaki*),[34] and "edicts of confirmation" (*andojō*),[35] provided vehicles for asserting greater control over maritime populations. The Noshima embrace of land-based forms of writing as cultural capital even extended to learning the intricacies of linked-verse poetry (*renga*).[36]

At the same time, although they did not identify themselves as sea people, sea lord bands did forge identities strongly connected to their ship-based livelihoods, which distinguished them from their land-based sponsors. Anthropologists have argued that sailors who spent long periods of time together aboard ship created bonds that united them against the dangerous world outside the fragile wooden walls. In this way, they developed a shipboard culture.[37] Although they acceded to land-based expectations and possessed edicts of confirmation following the traditions of lordship there, like Wang Zhi, Zheng Chenggong, Zhang Bao, and other so-called pirates in this volume, sea lords focused their economic and political interests on maritime trade networks. The Noshima Murakami controlled important ports and barriers such as Shiwaku and Kaminoseki, villages that produced salt, fish, seaweed, as well as other maritime products, and small island fortresses situated at chokepoints (these last included their home base of Noshima). Most of these places lacked significant value in terms of the grain-based productivity standard that defined land tenure paradigms dominant among land-based powers during this period.[38]

Sea lords insisted that recompense from patrons relate to their maritime power-base — even if labeled as "lands" or as "cash and provisions" in the documents.[39] In the early 1560s, the Noshima rejected a grant of land because of its inland location.[40] By maintaining such a maritime focus, sea lords could retain their autonomy and remain indispensable to sponsors by concentrating on the naval services which made them attractive to sponsors.

In addition, the accounts of land-based elite writers from Japan and other countries contain representations of maritime work cultures — as well as exoticization. A couplet in the tenth-century *Tosa Diary* illustrates how a shipboard life led to the development of unique skill sets: "Only sea-people/ Can readily discern/ The separation of sea and sky."[41] Korean records about pirates across the western Japanese littoral identify distinctive maritime gendered practices, forms of clothing and speech, and military tactics that differed significantly from cultural elements of "regular," land-based Japanese. These included diving under and drilling holes in ships, which may indicate roles for women — who did much of the diving in Japanese and Korean waters — on "pirate" ships.[42] Some observers noted significant similarity between the sea-going peoples of the Inland Sea and those of Tsushima. The 1420 Korean ambassador to Japan, Song Hŭigyŏng (1376–1446), described the Tagaya band dwelling on the Inland Sea islands of Kamagari as "pirates" (*haejeok*), "wicked and coarse in appearance, the same as those of Tsushima."[43] Despite the landlubberly invective, Song's description helps us appreciate that because both the Kamagari islands and Tsushima occupy chokepoints along the sea lanes and contain insufficient arable land to support an agricultural population, their inhabitants had to engage in non-agricultural, sea-based livelihoods.[44] In the fifteenth century, under the leadership of the Tagaya family, Kamagari denizens engaged in commercial shipping ventures; participated in overseas exchange networks; raided ports and performed other violent acts as mercenaries; and commanded protection businesses from sea-based toll barriers that secured their autonomy and maritime dominion.[45]

Toll Barriers and Protection

Japanese sea lords embraced the business of extracting protection money at sea-based toll barriers for several reasons. They could take advantage of its multivalent nature — like other forms of nonstate violence, toll-taking resonated with land-based patrons as both familiar and exotic, useful yet dangerous. Toll barriers and protection businesses, furthermore, represented extremely lucrative ventures that enabled sea lords to define the boundaries of their maritime domains because they established them at chokepoints. These narrow channels linked maritime regions and thus proved integral to the flow of traffic, but they also constituted border zones and provincial boundaries where the state's authority did not always hold sway. Fluctuations in political power on either the Shikoku or Honshu side of the central Inland Sea created the perception of provincial borders shifting in the sea in that period.[46] In 1371, the general and poet Imagawa Ryōshun found it "strange to think of crossing provincial boundaries at sea" when passing through the same region.[47] True power lay in the hands of those able to enforce their will over those spaces — namely, the sea lords.

Protection businesses and toll barriers exemplify sea lords' manipulation of land-based elites' ambivalent, dualistic perceptions of the sea. On the one hand, land-based authorities recognized that toll barriers had become ubiquitous by the fifteenth century, an accepted cost of doing business and a potential cause of conflict across the archipelago, on both land and sea. Shoguns and their wives, powerful religious functionaries, provincial governors, members of the imperial court, provincial warrior elites, village collectives, merchant bands, and others all tried to profit from erecting barriers and charging tolls. Protection tolls themselves carried a multiplicity of meanings, constructive as well as baneful — transaction costs, religious piety, temple reconstruction funds, protection, monies for local upkeep, and salaries, as well as extortion fees. Often, the strength of patronage determined the degree of popular acceptance of a toll barrier.[48]

On the other hand, land-based writers also specifically linked toll barriers to pirates. Some scholars have traced the origin of medieval piracy to seafaring communities attached to temples and shrines, which collected offerings for their gods from passing travelers. In return, the deities protected the travelers. It is possible that, especially during earlier periods, travelers may have believed that *kaizoku* could intercede with local maritime deities, giving them incentive to acquiesce to requests for the "donation of a gift" for them.[49] By the early fourteenth century, however, perceptions of this "otherworldliness" had changed. Some land-based officials considered *kaizoku* part of a larger category of protection-extorting "evil bands" (*akutō*); some even denoted them "a breed apart" (*irui igyō*) from normal people.[50]

At the same time, as commercialization and civil war grew over the course of the period, shoguns and *daimyo* increasingly depended on the maritime protection sold by sea lords from their chokepoint bases. By around 1400, the protection services of the Noshima and other sea lords extended to encompass escorting diplomatic missions and commercial vessels beyond as well as within Japanese waters.[51] Sea lords had made themselves and their protection services so pervasive that sobriquets in the fifteenth and sixteenth centuries included "Barrier-Erectors" and "Toll Barrier Captains."[52] This influence continued down to the seventeenth century; one definition in the 1603 Japanese-Portuguese dictionary entry for toll barriers linked them to pirate ships.[53]

Sea lords used toll barriers and protection businesses to expand their domainal boundaries and control over maritime trade from limited, regional and inter-regional networks in the fifteenth century to wider trans-Inland Sea networks by the sixteenth. Sea lords did so by using barriers and protection businesses as a means of practicing sea tenure by limiting access to maritime spaces and resources.[54] Scholars often assumed that land-based authorities solely possessed the instrument of tenurial rights. In premodern Japan, however, sea lords sought to "territorialize"[55] maritime space and resources using barriers and selling protection.[56] Even based on sea, ship, and island, maritime toll barriers delineated sea lords' domainal boundaries. Selling protection from their own and others' violence across a particular space influenced travelers to perceive it as part of a pirate's domain, and limited the ability of some travelers to use force against others.

By the early fifteenth century, for example, the Tagaya family and another (unclearly identified) sea lord band established protection businesses as a way of marking their division of the Kamagari region between them, such that they, not the shogun, held the true power in this area. The 1420 Korean ambassador to Japan explained in his travel diary:

> In this region live hordes of pirates; the writ of the King [shogun] does not extend here. ... In this region, there are pirates of the east and west. If a ship coming from the east has an eastern pirate on board, then the western pirates will not harm it. If a ship coming from the west has a western pirate on board, then the eastern pirates will not harm it.[57]

In contrast, by the 1560s, the Noshima Murakami had succeeded in expanding their domains across much of the Inland Sea partly by successfully developing such a well-established protection business that the Noshima no longer had to sail out and intercept ships in order to charge protection money. Instead, potential travelers, from *daimyo* to merchants, sent messengers ahead of time requesting protection from the Noshima in the form of pennants bearing their family's crest to assure themselves safe passage. In 1585, for example, one Noshima lord wrote in an edict accompanying one such pass for a recipient: "Regarding the crest pennant (*monmaku*), we send it according to the appeal you dispatched. It is to be used to ensure that nothing untoward occurs as you travel to and fro on the seas."[58] Instead of having members of their band physically ride along with or escort protected vessels, these flags flown at the masthead guaranteed the safety of ships on sea lanes over which Noshima laid claim (see Figure 3.1).

Figure 3.1 Noshima Murakami Flag-Pass
(Source: Yamaguchi Prefectural Archives, Japan)

This crest pennant system demonstrates the degree to which Noshima maritime lordship had become accepted. Based on extant sources, those who obtained Noshima flags came from all sides of the Inland Sea, from ports in Kyushu to Kii Province to Itsukushima Shrine, and included *daimyo*, merchants, and priests.[59] The wide geographical and occupational range of recipients suggests that land-based officials had ceded all responsibility for the Inland Sea to groups they knew as *kaizoku*. In addition, the ability to have these pennants accepted by such a diverse population from across western Japan represented an appropriation of powers formerly monopolized by land-based imperial and warrior authorities: the issuance of toll-exemption passes (*kasho*).[60]

Exploiting recognition received from both domainal inhabitants and external authorities[61] proved crucial for sea lords in successfully deploying protection businesses to expand maritime suzerainty over maritime networks. By requesting or accepting safe passage, travelers validated the legality of sea lords' protection business and their sea-based jurisdictions. Transformations in terminology used by both sea lords and customers for protection monies signified this acceptance; words for amenable payments replaced extortion: "protection rice" (*keigomai*); "thank-you cash" (*reisen*); "harbor tallies" (*sappo*); and "gifts" (*shukōryō*).[62] In addition, forms of recognition evolved as sea lords enlarged their realms. For the Tagaya and another band, institutionalizing reciprocal awareness of each other's suzerainty through a protection business legitimized their control over the Kamagari littoral in the fifteenth century. In the latter half of the next century, the Noshima Murakami's reputation for protection convinced regional lords, merchants, and other travelers to request crest pennants. In doing so, they accepted that the Noshima held sole sway over a large swathe of the Inland Sea, from Shiwaku in the east to Minogashima in the west. This assent extended well into the 1580s. Even after Toyotomi Hideyoshi (1537–98) had begun to unify Japan, the wider population continued to clamor for sea-lord protection. In 1586, the Jesuit Luís Fróis (1532–97) recorded a purported conversation in which Noshima Murakami Takeyoshi asked the Jesuits why they needed his protection if they had the goodwill of Toyotomi Hideyoshi. The Jesuits supposedly replied that only Takeyoshi could protect them on the seas.[63] As will be seen in other chapters in this volume, the use of protection businesses for establishing dominion was common among piratical groups in East Asia, including those of Wang Zhi, Zheng Chenggong, and Zhang Bao.

Mercenarism

Reputations garnered through protection businesses enhanced perceptions of the Noshima and other sea lords as valuable mercenaries in the long-running civil wars of the sixteenth century. Mercenarism constitutes part of nonstate, or "extraterritorial violence," in that it can mean, "enlisting in ... a foreign army."[64] Given the degree of autonomy achieved by sea lords, such a definition can help us understand the different ways in which sea lords and patrons perceived sea lord mercenarism and associated military tactics. In this period, *daimyo* and other competing state-level authorities recognized sea lord maritime operations as indispensable, but also at times, negative. Sea lords may have heightened this sense of "necessary evil" felt by their patrons by playing sponsors against one another in order to ensure their continued autonomy. In addition, the methods used by sea lord bands when engaging in mercenary naval enterprises often resembled those that they used in expanding their domains, spreading their reputations, and generating revenue through protection businesses: commerce-raiding and intercepting ships in chokepoints.

We can see the importance to sea lords of protection businesses as both a mercenary service and a reward in an examination of the licensed protection business the Noshima Murakami won in 1542 for switching sponsors from Kōno Michinao (d.1572), a *daimyo* in Shikoku, to Ōuchi Yoshitaka (1507–51), a powerful *daimyo* of western Honshu. The Noshima lord received legal protection for intercepting at the important religious and commercial island of Itsukushima and various inlets and bays vessels engaged in overseas trade, and then imposing "lading tolls" upon them to ensure the ships' safety.[65] Control of several chokepoints, especially the port and barrier of Shiwaku, made the Noshima ideally suited to regulate this traffic. By doing so, they worked to eliminate the shipping of Ōuchi Yoshitaka's competitors and protect his own, thus increasing protection costs for the Ōuchi's enemies and reducing them for the Ōuchi and their allies. The Noshima's mercenary protection business also helped stimulate further development of Itsukushima as a commercial entrepôt. Part of protection entailed escorting ships to Itsukushima,[66] where shipmasters, merchants, and other travelers found established markets for overseas luxuries such as silks.[67]

Noshima perceptions of their own autonomy, however, meant that attempts on the part of sponsors to change the deal risked violent retribution. Abrogation of the Itsukushima-based toll-taking privileges in 1552, by Sue Harukata (1521–55; Harukata overthrew Ōuchi Yoshitaka in 1551), caused the Noshima to reportedly "cause unforeseen incidents" using "pirate ships ... from Shiwaku."[68]

Sea lords demonstrated significant agency in exploiting *daimyo* dependence on their mercenarism. The record of the Noshima Murakami's participation in an on-again/off-again proxy war between 1561 and 1571 for two battling *daimyo*, Mōri Motonari (1497–1571) and Ōtomo Sōrin (1530–87) vividly illustrates the degree of autonomy inhering in sea lord mercenarism. Both *daimyo* employed sea lords to seize control of the chokepoint known today as the Straits of Shimonoseki. This narrow channel divides Honshu and Kyushu and, at the time, contained several busy ports, thus making it a highly strategic location for aspiring hegemons. Both the Mōri and the Ōtomo employed sea lord mercenaries to extend their influence into this maritime frontier zone, where they otherwise would have been unable to advance. Repeatedly, the Mōri specified in their letters to the Noshima the phrase "traffic lanes," meaning the chokepoint of Shimonoseki.[69]

For the Noshima, each stage of the conflict meant a new opportunity to negotiate with sponsors to secure the best deal, whether the confirmation of title to littoral holdings secured during the struggle, acquiescence to additional protection businesses, or sworn promises to seek adjudication in cases of disagreement.[70] The Noshima did not hesitate to switch sides multiple times during the conflict to gain the greatest benefit, even when dalliances with the Ōtomo led the Mōri to sponsor a siege of the Noshima home island that ended with Noshima sending hostages to the Mōri.[71] It should be noted that these reversals in and of themselves commonly occurred in Japanese society at that time,[72] but the case of sea lords suggests selling services to multiple sponsors as mercenaries instead of backstabbing for political gain. Even after suffering several incidences of Noshima side-switching in the 1560s and 1570s, the Mōri still entrusted the Noshima with management of part of the port of Akamagaseki, the most valuable on the Straits of Shimonoseki.[73]

Evidence from battles also shows how patrons and sea lords perceived military campaigns in different ways. Patrons viewed battles as sites where they sanctioned the deployment of violence for strategic purposes, whereas sea lords seem to have taken full advantage of them to enrich themselves while they weakened the patron's enemy. In one 1561 battle for the Straits of Shimonoseki, the Noshima and other Mōri-sponsored sea lords seized ships, prisoners (to sell as slaves), and horses.[74]

Sea lords performed many mercenary services that *daimyo* both disparaged as practices of "military irregulars" (*zōhyō*) and regarded as indispensable tools of war including piracy, arson, sneak attacks, and slave-taking as well as trading.[75] Obviously, many of these actions also had significant, maritime-work meanings for sea lords. Records of maritime ambush provide especially multivalent, dialogic descriptions, in that we can read them as significant for both sponsors' land-based discourse and sea lords' maritime practice. The diary of the Korean ambassador from 1420 contains a vivid example of multiple significations embedded in a portrayal of how seafaring bands fortified themselves within a chokepoint with the intent of catching potential prey by surprise:

> In the middle of the sea astride our path are stone islets resembling birds' heads ... It was here that in 1395 ... one pirate vessel hid behind this small island ... All the gifts and naval stores and even clothes were taken ... As our ship gradually approached the island, a small vessel emerged from it and raced towards us with the speed of an arrow. Our crew all clamored, shouting, 'They're pirates!'[76]

The ambassador also related how, on other occasions, travelers, sailors, and even other pirates employed for protection, often could not reliably determine whether a strange ship that they had spotted was a fishing smack or a pirate ship masquerading as a fishing boat.[77] For sea lords, the ability to catch ships by surprise and sow such confusion represented a valuable tool to employ in protection businesses — and thus sea tenure. By contrast, *daimyo* perceived the same as a naval tactical advantage, whereas the ambassador saw one more threat from the sea. The terror inspired by pirates' reputations and possible sea lord reprisals made any ship a potential threat for travelers, which further increased the capacity of sea lords to extort protection.

Conclusion

This volume focuses on the histories of seafarers labeled pirates across East and Southeast Asia, what we have called the greater China Seas region. In as much as many of those figures designated pirates throughout this volume employed nonstate violence, we ought not necessarily accept the terms outsiders applied to them. Rather, we can use the idea of border crossing, of "betweenness," as a way of considering how pirates viewed themselves. The case of the sea lords of the Seto Inland Sea in fifteenth- and sixteenth-century Japan suggests several ways that so-called pirates self-identified in this vein. Aware of land-based representations of the sea, sea people, and pirates, some leaders of seafaring bands were able to force acceptance of themselves as lords of maritime networks by using terra-centric forms of representation — especially of lordship — to their own advantage. To retain their autonomy, sea lords developed and purveyed forms of nonstate violence that played on land-based authorities' dual perceptions of the sea. By accepting the sponsorship of *daimyo* and other elites, they conformed to the land-based ideal of an incorporated and servile sea, but their independence and mobility in the deployment of violence substantiated land-based fears about a dangerous, exotic maritime world. Especially important for sea lords were the chokepoints that land-based authorities considered ambiguous border zones, but which sea lords used as bases for lucrative protection businesses. They used protection practices to define the limits of their domain; to receive external validation of their autonomous, sea-based power; and to become indispensable assets of land-based elites eager to expand their own military, commercial, and political dominion. At the same time, sea lord mercenaries sold these services to the highest bidder, playing sponsors one against another for maximum gain and maximum autonomy.

In the end, however, the instability engendered by a reliance on sea lord nonstate violence coupled with the transformation of the images of *kaizoku* from sea bandits to sea lords rendered the latter a threat to the new, early modern state that emerged in the 1590s. Toyotomi Hideyoshi and later the Tokugawa Shoguns (1603–1867) stringently outlawed the private exercise of naval violence. Although they lost their autonomous sea-based domains, many sea lords, including the Noshima Murakami and Tagaya, took advantage of the widespread acceptance of their self-representation in forms of land-based lordship to transform themselves into members of the warrior elite (minor *daimyo* and samurai) in early modern Japan.[78]

4

Merchants, Smugglers, and Pirates:
Multinational Clandestine Trade on the South China Coast, 1520–50

James K. Chin

Since the 1980s, the shadow or hidden economy has increasingly become a controversial topic among scholars and policymakers, but is hardly anything new since we can easily discover similar illicit activities in the history of the premodern world and, particularly, in maritime Asia. We can single out the first half of the sixteenth century, for example, as a crucial period in the history of maritime China, when numerous Chinese smugglers and pirates flocked to its southern coast, bartering with merchants from different countries. This period saw a new maritime economy and regional trade system emerging on the South China coast with joint ventures and emporia established through close collaborations between Chinese merchant-pirates and multinational smugglers from Japan, Ryukyu, Portugal, and port polities of Southeast Asia.

Based mainly on contemporary Chinese and Portuguese accounts, this chapter re-examines the smuggling trade along the southern coast of China during the first half of the sixteenth century, focusing on the years from 1520 to 1550. I take issue with the conventional views widely held among Chinese historians that have repeatedly condemned the smuggling trade and piracy on the South China coast and have perceived multinational traders as evil barbarian intruders.[1] Without doubt, piracy and kidnapping, closely associated with rampant smuggling, negatively or even destructively impacted the local social order. But here I would argue that booming illicit commerce on the South China coast, which lay outside the control of the imperial court and deviated from official political norms and formal economic institutions, had in fact greatly facilitated the development of a commodity economy in local society. Furthermore, clandestine trade supplemented what the legitimate and regulated imperial economy failed to provide. In other words, the shadow economy of sixteenth-century China, represented by the smuggling trade on the South China coast, contributed positively to the rise and formation of a new type of maritime economy in East Asia, though it only existed for a short period until the Ming government put it to an end.[2]

The Rise of the Smuggling Trade on the South China Coast

A large scale smuggling trade involving multinational traders on the southeastern coast of China did not appear until the 1520s. The coming of the *Feringhees* or Portuguese significantly influenced this change in the landscape of maritime China. Their first contacts with China occurred sometime in the early sixteenth century, shortly after a Portuguese fleet, led by Afonso de Albuquerque, had conquered Malacca followed by a number of merchant-adventurers who sailed for the South China coast in Southeast Asian native junks.

The earliest Portuguese visit to the South China coast dates back to 1517, when their first mission, led by Fernão Peres de Andrade, anchored in the Pearl River near the metropolis of Canton. A year later, a detachment of this squadron, under Jorge Mascarenhas, was sent to explore trading opportunities and the rumored gold mines on Ryukyu. On route to those islands, Mascarenhas stopped in Chincheo, perhaps part of today's Zhangzhou in southern Fujian, and stayed for several months. Unfortunately, no further mention exists of any subsequent trading voyages by the Portuguese to this region, leaving Mascarenhas' trip an isolated business venture.

When did the Portuguese start to shift their commercial activities from the Canton region to the Fujian and Zhejiang coast? It seems neither the Portuguese sources nor the official Chinese records clearly answer this question, but we can confirm that by 1540, the Portuguese had already well-established themselves on the Zhejiang coast. The actual period for the formation of an international smuggling trade emporium on the China coast and its relation to the early Portuguese commercial activities in China, nevertheless, remains quite vague and only appears in private Chinese sources. One of the Hokkien literati, Deng Zhong, wrote that, in 1524, when the chaos on the Zhejiang coast caused an overstocking of commodities for overseas trade at Shuangyu Island, many commercial ships roamed everywhere on the sea, including Portuguese vessels and junks from Japan and Ryukyu.[3] Another contemporary private Chinese record, written by Zheng Shungong, clearly pointed out that, Deng Liao, a Hokkien trader who had broken out of jail and fled to sea in 1526, initiated the maritime smuggling trade on the Zhejiang coast. Shortly afterwards, Deng led a group of "barbarian traders" (*fanyi*) to privately barter with the local populace.[4] In other words, between 1524 and 1526, a sizable smuggling trade, conducted jointly by Portuguese, Southeast Asian, Chinese, and Japanese merchants, established itself on Shuangyu Island off the Zhejiang coast (see Map 4.1).

Three factors support my previous contention and explain the reasons why the Portuguese found it necessary to move to the Zhejiang coast in the 1520s. First, an unfortunate conflict occurred in 1522 between the Portuguese fleet led by Martim Afonso de Melo Coutinho, Diogo de Melo, and Pedro Homem and the Chinese naval forces at Xicao Bay in Xinhui County off the Guangdong coast. The Ming government announced shortly afterwards a stern maritime trade prohibition

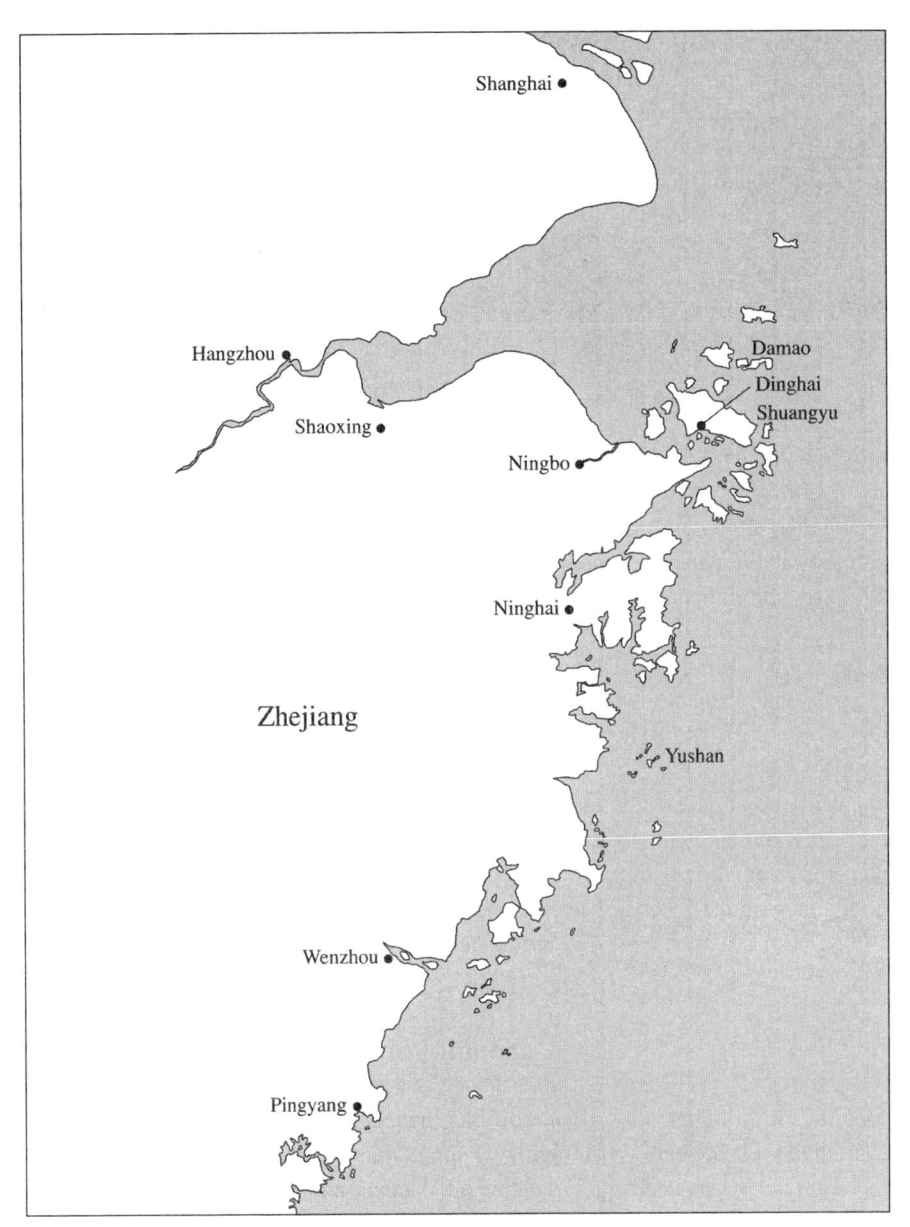

Map 4.1 Shuangyu Island and the Zhejiang Coast, c. 1550

targeted against the Portuguese, banning coastal Chinese from conducting business with the Iberians. Facing such a hopeless deadlock, the Portuguese had no choice but to seek new trade opportunities in other places. Second, in 1523, a serious armed battle between the Japanese tribute missions and the Chinese local government in Zhejiang suddenly broke out in Ningbo, resulting in the deaths of a large number of Chinese residents. Consequently, the regular tribute trade between China and Japan halted temporarily, and the Ming court issued a similar harsh order proscribing Chinese from trading with the Japanese. It not only forced Chinese sea merchants to engage in smuggling but also closed the former maritime market at Ningbo, an action that directly resulted in the formation of a popular international smuggling trade center at Shuangyu in 1524. Third, a direct and important reason for the Portuguese to shift their business to the Zhejiang and Fujian coasts stemmed from their desire to evade the tariffs levied by the Ming government. A private account by Yu Dayou, the Regional Military Commander, mentioned that the Portuguese went to Shuangyu because they wanted to avoid paying the heavy maritime duties imposed in Guangdong.[5] In other words, immediately after the conflict between China and both the Portuguese and the Japanese on China's southeastern coast, and sometime around late 1523 to early 1524, a burgeoning international smuggling trade emporium emerged on Shuangyu Island. Large numbers of maritime traders from China, Japan, Southeast Asia, and Europe flocked to the island to do business. During this period, the Portuguese started to move their illicit trading activities from Guangdong to Zhejiang and Fujian.

Apart from Shuangyu, the smugglers also used a number of other islands and harbors scattered along the Zhejiang and Fujian coasts as trading posts, among them, an important base on the small island of Damao, near Shuangyu. On the Fujian coast, islands inhabited for short periods by multinational smugglers, included Dadan, Wuzhouyu (today's Jinmen Island), and Nan'ao, as well as a wide range of tiny islands that dotted the coast, such as Meiling and Zoumaxi.

The Formation of an International Smuggling Entrepôt on Shuangyu Island

A profusion of small ports and anchorages along the Fujian and Zhejiang coasts served as temporary smuggling settlements by the sixteenth century. Principally because of the arrival of Portuguese traders, with their exotic commodities and tropical Southeast Asian products, Shuangyu quickly rose above the other numerous obscure offshore islands, and developed into a flourishing smuggling entrepôt between 1524 and 1526. It functioned as a smugglers' mart for roughly twenty years until the Ming forces under Zhu Wan completely destroyed it in 1548. During the first decade, according to Chinese records, Shuangyu merely operated as a seasonal trade outpost, where Chinese smugglers and their Portuguese counterparts erected temporary matsheds to house themselves and their goods during the trading season. Afterwards, they burned or dismantled their sites before they sailed away with the monsoon. Nevertheless, facilitated by the new commercial opportunities brought in by Portuguese traders, the center of China's private maritime trade began to shift from southern Fujian to the Zhejiang coast.

The situation changed considerably after 1539, when a number of Chinese smugglers and traders from coastal Fujian started guiding foreign merchants from Patani and Malacca to barter at Shuangyu Island. Soon, they were occupying the island. In that year, a Hokkien merchant, Jin Zilao, piloted a group of Westerners to Shuangyu, and, in the following year, another notorious Hokkien smuggler-pirate, Li Guangtou (Baldy Li), joined him. Together, they led an assortment of foreign traders and adventurers, including Portuguese, to the island.[6]

Around the same time an influential Chinese sea merchant syndicate headed by the Xu brothers moved its commercial base from the Malay Peninsula to the Zhejiang coast, and established settlements at Shuangyu and Damao. Again, a band of Portuguese traders and Southeast Asian businessmen accompanied the Chinese smugglers.[7] As the Xu brothers' cartel demonstrated financial power, and maintained a close partnership with the Portuguese, more and more small smuggling groups started to submit themselves to the Xu brothers, in turn triggering a wave of internal mergers among the Chinese smuggling groups, including the one commanded by Li Guangtou. As a consequence, the Xu brothers' syndicate became the most powerful smuggling bloc on the South China coast by 1542.

Fearing that smuggling on the Zhejiang coast had become uncontrollable, in 1543 the Ming government sent war junks to eradicate the clandestine activities centered at Shuangyu (see Figure 4.1). However, the smuggler-traders led by the Xu brothers seriously checked the military campaign, wounding and killing many of the soldiers and officials.[8] Judging from the advanced types of guns and cannons used by the smugglers, the Portuguese very likely participated in the naval battles, and probably, even fought for the Xu brothers.[9] The victory the multinational smugglers achieved in their clashes with the Ming coastal forces paved the way for smugglers to create a sizable community at Shuangyu. From that time onwards, they not only established trading settlements on islands off the Zhejiang coast, but gradually expanded their activities to markets in southern Fujian, eastern Guangdong, and even to the city of Nanjing. Shuangyu served as their smuggling business hub.[10] Headed by the Xu brothers, thousands of smuggles and petty traders from fishing villages and towns of South China congregated on a number of islands near Dinghai in Zhejiang.[11] Along with the Portuguese and other overseas merchants, Chinese smugglers enjoyed lucrative profits while inadvertently making contributions towards building a commercial economy using clandestine methods.

Figure 4.1 Ming Dynasty War Junk
(Source: Zheng Ruozeng, *Chouhai tubian*, 1562)

The heyday of Shuangyu Island as an international smuggling entrepôt, however, did not arrive until 1544, when Wang Zhi led a band of adventurers from Kyushu and joined the Xu brothers syndicate. Wang Zhi's alliance with the Xu brothers became especially significant for the rapid expansion of the smuggling trade in the open waters of East Asia. It not only underlined the importance of the formation of a forceful smuggling consortium comprising individuals from different Chinese dialect groups, particularly those from southern Fujian and Huizhou (in today's Anhui Province), but it also marked the opening of a new Chinese clandestine trading market in southern Japan. As Wang Zhi had already established himself in Kyushu before he moved back to the Zhejiang coast, his return with his Japanese business partners consequently helped the smuggling traders based at Shuangyu easily extend their informal commercial activities to Japan, which, in turn, created an important linkage connecting two major regional maritime trade zones.

Also, in 1544, as explained in Igawa Kenji's chapter, a Japanese tribute mission arrived in Zhejiang, but the Ming court refused to meet them. The Japanese private maritime traders who sailed to China with them had no choice but to barter with multinational smugglers based at Shuangyu. After completing the transactions, Wang

Zhi led a group of Chinese smuggler-pirates together with the Japanese mission back to Japan to conduct business.[12] The following year, more private Japanese sea merchants traveled to Shuangyu guided by Wang Zhi.[13] Thereafter, until its demise in 1548, more and more Japanese traders made their way to the Zhejiang coast, and Shuangyu quickly developed into the biggest smuggling entrepôt in maritime East Asia with commodities imported from Europe and Asia.

Chinese Clandestine Traders

In the sixteenth century a large number of petty traders, fishermen, and local inhabitants took part in the flourishing smuggling trade on the South China coast. From contemporary accounts, we can discern three groups of Chinese smugglers and pirates active in the waters of the greater China Seas region: one, those based in Southeast Asia, two, those based in Kyushu, and three, those based in South China.

Chinese smuggler-traders based in Southeast Asia. From the fifteenth through the seventeenth centuries, a number of Southeast Asian emporia, such as Malacca, Patani, Pahang, and Manila, became booming trading ports frequented by Chinese smugglers, pirates, and merchants (see Map 1.1 on p. 4). Because the Ming government prohibited the coastal Chinese from sailing overseas, and banned those who had ventured out to sea from returning home, a large number of Chinese maritime merchants involuntarily turned into smugglers and established their commercial bases in overseas trading ports. Among these adventurers, the Hokkien merchants Deng Liao and the Xu brothers led the earliest smuggling groups.

According to Zheng Shungong, a Guangdong merchant whom the Ming government had sent to investigate the *wakō* situation in Kyushu in 1556, the smuggling trade started on the Fujian coast in the early 1520s. The Xu brothers founded and controlled, he said, the most influential smuggling group. The Xu family had four sons (Xu Song, Xu Dong, Xu Nan, and Xu Zi). Like Deng Liao, they participated in maritime trade-cum-piracy. Xu Dong (or Xu Er, the second brother)[14] and Deng Liao had been arrested and jailed in Fujian in the early 1520s. Sometime around 1526, they managed to escape with a group of smugglers and fled to sea. While Xu Dong established himself in Patani, his young brother, Xu Nan, went to trade in Malacca, and both of them married local women. Soon afterwards, the eldest brother, Xu Song, and the youngest brother, Xu Zi, sneaked out to join them, and together the four brothers built up a huge smuggling business with headquarters on the Malay Peninsula.

The Xu brothers actively conducted their maritime trade in Southeast Asia for more than ten years until 1540, when they directed the Portuguese to trade clandestinely on the Zhejiang coast. Collaborating with them, the Xu brothers established temporary trading settlements on offshore islands such as Shuangyu and

Damao. Similarly, in combination with the Hokkien smuggler-pirate, Li Guangtou, they plundered coastal villages in Fujian and Zhejiang while also trading with private Japanese merchants in Hakata on Kyushu.[15]

After the Xu brothers shifted their businesses to the China coast and Kyushu in the 1540s, another group of Chinese merchant-pirates controlled by He Yaba and Zheng Zongxing emerged in Patani. He and Zheng both came from Dongguan County, near the bustling metropolis of Canton. In 1554, they led a few hundred sojourning Chinese merchants and a group of Portuguese traders from Patani to barter with the Chinese on the coasts of Guangdong and Fujian. However, this venture failed, ending up with the deaths of 26 and the arrests of 119 smugglers by Ming coastal forces near Macau, and the further apprehension of He Yaba. The rest of the smugglers fled back to Patani.[16] The Chinese navy possibly also killed and captured some Portuguese during this campaign, but the Chinese sources remain silent on this matter.

Pahang also operated as a key trading port in the sixteenth and seventeenth centuries. Lin Jian, a venturous Chinese merchant-pirate, established his base there. Although sources give us no detailed information on Lin's background, Ming records indicate that he headed a sojourning Chinese commercial community in Pahang in the early sixteenth century. He controlled a large junk fleet that frequently plied between different trading ports in Southeast Asia, either doing business or plundering on the sea. In 1547, for instance, in collaboration with the Xu brothers, Lin led a fleet of over seventy junks from Pahang to raid the Zhejiang coast.[17] Very likely, a number of Malay or Siamese maritime traders participated in the fleet, though the contemporary Chinese records only vaguely depict them as "pirate gangs" (*zeizhong*).

Chinese smuggler-pirates based in Kyushu in southern Japan. Traditionally the island of Kyushu served as the hub for Chinese maritime trade in northeast Asia. The feudal lords of Kyushu actually welcomed and protected the smuggling trade on the island, since they eagerly wished to strengthen themselves economically by fostering overseas trade with Chinese merchants. Gradually, at least seven Chinese commercial sojourning communities emerged on the island of Kyushu, particularly in Bungo-no-kuni, Hirado of Hizen, and Satsuma (see Map 5.1 on p. 61). The Chinese maritime traders came mostly from southern Fujian and coastal Zhejiang.

Of those Chinese merchant-pirates based in Kyushu in the sixteenth century, without doubt, Wang Zhi stood out as the most important.[18] He hailed from Huizhou, and had operated as a wealthy salt merchant for years before the Ming court forced him to venture out to sea and became a merchant-pirate, known by the name, Wang Wufeng.[19] He started his maritime career in 1540, when the Ming court temporarily relaxed its control over private maritime trade. Wang traveled to Guangdong with several business partners including Ye Zongman, Xu Weixue, and Xie He, where they built huge trading junks. Together they traded in Japan,

Siam, and other emporia of Southeast Asia with goods purchased in China, such as saltpeter, silks, cotton textiles, and rhubarb.[20] Within five or six years, Wang rose to prominence among the Chinese maritime merchants, respected by his peers, who called him Captain Wufeng.[21]

It should be observed that Wang's advancement originated in his links with the Xu brothers. Earlier in his maritime career, Wang worked for his fellow-townsman and renowned merchant-pirate, Xu Dong (Xu Er), and he helped the Xu brothers run their routine overseas trading concern. Because of his exceptional abilities in business management and maritime transactions, shortly afterwards, the Xu brothers elevated Wang to financial supervisor (*guanku*) for their family on Shuangyu, and, before long, they again promoted him to the positions of commander of the armed fleet (*guanshao*) and councilor on military affairs (*liaoli junshi*). As John Wills has pointed out, Wang's foreign contacts and control of Xu Dong's wealth aided his emergence as the new leader of Xu's organization in 1548–49, after Xu Dong fled China.[22] Additionally, one should note that Wang Zhi had already controlled the Xu brothers' vessels prior to that time, which helps to explain why Wang did not face any opposition to his assuming control of the Xu syndicate. While Wang Zhi remained a key merchant-pirate based in Kyushu in the mid-sixteenth century, interestingly, he never personally commanded an attack on the coast of South China, but he always stayed on his island bases or in Kyushu. His partners or subordinates usually led the pillaging expeditions.

Xu Hai also deserves mention as an influential merchant-pirate based in Kyushu in the mid-sixteenth century. Xu Hai, like Wang Zhi, also came from Huizhou. However, unlike Wang, Xu started his career as a monk at Hangzhou's famous Lingyin Temple when he was young, and stayed there for many years. His younger brother, Xu Hong, took part in the cloth business in Wuxi, and his uncle, Xu Weixue, ran an overseas smuggling business as Wang Zhi's partner. Xu Hai left the temple and joined his uncle in 1551; and people in Kyushu warmly welcomed and respected him because of his former role as a Buddhist monk. Around this time, however, after Ming troops killed his uncle on Nan'ao Island, Xu Hai became a pirate in order to pay off his uncle's debt to a Japanese business partner in Osumi. Collaborating with Japanese merchant-pirates from Izumi, Satsuma, Hizen, Higo, Tsusyu, Tsushima, Chikugo, Bungo, and Kii, Xu Hai led a huge naval fleet to plunder the Zhejiang coast between 1554 and 1556. Assisted by Ye Ming, Chen Dong, and a Japanese chieftain, Shingoro, Xu's forces expanded rapidly in the mid-1550s. During the heyday of his piracy, contemporary accounts recorded that he controlled more than one thousand junks with no fewer than sixty thousand pirate-smugglers.[23]

Chinese merchant-pirates based in southern China. The majority of the Chinese merchant-pirates actually roamed actively along the South China coast, using offshore islands as their smuggling trade centers. Relatively few based themselves in entrepôts in Japan and Southeast Asia. Among the large number of South China-based merchant-pirates, three prominent Hokkiens merit notice, Xie He, Hong Dizhen, and Zhang Wei.

Xie He, an experienced maritime trader from Zhangzhou in southern Fujian, began his smuggling career with Wang Zhi. Xie lived for a short period on Goto Island in Kyushu prior to his return to China with Wang in 1557. Joining Xu Chaoguang, a Chaozhou merchant-pirate, and other bands of pirates and bandits, Xie launched a large-scale pillaging raid on the port of Yuegang in Zhangzhou in the summer of 1557.[24]

Hong Dizhen, Xie's fellow-townsman, also took part in Wang Zhi's syndicate, and had engaged in the smuggling trade for many years. Hong joined Xie in late 1557, after Wang had been tricked into surrendering to the Ming authorities and was later executed. Hong and Xie established themselves on Wuyu Island off the Fujian coast, and directed a fleet with more than three thousand pirates to plunder coastal villages and towns. Hong's conversion to piracy provides a revealing example that helps explain why many coastal Chinese became pirates. According to the local gazetteer, Hong made his fortune operating in the maritime trade between the smuggling ports of south Fujian and east Guangdong. He assisted coastal residents in bartering clandestinely with foreign traders, which offended the Ming government. But local Fujian officials failed to capture Hong, whom coastal inhabitants protected and supported. As a result, the government imprisoned his family members as a punishment, which, in turn, forced Hong into piracy.[25] Simply put, as in Hong's case, the Chinese government had actually forced large numbers of Chinese maritime merchants of the sixteenth century to join the pirates and bandits.

In another example, Zhang Wei, a minor Hokkien trader from Yuegang, led a large uprising against the Ming government. Historically it was a common practice among coastal Hokkien residents to venture out to sea to pursue high profits by conducting maritime trade. Pooling capital together, in 1557, twenty-four petty traders led by Zhang Wei built a junk in hopes of making profits through transactions with overseas foreign traders. Because of the Ming sea bans, the government did not tolerate such activities, and sent three hundred soldiers to arrest them, thereby triggering a wide-scale popular revolt. Again, unsurprisingly, government actions compelled Zhang Wei and his cohorts to join the pirates, and to organize local residents to attack the Fujian coast with the assistance of other bands of raiders.[26]

Collaborations between Multinational Traders and Coastal Chinese

For more than twenty years, multinational smuggling led by the Portuguese enjoyed a booming and successful trade along the Fujian and Zhejiang coasts, primarily due to the support and assistance of Chinese coastal residents, local gentry, and even some Ming officials. People in the region openly traded with and supplied smugglers and pirates. Chinese merchants and gentry frequently played the role of business brokers. While the area's literati and traders were quietly doing business with the Portuguese, its fishermen acted as pilots for Portuguese vessels. Officials and their underlings sometimes collaborated with smugglers in exchange for a share of the profits.[27]

As shown previously, Ming sources clearly demonstrate that Chinese maritime merchants took part in the smuggling trade and they directed the Portuguese to trade on the China coast in the sixteenth century, routinely handling the actual business for the Portuguese in their capacity as commercial intermediaries. Since the Portuguese did not understand the Chinese language or customs, they could not easily conduct transactions with local Chinese. As a result, having no other alternatives, the Portuguese trusted prominent Chinese merchants, making them their business brokers or agents, and asking them to sell commodities brought in from tropical Asia on the Portuguese's behalf without paying any security deposit. When Chinese merchants had sold or bartered all the goods with coastal residents, they would then return to Shuangyu Island, distribute the products they had acquired to their Portuguese partners, and divide the profits. The Xu brothers, for instance, usually had credit-sale agreements with their Portuguese associates and could thus obtain all the imported goods from them without a guarantee. Xu Dong and his brothers bargained with the residents of Ningbo and Shaoxing, two wealthy regions in Zhejiang, and afterwards, repaid the Portuguese upon completion of the entire business venture.[28]

People based in the ports of Southeast Asia normally traded on the Zhejiang coast with pepper, sapanwood, ivory, and clove consigned by Portuguese merchants. Surprisingly, on occasion, the Portuguese even provided the Chinese traders with guns and swords in order to guard against pirates.[29] The credit-sale mechanism, to a large extent, helped the Portuguese and the Chinese merchants form a mutually beneficial business partnership. Nevertheless, it also laid the foundations for a crisis that eventually led to the demise of Portuguese commercial activities along the Zhejiang and Fujian coasts. When the Chinese merchants went bankrupt or lost their cargoes and, as a consequence, could not pay off debts borrowed from their Portuguese business counterparts, it would inevitably trigger an internal armed conflict, causing the local government great concern, and finally, inviting military intervention and a crackdown from the Ming court.[30]

Not only private traders, but also local Ming officials and soldiers participated in the smuggling trade and accepted bribes from the Portuguese. Collaborating with maritime traders from different countries, authorities profited from the smuggling trade despite the continuous prohibitions issued from the imperial court. In Ningbo and Shaoxing, for example, local officials collected rice, money and other official commodities from government storage under the guise of official business and traded these items with the Portuguese anchored at Shuangyu.[31]

Among the different groups, the Hokkien merchants from Quanzhou and Zhangzhou in Fujian remained the most active.[32] To escape the monitoring of government authorities, Hokkien merchants usually ordered their junks built in Gaozhou or Chaozhou in eastern Guangdong. Afterwards, they sailed to Ningbo and Shaoxing in Zhejiang to purchase cargoes before setting out to sea. Likewise, merchants from Zhejiang and Guangdong chose Zhangzhou and Quanzhou of southern Fujian as the places to construct their junks and to buy their goods.[33] Moreover, these smuggler-merchants often deposited their merchandise at the homes of local fishermen, and later sold them when the Portuguese arrived.[34] In such a clandestine way, Chinese smugglers successfully managed to act as brokers for the Portuguese. The first groups of Chinese to become acquainted with the Portuguese and to establish business links with them included merchants from the coastal regions of Guangdong, Fujian, and Zhejiang. Around 1557, when Macau officially opened as the key trading emporium for the Portuguese in maritime East Asia, a large number of Hokkiens, Cantonese, and Zhejiang natives moved there to become commercial interpreters for the Portuguese.[35]

During this period, the first group of Portuguese reached Japan with Wang Zhi's assistance. Understandably, Satsuma and the nearby island of Tanegashima played special roles in the Kyushu trade and maritime traffic in the early sixteenth century. In 1542, three Portuguese merchants, António de Mota, Francisco Zeimoto, and António Peixote, traveled on board a Chinese junk that had set off from Siam. They intended to head for Canton but the junk floated down to the "Chincheo" coast (probably the area around Zhangzhou) in southern Fujian. With the cooperation of local Chinese authorities, they succeed in bartering with Hokkien merchants and set sail again. Unfortunately, a storm blew them off course, and they drifted ashore near Cape Kadokura on the southern tip of Tanegashima Island.[36]

Although the Portuguese source does not specify on whose junk they made this trip and "discovered" Japan, contemporary Japanese documents mention Wang Zhi's name when describing the ways the Portuguese introduced muskets into Tanegashima. According to *Teppōki* or *Account of the Guns*, in the eighth lunar month of 1543, a huge disabled junk reached Tanegashima with more than one hundred passengers on board, among them, one of the Chinese literati, Wufeng (i.e., Wang Zhi). Since local residents could not understand the language spoken by them, Wufeng communicated with the village head by writing Chinese characters on the sand with a stick. He told the islanders that on his junk, the passengers included three foreigners — barbarian traders from the southwestern part of the world, who had no knowledge of local customs. With the help of Wang Zhi, the Portuguese merchants not only established friendly relations with the people there, but also introduced Western firearms, called *teppō* or iron guns, to Tokitaka, the feudal lord of Tanegashima. Since then, every year, Tanegashima has held the *Teppō Matsuri* (Gun Festival) to commemorate the arrival of the first group of Portuguese.[37]

In short, Chinese smugglers contributed considerably towards the Portuguese maritime activities in Asia. They not only induced the Portuguese to trade on the coast of South China, but also brought them to Japan. With the help and guidance of Chinese traders, fishermen, and smugglers, more and more Portuguese merchants started to gather at the clandestine trading settlements along the Zhejiang coast, especially at Shuangyu.

It requires emphasizing, however, that the Portuguese did not always treat the Chinese merchant-pirates as their business partners. They disposed of the Chinese once the opportunity permitted or if they threatened their business interests. For reasons unknown to us, sometime around 1548, Portuguese forces annihilated Lin Jian and his followers off the Chinese coast. Interestingly, this account does not appear in official Ming records, but rather, in the private letter of an influential Hokkien gentry, Lin Xiyuan, which mentions that the Portuguese helped the Ming government to pacify the pirates.[38]

Lin Xiyuan also provided the following description of the daily business activities of the *Feringhees* or Portuguese along with their relations with local Chinese society:

> The *Feringhees* who came [to Fujian], brought their local pepper, sapanwood, ivory, thyme-oil, aloes, sandalwood, and all kinds of incense in order to trade with our coastal residents, and the price of their goods were particularly cheap. Their daily necessities, such as quantities of rice, flour, pigs, and fowls, were provided by our people. The prices which they paid for them were double the usual amount, and therefore our coastal residents were happy to trade with them. They did not invade our frontier region, nor did they slaughter or plunder our people. Moreover, in fearing that pirate activities might hamper their business they even helped us to expel pirates when they first came here. As a consequence, pirates are all scared of them and dare not to plunder anymore … Given such facts, we could say that the *Feringhees* have never been pirates; instead they expelled pirates for us. They have never been a threat to our people. On the contrary, what they did is good for our people. While our government desperately plans to expel them, I do not think this is a correct decision.[39]

Without doubt, local Chinese on the Zhejiang and Fujian coasts welcomed the arrival of the Portuguese, and believed that they were their friends, protectors, and business partners. The quote detailed above not only expressed one Hokkien gentry's opinion, but indicated the general view of maritime society in South China at that time. Unfortunately, however, Chinese historians have frequently criticized such a representative comment from a contemporary private Chinese record as politically incorrect.[40]

The previous descriptions clearly show that the smuggling trade conducted along the Zhejiang and Fujian coasts from the late 1520s to 1550s, with Shuangyu Island as its center, actually formed a shadow economy. Apart from the Chinese, Portuguese, Japanese, and Ryukyuan smugglers, a large number of traders from Southeast Asian port-polities such as Siam, Cambodia, Java, and Pahang also appeared in the relevant historical sources. While Portuguese merchants primarily led the smuggling trade of the mid-sixteenth century that revolved around the South China coast, a plethora of Asian traders, either from China, Japan, or Southeast Asia, also participated. In this sense, such a joint business effort resembled an international one, although it ultimately failed due to the restrictive maritime policies adopted by the Ming authorities.

Conclusion

From approximately 1520 to 1550, for nearly thirty years the Portuguese and other foreign traders conducted clandestine business activities along the South China coast, having shifted their main operations from Guangdong southward to Fujian and Zhejiang. Assisted and guided by private Chinese maritime merchants and smugglers, multinational traders not only established themselves on islands off the Zhejiang coast, especially at Shuangyu, but also formed a sizable international trading network throughout maritime Asia.

The credit-sale mechanism, as briefly discussed above, contributed to the formation of business partnerships between the Portuguese and the Chinese smuggler-traders. When unexpected business failures occurred, however, the same mechanism resulted in unfortunate consequences. The Chinese smugglers who could not collect their payments and dared not face their Portuguese business partners simply fled or sought aid from local authorities at the expense of the Portuguese. Commercial disputes caused by business debts, not guaranteed by written legal contracts, eventually led to conflicts and Ming military crackdowns, which ended the once prosperous international trade emporiums. The experiences of the multinational traders on the South China coast during this short period proved tragic insofar as it concerned the development of maritime Asia in the sixteenth century.

As economists have convincingly argued, the shadow or hidden economy importantly impacts all societies. It has been operating alongside or underneath the visible, formal economy for many centuries, and has become a central and integral feature of the official, regulated economy. We cannot overlook the contributions made by its activities.[41] Similarly, the shadow economy of sixteenth-century China, as represented by the smuggling trade on the South China coast, did add to the rise and formation of a new type of maritime economy in Asia, which also merits attention.

That shadow economy produced three discernible tiers of maritime trade on the South China coast. The first tier concerns the coastal trade that involved traders from China, Portugal, and a number of Southeast Asian countries. The second tier reveals that Portuguese and Chinese smuggler-traders expanded a business network to include those based in Kyushu in southern Japan, while making Shuangyu Island into their regional business headquarters. This, to some extent, increased the importance of the Portuguese presence and their commercial activities on the China coast. The third tier moves beyond the boundaries of China and the East China Sea. With the joint efforts of maritime traders from remote marts and kingdoms of Southeast Asia, this tier connected with the larger trading network centered in the greater China Seas area. If we take global and regional maritime trade systems into account, multinational traders brought with them various new international and regional elements as they bartered on the southern coast of China. A new type of maritime economy, outside the control of the Ming government, thus gradually formed on the South China coast. In one sense, therefore, we should evaluate more positively the smuggling trade or shadow economy in sixteenth-century China.

5
Pirates, Gunpowder, and Christianity in Late Sixteenth-Century Japan

Maria Grazia Petrucci

In the late sixteenth century, more than sixty domains, each ruled by a warlord, and often in conflict with each other, divided Japan territorially. In southern Japan, the disputes among warlords incited political and social instability, but as this coincided with the arrival of Chinese outlaws and Portuguese adventurers, it also brought about economic opportunities for the lower strata of the population, particularly ambitious warriors, mercenaries, and pirates. They exploited the period of warfare by finding diverse occupations, by switching their loyalties, and by engaging in profitable activities, such as trade and smuggling. The participation of Japanese warlords in international trade, who used the pirates' services to sustain their wars of conquest, further augmented their window of opportunity.

I contend that the strong *daimyo* or warlords of southern Japan, acting as catalysts for Chinese outlaws, Japanese pirates, and Portuguese traders, created ideal conditions in their territories for the upward social mobility of local Japanese pirates. In fact, by seeking to expand their trading zones throughout the greater China Seas region, powerful Japanese *daimyo* allowed both Chinese marauders and Japanese pirates to advance to positions of authority and relative independence within Japan's feudal domains. Three factors help explain this rise in social standing: Chinese brigands found a niche for their exports in Japan, supplying materials for the newly imported Portuguese warfare technology; the *daimyo* managed to sustain local weapon production; and the Japanese pirates benefited from the expansion in trade by becoming low-ranking retainers of powerful *daimyo* because of their newly acquired warfare and nautical skills. Hence, the *daimyo* later legitimized the positions that Japanese pirates had often won by force. This gave the pirates the opportunity to fulfill various occupational roles, and to accelerate the economic expansion taking place by revitalizing sea routes and harbor towns along the paths of their activities.

Goto and Bungo between Chinese Outlaws and Portuguese Traders

The Japanese and Chinese pirates, known in the sixteenth century by such terms as *kaizoku* and *wakō*, operated during a period of early international economic globalization in which Western expansion clashed with East Asian domestic and foreign policies. In the 1550s, China, eager to protect its coast from foreign raiders and keen to maintain official trading under the umbrella of its tributary system, issued a series of bans on maritime trade that, however, had the unintended consequences of increasing piracy on the South China coast, and causing some of the major "piratical" gangs to relocate elsewhere in Asia (as Igawa Kenji explains in the following chapter). In southern Japan, the *daimyo* of the Matsuura, Ouchi, and Ōtomo families, welcomed the foreign traders, who brought economic benefits to their fiefs (Goto, Hizen, Bungo, and Nagato). These *daimyo* effectively achieved a symbiosis with both external and indigenous pirates (see Map 5.1).

The period between the 1550s and the 1590s proved crucial for understanding piracy in light of the geopolitical and economic changes occurring in China and Japan, on both domestic and international levels. Sakurai Eiji has shown that marginal geographic and economic circumstances had often forced individuals to lead lives of crime and turn into pirates. Sakurai's original work also claimed that the pirates, whom he labeled *kaizoku*, played dual roles as "sea robbers" and "maritime guards."[1] Fulfilling these various functions, Japanese pirates assumed multiple positions in society. There, many pirates who began as petty looters managed to expand their fleets and extort passage fees along important bottleneck straits in the Seto Inland Sea, elevating their standing to what Peter Shapinsky has called "sea lords," with rights and duties similar to those of land-based lords.[2] Of course, not all Japanese pirates became successful sea lords. However, in this period of economic expansion and maritime bans, skilled individuals in lower social echelons could rise in status by taking advantage of the many possibilities offered by the changing economic needs of Japanese warlords, such as the Matsuura, Ōtomo, and Ouchi, and the determination of Chinese outlaws to engage in trade.

In China, the Ming government made an effort to eliminate the pillaging of coastal areas by issuing stringent bans on sea trade, but these were loosely enforced before the 1550s, thereby giving private merchants the opportunity to sail abroad and trade, even though it was nominally illegal. One of these merchants who turned pirate was Wang Zhi. According to the *Illustrated Compendium of Seaboard Strategies* (*Chouhai Tubian*), written in 1562 by Zheng Ruozeng, Wang came from a family of salt merchants, natives of Huizhou (Anhui). He had initially cooperated with the coastal patrols until the 1550s, when the Ming government began to enforce the sea bans by sending coastal guards to halt illicit, non-tributary trade, and by prohibiting merchants such as Wang from going outside China to trade. Zheng

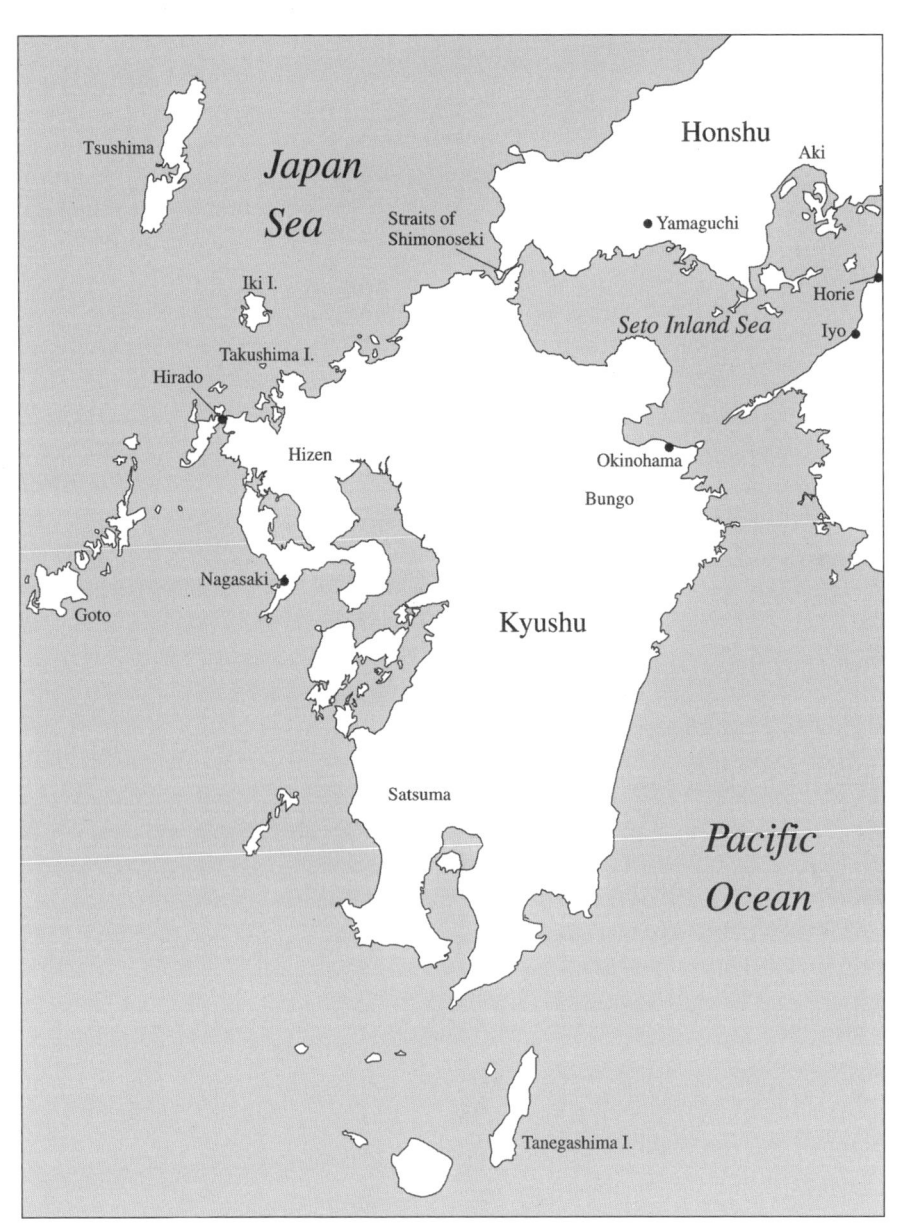

Pirates, Gunpowder, and Christianity in Late Sixteenth-Century Japan 61

Map 5.1 Southwestern Japan in the Late Sixteenth Century

Ruozeng justified, to a certain degree, Wang's involvement in piratical adventures, since he would not have resorted to piracy had the government permitted trading.[3]

Zheng also reported Wang Zhi's association with Japanese fighters on his ships at Shuangyu Island, and related how the petty merchants entrusted Wang with their goods to transport and sell in Japan.[4] But Zheng further mentioned that merchants such as Wang Zhi sought the assistance of "Japanese pirates" because Chinese pirate gangs had repeatedly plundered their junks. These merchant ships hired war-hardened Japanese thugs to defend them against pillaging and looting. Chinese villagers had no other choice but to emulate them in order to protect their property and their lives; the situation soon spiraled out of control. Zheng continued saying that many coastal people admired Wang, and helped him by providing the pirates with daily necessities, including women. People also even pledged their own children. Many youngsters willingly joined not only Wang's organization, but also other piratical groups in Zhejiang.[5]

As Wang's group defeated other rivals and increased the size of his own fleet to more than one hundred vessels, his foreign connections brought wealth to the villages of Shuangyu. Local residents willingly aided Wang and other gangs by "melting copper coins to make shot, using saltpeter to make gunpowder, iron to make swords and guns, and leather to make their armor," suggesting that Wang managed to support himself and sustain entire villages — which had previously engaged in subsistence agriculture and fishing — with his entrepreneurial piratical skills.[6] In the villages of Fujian and Zhejiang, because of the poor quality of its soil, individuals could not survive on farming alone, forcing them to supplement their livelihoods by other means. Most villagers worked as fishermen who occasionally engaged in piracy in times of economic difficulties.[7] However, professional, long-haul merchant-pirates like Wang Zhi carefully selected their bases among villages on relatively secluded islands, as for example, Shuangyu, that dotted the Chinese littoral. When Wang Zhi became an outlaw and a wanted man by the Ming government, he decided to resettle in Japan.

In 1545, Wang Zhi began trading in Japan with the Matsuura domain, where he joined a wealthy merchant, Sukezaemon, who belonged to the mercantile oligarchy of Hakata city, a trans-shipment harbor ruled by well-to-do business families.[8] Wang chose to live in Hirado, under the patronage of the *daimyo* Matsuura Takanobu, and because of Wang's reputation and rapidly developing networks, he quickly attracted many other traders from various countries. To protect his illicit business dealings, he created a band of "security guards" drawn from among his key henchmen.[9] As Tanaka Takeo explained, Wang offered protection not only to Chinese merchants, but also to Japanese and Portuguese traders. The Japanese copied this type of security organization to protect their sea routes to and from Kyushu.

Even more importantly, Wang brought to his organization a group of Japanese willing to trade, even illegally, in China. In particular, three merchants, including

Sukezaemon, went with Wang to Shuangyu to initiate trade with Chinese and Portuguese smugglers. By the 1570s, Wang's successors were trading in twelve of the thirty-six islands ruled by Matsuura Takanobu. By increasing the competition to obtain foreign goods, Wang's group greatly augmented the revenues of the Matsuura domain. But the Matsuura did not represent the only *daimyo* that benefited from Wang's trade. Wang succeeded in finding his own market in Japan, mainly due to the introduction of Portuguese weapon technology, such as the musket, that required steady supplies of gunpowder.

Piracy, the Gunpowder Trade, and Labor Specialization

Individuals in China discovered gunpowder in the seventh or eighth century, but, at that time, had not used it as an explosive. As gunpowder technology developed, it traveled via the Arab world to medieval Europeans, who improved on it by developing instruments that could contain and release its explosive charge. Cannons and muskets changed the outcome of battles and the nature of warfare.[10] The interaction between Chinese outlaws and the Portuguese intensified with the arrival of the first junk in 1542 on Tanegashima Island, where the Portuguese introduced muskets to Japan. This junk belonged to the Chinese outlaw Wang Zhi. He transported the Portuguese sailors who brought the knowledge of the first musket to the "King" of Ryukyu.[11] The Japanese, whose incessant wars necessitated increasingly advanced weaponry, quickly adopted Western firearms (see Figure 5.1). But the muskets were not only acquired by warlords. Wang Zhi's Japanese acquaintances in Goto, such as Shingoro,

Figure 5.1 Samurai Drilling with Firearms
(Source: Goyoda City Provincial Museum, Japan)

who lived the life of a pirate, and others in Satsuma and Hyuga, benefited from the new technology.[12] By 1549, this technology returned to China, where pirates and some gentry adopted it.[13]

Black gunpowder consisted of potassium nitrate or saltpeter (seventy-five percent), sulfur (ten percent), and carbon (fifteen percent), and required manufacture.[14] Saltpeter and carbon were abundant in China, but sulfur had to be imported from Japan to produce large quantities of high-grade gunpowder. At the same time that Wang Zhi exported saltpeter and carbon from China to Japan, he imported sulfur from Japan, to make gunpowder, particularly black gunpowder, using the technological skills taught by the Portuguese. Ōta Kōki, a Japanese scholar, explained that the gunpowder components could have arrived along diverse routes involving the Wang group, Portuguese traders, and Japanese merchants and *daimyo*. The Portuguese could have sold muskets and cannons to Wang Zhi, who in turn would have resold them to the Japanese. He purchased sulfur from Japanese merchants and then resold it to Chinese or Japanese pirates at various locations. Saltpeter would have followed the reverse course from China to Japan.[15] This trading structure also caused specialization in the production, extraction, and export of the necessary minerals. The manufacture of black gunpowder concentrated strategically in Kyushu, the location of sulfur extraction, largely within the domain of the Ōtomo family.

The Ōtomo family had been exporting sulfur from their domain in Bungo since the 1450s, at first trading in a tributary relationship with the Ming government and with Korea. They often used the services of pirates to ensure the safety of their commercial enterprises. In 1471, the Korean envoy, Park So Sen, wrote in his diary about the pirates he encountered in Bungo, who belonged to the Tomiku, Kibe, and Kushiki families. Park mentioned explicitly the Kibe family, who functioned as "magistrates" for the Ōtomo and, as such, administered coastal defense. He said they received a free hand to use violence in coastal areas. In 1510, those pirates became Ōtomo's retainers.[16] Pirates under their rule held the responsibility for the defense of commercial ships and maritime routes within their territories. Those pirate families corresponded, for all intents and purposes, to retainers who fought on the sea to protect the various commercial and military interests of their *daimyo*.

In the fifteenth century, the Ōtomo family began to extract sulfur in large quantities from Bungo, Yamato-bu, in northwestern Kyushu. The government included sulfur among the official tributary items it regulated, and, as such, shipped it to the harbors of Kita on Kyushu and to the Kinai regions via the Inland Sea routes, and then sent it as part of tributary missions to Ming China. In fact, China used sulfur both for medicinal purposes and in weaponry, such as poison smoke balls that they had developed as early as the Song period (960–1279).[17] In 1434, however, the Japanese government prohibited the exportation of sulfur, in the vain hope of regulating trade.[18]

By the sixteenth century, the Ōtomo family became well known among traders as "dealers in sulfur," and Ōtomo Yoshishige increased his wealth by taking advantage of the trading skills of his wholesaler merchants, allowing them to operate within his territory in exchange for fees and military information. In this manner, his financial power grew, and he reinvested his money in expanding his business. He directly controlled trade, particularly the sulfur trade, by allowing his trusted merchants to sell it from the places of extraction, located within his domain.[19] Yoshishige, in the process of enlarging his mercantile operations, often did business with Chinese pirates such as Wang Zhi and with the Portuguese in Bungo and Yamaguchi.

Ōtomo Yoshishige and his brother, Ouchi Yoshinaga, sought to trade with China by gaining recognition in the Chinese tributary system as Japanese "kings" and by acquiring official seals that allowed them to trade legally. Yoshinaga succeeded first in 1557; one year later, Yoshishige received permission after he formally apologized to the Ming court for harboring Japanese and Chinese pirates in his fief. Even after he obtained his seal, however, Yoshishige continued trading with Wang Zhi, as well as buying weapons and gunpowder from Portuguese traders, which his retainers then redistributed to his army. Furthermore, Hu Zongxian, the Ming supreme commander in southeastern China charged with the task of stopping piracy,[20] allowed Yoshishige to trade in several harbors where officials did not enforce the sea bans, doubtless to the great joy of Wang Zhi and Yoshishige, who promoted them as free trading ports.[21]

Evasion of the Ming bans on maritime trade seemed to have been relatively easy. Although the Ōtomo, as well as the Matsuura, tried to secure legal rights to trade with China, the Ming did not carefully enforce the sea bans. Japanese lords simply paid lip service to the Ming court, and subsequently carried on with pirates, just as before.

Chinese pirates had close relationships with local Japanese pirates in the Inland Sea area. They established their own trade communities in several ports. They also used these free trading ports for the exchange of large quantities of contraband goods bound for export, such as sulfur, and for import, such as saltpeter. This constituted an important trade, because the Ōtomo, as well as other *daimyo*, required importing saltpeter in order to produce good-quality gunpowder so they could defeat their enemies, using the latest military technology.

In a 1567 letter to Bishop Belchior Carneiro, stationed at Macau, Ōtomo Yoshishige requested the bishop's help in prohibiting all exports of saltpeter to Japan, except for his domains. He wanted to reconquer his territories that the Mōri family had taken.[22] In essence, Yoshishige was asking for a monopoly on saltpeter so that he would become the only *daimyo* capable of trading large quantities of it in Japan. He wrote, "The captain major may bring me ten piculs of good saltpeter every year, for which I will pay him one hundred taels or whatever your Lordship may desire." The following year, Yoshishige sent his regrets that the bishop's gift of a cannon had been lost at sea when a Portuguese ship sank in Malaccan waters.[23] Those letters not only attest to the importance Yoshishige placed upon the illicit saltpeter trade, but also to his belief that the Portuguese bishop could control its distribution. Ironically, of course, he himself was dealing in sulfur with Chinese and Japanese pirates, and though the Portuguese were competing for trading harbors in Japan, they would have had difficulty controlling that trade on their own. Nonetheless, documents show clearly that Yoshishige had access to large quantities of gunpowder, which he reported distributing among his retainers.

In another letter, written in 1575, sent by Ōtomo Yoshishige to Maki Hyogonosuke, a retainer of the Amako pirate family of Shikoku, Yoshishige mentioned sending, as gifts for services he would perform, an ink stone slab useful for writing and a gourd of gunpowder.[24] The interesting use of valuable supplies as gifts merits notice, as both the Amako and the Maki families in reality acted as local retainers involved in piratical activities. As such, they had access to and could contact other pirates in the Seto area in case of need.

Ōtomo's trade in sulfur and its shipment from Bungo followed the so-called Kuroseto route that passed through the Seto Inland Sea, a region in which pirates had secured their strongholds since the Kamakura period (1186–1333). Therefore, whoever controlled the various passages of the Inland Sea could gain great power and authority over the surrounding coastal areas, as well as the main trade routes. Between the 1550s and the 1590s, various portions of the Inland Sea fell into the hands of different lords: the Ōtomo, Ouchi, and Ōmura in Kyushu. Regarding the latter group, letters by a Jesuit priest, Pedro Reimão, mentioned Ōmura Sumitada (baptized as Don Bartholomew) and his brother-in-law, a man identified as Fucaforidono. Reimão described the latter as a "public pirate and a great corsair, who captured on the sea not only the vessels belonging to his own people [Japanese], but also of the poor Chinese merchants who come to deal in business."[25] The Jesuit father here clearly indicated the increased number of Chinese traders free to operate in any harbor, not confined by naval technology to bigger ports, or limited in their business. But his letters also showed the presence of contended territories between the Japanese and Chinese piratical gangs as well as the Portuguese, who, as early as 1561, had expressed the desire that their merchants trade only with Japanese who had converted to Christianity.

The Portuguese merchants' correspondence never mentioned the involvement of the Jesuits in trade negotiations, but it is likely that the merchants, grateful for their help, contributed to their cause by donating substantial sums of money to support their proselytizing work in Japan. The Jesuit priest, Luys D'Almeida, clearly documented this in a letter written from Yamaguchi on October 21, 1561. He rejoiced in the news that a retainer of Matsuura Takanobu, one Kotera Yasumasa (known to the priest as Dom Antonio Kotera), had allowed the Jesuits to build churches on his islands of Iki and Takushima.[26] The merchants' contributions to the Jesuit missions also likely derived, at least partially, from illicit commerce, particularly the business in gunpowder and saltpeter. The introduction of Portuguese military technology created a complex division of labor between China and Japan, which in turn necessitated a contraband trade in the materials needed to produce gunpowder and firearms. As a result, in order to do business with the Portuguese who supplied the musket technology, many Kyushu *daimyo* converted to Christianity; among them, Matsuura Takanobu, Ōtomo Yoshishige, and Ōmura Sumitada.

By this time, many Portuguese captains trafficked only through the Jesuit interpreters in authorized harbors. Initially, because of fierce competition to trade with the Portuguese, each domain had an interest in protecting its commercial privileges and routes. To accomplish this, Japanese *daimyo* and merchants recruited men-at-arms capable of piloting vessels. Pirates proved to possess the ideal qualifications, and ably guarded their sponsors' merchandise, enabling their families to become active participants in the economic life of the region, and to achieve high military rank as hired warriors. It also permitted the latter to become lower-ranking retainers whose services the local *daimyo* deemed valuable.

The Shirai: Wealthy Pirates, Merchants, and Maritime Security

The Ōtomo family established their own maritime security (*keigōshū*), as many other *daimyo* had done previously. In Kyushu, the Ouchi family, too, was trying to expand its domains in the Seto area, also using maritime security. The Shirai family, one of Ouchi's groups of retainers, worked as coastal guards. Their importance derived from their dual role as both pirates and coastal security agents. The Ouchi had defeated the Takeda *daimyo* in the region of Aki, and inherited their retainers. The Shirai, now Ouchi retainers, rendered their new lords invaluable services, including vanquishing the Iyo pirates of the Inland Sea in the 1540s. On that occasion, the Ouchi awarded them lands with an annual maximum rental fee of three hundred *koku*.[27]

The Shirai mainly engaged in providing maritime security, controlling certain trade routes, and ensuring that the Ouchi's coastal territory remained free of other piratical gangs. In fact, their activities did not differ from those of other pirates. According to the *Nankai Jiranki*, minor differences existed between coastal guard security and piratical activities; wealthy mercantile houses or groups often hired pirates to defend their boats while transporting goods from place to place — the role of coastal security.[28] Therefore, as we can see, the Shirai also held twin positions as coastal security patrols and pirates.

In the *Record of Military Families* (*Buke Mandaiki*), written in 1644, it is recorded that by the 1550s, the Shirai Governor of Etchu was a pirate in Ōshima who, with help from the neighboring Ugashima, commanded a fleet of five hundred boats.[29] One historian, Udagawa Takehisa, estimates the Shirai's naval strength as equivalent to that of Kobayakawa Takakage of the Mōri family, who possessed the strongest naval force of that period. Although the Shirai disbanded after the Battle of Itsukushima in 1555, soon afterward they regrouped, as they were recruited for service elsewhere. Scholars consider the Battle of Itsukushima a major turning point in the piratical history of the Seto Inland Sea, since the Ouchi had controlled the western Seto maritime region until then. Afterward, control passed to the powerful Mōri family, who also absorbed the naval forces of the losing parties under their command. The Shirai therefore came to serve the Mōri family in their capacity as maritime security specialists.[30]

The resilience of the Shirai in retaining their status as maritime security professionals and pirates derived from their technical skills as seafarers and their ability to build and maneuver massive warships, called *atakabune* (see below). The Shirai had acquired this expertise while in the service of the Takeda family, one of the first *daimyo* clans ever to possess such large and more easily defended ships.[31] Over the course of a century, the Shirai transferred their loyalties at least three times to diverse *daimyo* groups because of their maritime skills. In addition, the *Buke Mandaiki* reported that their sailors had trained in the use of muskets.[32] This made their services even more valuable, considering that Japan had just begun to produce and use such advanced military weaponry. In serving the Mōri, the Shirai were relocated elsewhere in the Seto Inland Sea and by 1565, had been resettled close to Osaka.

Jesuit sources reveal an interesting side of the Shirai family. The Shirai of Kawachi worked for Miyoshi Chōkei, the regent for the shogun, in the fortress of Iimori. As a result, the Shirai possessed a small fief near Osaka called Sanga, an island situated on Osaka's main river estuary.[33] Iimori had a fortress that served as one of the last toll barriers before travelers crossing the Inland Sea could reach the capital of Kyoto or the wealthy mercantile city of Osaka. Therefore, it stood as an important outpost for the security of the capital. By 1564, the Shirai had converted to Christianity. From that point onward, the Shirai leader became known to the Jesuits as Don Sancho Sangadono. In 1565, he hosted Father Vivera and Luys D'Almeida, the Portuguese merchant-turned-missionary, traveling to Kyoto.[34] Sangadono allowed the Jesuits to build churches in his domain. The Jesuits recorded that:

> Three miles away from Okayama there is an island called Sanga, and its lord is Christian with all his people a total of 1,500 persons. This place is very pleasant and strong as it is situated on a big lake; and the lord of this place is one of the best and oldest Christians that we have here and with his ingenuity he has built a beautiful church with a house to maintain the fathers.[35]

Their supporters considered the Shirai coastal security guards while their enemies viewed them as pirates, but also, the Jesuits considered them as Christians. From 1565, and over the course of many years, Sangadono helped the Jesuits set up meetings with important Japanese rulers, such as the Miyoshi, the Mōri, and Oda Nobunaga.[36] Since the Shirai operated as pirates, Christians, and maritime security specialists, they benefited greatly from their military connections as well as their trading and religious networks with the Portuguese. They escorted the Jesuits wherever they needed to travel within the Inland Sea. For instance, Vicente, referred to by Father Organtino as the son of Sangadono, came from an important mercantile family in Sakai and also converted early to Christianity.[37] He served the Mōri, and helped facilitate the transportation and protection of the Jesuits and their trade within the Inland Sea; in addition, he aided them in their missionary work.

Participation in these networks allowed the Shirai to familiarize themselves with firearms, and they put this knowledge to good use aboard the Mōri warships, known as *atakabune*.[38] These warships were top-of-the-line naval vessels that were larger and sturdier than most other warships and were equipped with cannons and muskets. Because of their well-known naval skills, the Shirai most likely would have commanded these warships. Using their abilities and business connections in the Inland Sea, the Shirai family assisted Portuguese and other merchants, thereby helping increase trade throughout the entire area.

Piracy and the Economic Development of Coastal Towns

Pirates who functioned as sea lords facilitated navigation through their wealth, influence, and authority. They worked at regulating the flow of goods and taxes of various trading groups between domains and institutional centers, such as temples and shrines. Pirates in the Inland Sea notably transported taxes in the form of rice paid by the local islanders to temples and shrines, which served as collection points for onward transmission to the capital. In offering such shipping services, pirates perpetuated their existence and their commercially centered activities by encouraging the development of coastal towns, which, in fact, they often controlled. According to Tanaka Takeo, in Japan, by the 1550s — the period in which Wang Zhi resided in Hirado — at least forty-nine towns were connected to piratical activities.[39] Indeed, Tanaka's study likely understates greatly the number since it reflects only those towns that surviving documentation verified.

Castle-towns sprang up between 1550 and 1590, particularly in the Inland Sea area. As Yamauchi has shown, the Jesuits and Portuguese in the Inland Sea during that time often used castle-towns as harbors. When Vilela visited Japan in 1559, he traveled from Okinohama in Kyushu to Kyoto by way of stopping at various coastal towns along his path. It took him ten days with contrary winds simply to cross the strait from Miyajima to Horie in Shikoku. In contrast, seven years later, the voyage of Father Luís Fróis and Father Luys D'Almeida between Bungo and Horie took only three days, due to better inland transportation routes and improved political and economic conditions in coastal settlements.

Between the 1550s and the 1590s, the Inland Sea region experienced an economic boom as various individuals began to settle in the many burgeoning coastal towns. Fróis mentions his encounter with Kamo Manuel Akimasa, a Japanese astrologer who had converted to Christianity and settled in the port of Horie during his journey from Kyoto to Bungo. Horie, a castle-town and deep-water port, was conveniently located on the route controlled by the Kōno pirates of Iyo. It served as a naval base, whose importance increased steadily among the pirates and the navy.[40] Other deep-water harbors that offered natural protection for large, long-haul vessels developed during this period.

The era presented great opportunities for smaller pirate gangs who sought to profit from robbing foreign as well as Japanese vessels. Piracy in itself did not disappear, but the pirates diversified into sea lords. They contended for the biggest share of territorial waters by allying themselves with landed lords while assuming the function of tax collectors, even for large temple complexes. Small piratical bands looked elsewhere for sources of fresh revenue, competing closer to the coast and to the capital for more booty. In the 1580s, individuals traveling from Kyoto to Muro or Koto, once past the Murakami territory, could not assume their own safety, and their lives and property depended on the strength and competence of security coastal patrols and local lords. The farther one ventured from the centrally governed territory, the more dangerous it became. Outside the purview of the central government authority, represented by Toyotomi Hideyoshi's regime, the pirates still ruled, in more ways than one.

Conclusion

The pirates of the sixteenth century in China and Japan had close relations with local authorities, and often used those connections to create their own power hubs. Wang Zhi, who set up a trilateral trading network based upon the production of gunpowder for muskets in collaboration with the *daimyo* Matsuura of Hirado, exemplified this phenomenon. The Portuguese introduced the musket and re-exported it to China. Japanese wars and subsequent innovations in weaponry fostered the creation of an industry that helped other groups defeat their enemies. Those who lacked the more advanced weapons (muskets and cannons) and ammunition (gunpowder) lost, both in Japan and China. The Chinese and Portuguese, who traded illicitly, hired Japanese fighters and thugs to protect their trade. In the meantime, *daimyo* such as

Ōtomo Yoshishige and Ouchi Yoshitaka participated in the gunpowder trade, using their piratical associations within their own territories to enhance their power on local sea routes, as for example, on the Inland Sea. Ōtomo and Ouchi desired to establish trading relations with China within the Ming tributary system, but their initial failure to do so led them to resort to employ local pirates to increase their wealth and authority.

Between 1550 and 1590, one major pirate clan successfully absorbed all the less-powerful pirates in the Inland Sea region. The Murakami, under the leadership of Murakami Takeyoshi, emerged as the principal pirate power controlling smaller piratical families who eventually played multiple roles as coastal guards, genuine pirates, and merchants. Japanese and Jesuit documents reveal how the Shirai family became cleverly involved in trade and piracy during the period of Japanese territorial unification under Toyotomi Hideyoshi.

As required by circumstances, pirates assumed diverse roles, which distinguished this wave of piracy, both in China and in Japan, at the end of the sixteenth century. While Japanese pirates took on various functions in order to survive the political and economic changes taking place in their territories, Chinese merchant-pirates gradually, in the next century, transformed into Ming loyalists and rebels in opposition to the Manchu invaders. As this and other chapters in this volume demonstrate, Chinese and Japanese pirates accelerated the economic expansion taking place and revitalized sea routes and harbor towns along the paths of their expansion.

6

At the Crossroads:
Limahon and Wakō in Sixteenth-Century Philippines

Igawa Kenji

In the sixteenth century, the Philippine Islands occupied a crossroads of culture, trade, and piracy. Many Chinese and European sources clearly show that these islands drew upon a well-established maritime network linking Japan, Borneo, Vietnam, Thailand, and South China. After the Spanish occupied Manila, it added Mexico to this network. Even before the Spanish arrival, the Philippines represented one of the most important trading hubs in the greater China Seas region; in fact, in the late fourteenth century, the islands had sent tribute missions to China. However, with the sea bans in China, political instability in Japan, and the intrusion of Europeans into the region, piracy became closely tied to commerce and, as we shall see, to the development of major trade routes. The Chinese pirate, Lin Feng or Limahon, and bands of *wakō* raiders were particularly active in and around the Philippines in the later part of the sixteenth century.

Although Japanese scholars have written much on the Philippines, little of their research focuses on the significance of the islands as an international crossroads and its links to piracy. To date, most recent studies dealing with the sixteenth century have analyzed narrow topics, such as Spanish missionary activities in the Philippines, the role of South American silver in Chinese-Philippine relations, and unilateral trade links between the Philippines and Japan.[1] While they have added greatly to our knowledge of this period, each displays a fundamental inability to further advance the argument beyond simple one-sided relationships, particularly those between the Philippines and Japan. Moreover, they show a complete lack of appreciation of the Philippines as a crucial international crossroads in the sixteenth century. The complexities surrounding historical materials further hinder understanding. To create a complete picture of the Philippines, we must examine all relevant sources in Asian and European languages.

Needless to say, scholars confront a difficult task in reconstructing the history of Philippine foreign relations in this period. In this chapter, I will explore three sets of key questions using a multilateral perspective. First, when and why did the

Philippines become a crossroads? Second, who were the pirates and what role did they play in the development of the Philippines as a crossroads? Third, how did piracy and trade relate in this period, especially with regard to the interaction between the Philippines and Japan? In addressing these questions, I hope to explicate the status of the Philippine Islands in Asian international relations in the sixteenth century, and to show how piracy factored critically in the development of the Philippine crossroads.

The Making of the Philippine Crossroads

In the late fourteenth century, the Philippines were emerging as a major geopolitical area within the greater China Seas. As an indication of its rising stature, according to the *Ming Dynastic History* (*Ming Shi*), Luzon sent tribute missions to China in 1372 and 1410. Although this source does not further mention the islands until 1576, we can find additional references to intra-Asian trading networks in various European documents. Clearly, by the sixteenth century, the Philippines had already become an important crossroads in the greater China Seas region, with a web of sea routes that stretched from China to Southeast Asia, and, with Portugal and Spain, to far-away Europe and the Americas.

The book, *A Suma Oriental*, written by Tomé Pires, is an essential source. Many years before Ferdinand Magellan reached Cebu (1521), Pires wrote that it took ten days to travel from Luzon to Brunei.[2] The description clearly indicates that a maritime route from Luzon to Brunei existed at that time. Further, it might have extended to Malacca since Pires wrote his book there. In fact, the author provided another key piece of evidence by mentioning a man from Brunei who traveled between Malacca and Luzon buying and selling various local products. From this account, we learn of possible trade links in which Luzon exported foodstuff and beeswax to, and imported clothing and other items from, Malacca. This information is interesting not only because it tells us of the maritime network of Luzon, but also that Malacca had contacts with Luzon, but not Mindanao or Cebu, at the time (see Map 6.1).

With the voyage of Ferdinand Magellan, Spain developed a greater interest in the western Pacific region. António de Morga, in his monumental *Sucesos de las islas Filipinas* (1609), includes some useful material. It is well known that natives of Mactan Island in the Philippines killed Magellan after he arrived there during his voyage around the world. De Morga continued his description, recalling that Magellan's fleet managed to reach the Moluccas without their captain, but could not stay there for long because of Portuguese interference, and ultimately, they returned to Spain.[3] After other similar occurrences involving Juan Sebastian del Caño and Comendador Loaisa, a flotilla commanded by Ruy López de Villalobos departed

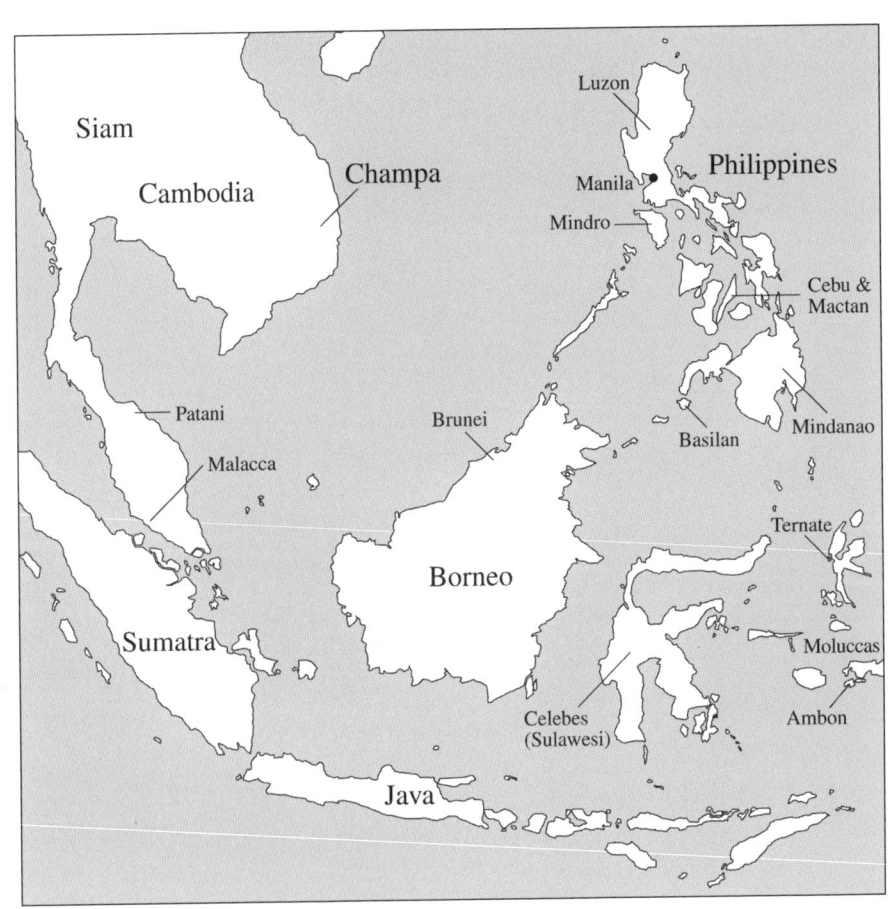

Map 6.1   The Philippines and Southeast Asia in the Sixteenth Century

from Mexico and arrived in the Moluccas in 1543. They sailed past Cebu Island to reach their final destination. In the Moluccas, they became embroiled in a conflict with the Portuguese, but eventually managed to return to Spain.

As de Morga hinted, a maritime route already snaked its way from the Philippines to the Moluccas in this period. We have a detailed account of the voyage of Villalobos, whose fleet reached Mindanao on January 29, 1543, according to a letter by Geronimo de Santisteban to António de Mendoza, dated January 22, 1547. In the report, the author described the island and its inhabitants, a thickly populated one, rich in gold, whose people came from the Celebes (known today as Sulawesi). Three kings, Sarripara, Butuan, and Biçaya, ruled — the first, the most powerful, but the second, the richest. The island produced, among others, great amounts of ginger, sandalwood, rice, sago, palm, myrobalan (a medicinal herb), pork, animals, and fruits. The Spanish sent an embassy consisting of a ship, the *San Juan de Letran*, and sixty men to Sarripara, taking with them decorated chairs, Venetian glass, and other items. Later the vessel returned to Mexico with rice, sago, chicken, pork, and other typical regional foodstuff. Soon afterwards, the Portuguese arrived in Mindanao.[4]

Chinese merchants, and probably pirates, visited Mindanao and found some gold in 1543. Another naval dispatch, entitled *Relación de García de Escalante Alvarado*, stated that in Cebu, in 1544, a number of the Spanish who had gone there in the period of Magellan to sell gold and gems to the Chinese who still remained behind.[5]

From these European sources, we know that several sea routes from the Philippines to Southeast Asia had already existed in the first half of the sixteenth century. Tomé Pires described one from Luzon to Malacca by way of Borneo. The accounts of Villalobos's ships show that the southern Philippines had a route to the Celebes. Most significantly, the two fleets of Magellan and Villalobos sailed to the Moluccas from the southern Philippines. While traveling there, Father Cosme de Torres sent a letter to Ignatius Loyola, founder of the Society of Jesus or Jesuits, explaining that he met Francis Xavier on Ambon Island, and accompanied him to Japan.[6]

António Galvão, a Portuguese captain in the Moluccas, described the Philippines in the same period, but from a different perspective. In *Tratado dos Descobrimentos* (1563), he wrote that Francisco Serram and some Portuguese had been captured on Mindanao in 1512.[7] They had arrived in the Moluccas nine years earlier than Magellan's fleet. De Morga also covered the same events. After the European "discovery" of the Moluccas, Serram returned to Malacca, and sent letters to his friend Magellan, providing him with important information in preparation for his voyage.[8] In 1538, Francisco de Castro landed there and baptized six "kings." According to Galvão, in February 1543 (not January as de Morga said), Villalobos reached Mindanao, and consequently named the islands as the Philippines.[9]

Galvão continued his narrative. In June 1545, a Portuguese, Pero Fidalgo, departed from Borneo and arrived in Luzon by junk. He described the location as between Mindanao and China. Although Tomé Pires had referred to Luzon thirty years earlier, it seems that this represented the first visit of a Portuguese to Luzon. He wrote that the island bordered upon China, and produced gold and silver.[10]

These accounts of the routes used by the Portuguese and the Spanish give some ideas about the presence of Luzon's maritime passages to Borneo, the Moluccas, Mindanao, and China. The usage of a junk by Fidalgo suggested that Chinese sea merchants had recently established a maritime route from Borneo to Luzon. According to Galvão, they disembarked at Luzon, somewhat later than at Mindanao. He also recorded the arrival of a Portuguese named Francisco de Castro before the Spanish "discovery." However, we must approach such a claim cautiously since it is likely that Galvão wrote his book to counter and contest the discovery reported by Villalobos.

In another interesting account, Father Luís Fróis detailed the presence of cinnamon and gold in Mindanao and Basilan. In a letter dated November 19, 1556, at Malacca, he wrote that because the people had lost their souls, they received the Christian faith easily.[11] This letter suggests that members of the Society of Jesus went to Mindanao, returned to Malacca, and passed on this information. But we know little else about the events of this decade. De Morga also revealed that when the vice-king of Nueva España, Luis de Velasco, was preparing a voyage to the Moluccas, he instructed the Spaniard, Andres de Urdaneta, to cooperate with Miguel Lopez de Legazpi. After the former's death, the fleet of Lopez de Legazpi departed from Mexico for the Philippines.[12]

In addition to the sources above, Florence houses other useful information including the last part of a letter, dated February 13, 1558, by Francisco Vieira to Diego Laínez, the superior-general of the Society of Jesus. Vieira, who came from the suburbs of Lisbon, reached Goa in September 1554 and Ternate in October 1557. He stayed in the Moluccas until his death in 1560. In his letter, he pointed out the possibility of opening a maritime route from Ternate to Japan.[13] What does this suggest? While no proof exists to confirm that the Portuguese had in fact used this route to Japan, nonetheless, a good possibility of its presence does remain.

By the middle of the sixteenth century, the route from the Moluccas to the Philippines had certainly become well-established since two Spanish fleets went to the Moluccas from the Philippines. Sea routes were also very likely to be extended to Malacca, Brunei, Borneo, Celebes, and possibly even to Japan. Further, Chinese merchants had gone to the Philippines to trade or seek gold; Garcia de Escalante Alvarado wrote that Chinese visited Mindanao, and found some gold there in 1543, and, in the following year, some Chinese merchants had traded with the Spanish on Cebu Island. As mentioned above, Galvão described Luzon as China's neighbor. (For an overview of this large area, see Map 1.1 on p. 4.)

The Activities of the *Wakō* and Limahon

Maritime routes between China, Japan, and Southeast Asia settled firmly in place by the second half of the sixteenth century, which also witnessed the beginnings of persistent naval operations against the pirates along the coast of China. Not coincidentally, *wakō* pirates, who were fleeing suppression campaigns in China, appeared in the Philippines at this time, and by 1567, a sea route probably came into existence between Japan and the Philippines as well. Who were these pirates? What were their relationships to the Philippines?

During the sixteenth century, pirates, commonly known as *wakō*, had spread throughout the greater China Seas, and by the latter half of the century, they had come to play a key role in shaping Philippine history. Although the word *wakō* itself denoted Japanese pirates, they actually came from miscellaneous groups of mixed ethnic origins, including Chinese and Southeast Asian pirates, besides Japanese. In fact, as James Chin shows in his chapter, it is better to describe them as merchant-pirates with multinational connections rather than simply pirates. One Chinese chief, Wang Zhi, established a trading base in the Japanese port of Hirado and shipping networks in Southeast Asia as well as China. Another Chinese pirate, Limahon, had close connections with Japan, Taiwan, the Philippine Islands, and other areas of Southeast Asia.

Although the mention of *wakō* raids on the China coast dated back to the Mongol period, they only became a serious problem in the early sixteenth century.[14] In 1540, Wang Zhi traveled to Guangdong with Ye Zongman and several other colleagues, where they constructed large trading ships for their ventures in Japan, Siam, and other Southeast Asian countries. By then, Wang already had been trading sulfur, saltpeter, and cotton for over five years. Later, he went to Shuangyu, believed to be the island of Lianpo in European sources, where he met representatives of an unofficial Japanese tribute mission in 1544, and subsequently journeyed to Japan (see below).[15]

Tribute missions of Japan sometimes became involved in piracy. One Japanese source, the *Teppōki* (1606), written by Bunshi Genshō, contains a famous description of the first arrival of the Portuguese in Japan, as well as a section on a Japanese deputation to China. Genshō wrote:

> I heard a story from an old man. He said in 1542–1543, three big ships of a tribute mission were going to China. Therefore, a thousand of the richest people in western Japan and hundreds of ship's crew assembled like gods. They prepared the ships and waited for the time to depart. After they departed, however, a storm arose at sea, and the huge waves broke up the ships. Losing its masts and rudder, the first ship of this fleet sank into the sea. The second ship managed to arrive in Ningbo. The third ship could proceed no further and returned to Tanegashima.

Although very well-known in Japan, scholars seldom use this source to study the tribute missions to China. The ships mentioned in the *Teppōki* presented an extraordinary case since, generally, tribute mission fleets were prepared in Hakata or Sakai, the large international ports of those days. Additionally, no significant record of this mission now exists. In fact, the Chinese court refused to treat it as an official embassy, probably the reason for the dearth of records. I have dealt with this tribute delegation previously,[16] and so here, I wish to discuss its relationship with *wakō*.

Only the second tribute ship reached Ningbo, as confirmed in a Chinese source, the *Chouhai Tubian*, which states that in the sixth lunar month of 1544, a barbarian vessel arrived with the ambassador monk, Jukō, and 158 crew members. They came to China under the pretense of seeking official recognition, but without a letter from the Japanese "king," which did not follow Chinese regulations regarding the appropriate intervals of missions. Therefore, the Ming court refused to treat them as an official contingent.[17] Ming official records state that they stayed in China for about a year.[18] The merchant-pirate Wang Zhi returned to Japan with this group, and at approximately the same time, another merchant-pirate, Xu Dong, began trading with the Japanese.[19] This extraordinary mission was important because, in a sense, it marks the practical beginnings of the clandestine trade relations between Japan and China.[20]

Apart from Wang Zhi, other merchant-pirates traveled to Japan in these years, including, in the 1530s–1540s, nine illegal missions which were not official Chinese embassies.[21] In addition, the *Choseon wangjo sillok* reported many examples, so-called "drifting ships" (*hwangtang seon*), or clandestine Chinese vessels, found around the Korean Peninsula. The majority of them, however, headed for Japan.

Another difficulty surfaced in the 1540s. In 1546, the Chinese general, Zhu Wan, commenced naval operations against the *wakō* off the Zhejiang coast, beginning a protracted period of military conflict with the pirates on the coast of China. Zhu sent Lu Tang and Wei Yigong to Shuangyu Island, where they captured a *wakō* boss, Li Guangtou (Baldy Li), in the fourth lunar month.[22] In his chapter, James Chin mentions that it is likely that the Portuguese aided the pirate-smugglers, and a letter from Francis Xavier, dated January 25, 1549, provides evidence supporting this contention.[23] However, military operations in and around Shuangyu continued into 1548, when approximately at that time, Xu Dong, without choice, fled for his life, allowing Wang Zhi to become the major *wakō* captain.[24] General Zhu Wan committed suicide in 1549 because of criticism of his operation.

The 1550s marked a well-known period of *wakō* exploits. The historian, Zheng Liangsheng, described in detail the great pirate onrush between 1553 and 1561. For example, during one raid in Zhejiang in May 1556, the pirates assembled over twenty thousand people.[25] At the end of the year 1559, Wang Zhi surrendered, but was put to death, after which *wakō* activities diminished somewhat. During this period, Francisco Vieira suggested the possibility of developing a trade route from Ternate to Japan.

The 1560s clearly signified a period of important changes for the Philippines, as pirate-merchants increasingly made their way into their waters, seeking refuge in the islands from the persistent suppression campaigns in China. Although some tentative sea routes had existed between China and the Philippines since at least the 1540s, two decades later, trade was already flourishing. Miguel Lopez de Legazpi reported, in a letter dated July 23, 1567, that Chinese and Japanese visited Luzon and Mindoro every year bringing silk, wool, bells, porcelain, perfume, tin, and cotton cloths. They also took away gold and beeswax — the first conclusive evidence of the existence of a route from Japan to the Philippines.[26] Therefore, although we do not know for certain when the links started, we do know without doubt that, at the latest, they operated in the 1560s, because Lopez de Legazpi wrote that Japanese had visited the Philippines every year. Another dispatch, purportedly written in 1570, stated that forty married Chinese and twenty Japanese lived in Manila.[27] Due to China's ban on private sea trade, many of these merchants and sojourners in the Philippines necessarily took on the additional role of pirates.

Lin Daoqian and Lin Feng, known respectively as Vintoquián and Limahon in European sources, were two renowned *wakō* captains during this period. Although some scholars claimed that they were the same person, this was not the case.[28] After being driven out of Taiwan in 1563 by the Chinese navy, Lin Daoqian fled to Champa; this is the first mention of his name in the historical records. Afterwards, Li You again defeated Lin, and he escaped to Luzon.[29] Soon after that, he returned to Zhaoan, on the South China coast, where Qi Jiguang vanquished him in the tenth lunar month of the same year.[30] Although one source contends that Lin Daoqian escaped to Cambodia and did not come back to China,[31] we know that in the fall of 1578, he was again pirating and trading along the southern coast of China.[32] It was reported that he later died in Patani, in southern Thailand, and in fact, his tomb is located there.[33]

How did Lin Feng operate at this time? He deserves more attention for the purposes of this chapter, not only because he appeared in European sources, but also because he exemplified the clandestine relations between South China and the Philippines during this period more clearly. In the tenth lunar month of 1571, Lin Feng attacked Shenquan and in the following year, sailed to Chenghai, both on the Guangdong coast, where he was defeated. He fled to Luzon where he established a fortified trading base. Chinese General Liu Yaohui requested the local "king" to attack the pirates and burn their ships. Liu also sent a fleet that drove Lin from Luzon, but he escaped to Danshui in Taiwan.[34] In the spring of 1574, he was once again pirating along the Chinese coast around Qinglan on Hainan Island.[35]

In November 1574, Lin Feng's forces raided Manila.[36] Reports claim that his fleet consisted of seventy ships and three thousand pirates with an additional four hundred Japanese soldiers sent by Sioco to help them.[37] Juan Gonzalez de Mendoza, the author of *Historia de las Cosas Mas Notables, Ritos y Costumbres, del Gran Reyno dela China* (1585), carefully described how they viciously assaulted Manila.[38] A Spanish armada led by Juan de Salcedo successfully expelled the pirates from the Philippines, while a Chinese fleet under Wang Wanggao, in cooperation with the Spanish, carried out mopping-up operations against Lin Feng. Afterwards, the combined force sailed for Quanzhou in July 1575.[39] According to Spanish sources, it seems that the problem of piracy was solved. However, they failed to destroy Lin Feng and the remnants of his followers probably escaped to Guangdong and, subsequently to Taiwan.[40] The *Ming Veritable Records* claims that Lin surrendered to the "barbarians" with more than two thousand men in 1576. However, after further fighting with Chinese and Spanish forces, Lin joined forces with Li Mao and Chen Dele to ravage the coast of South China in 1589. At this point, Lin Feng disappeared from the historical records.[41] Map 6.2 shows the areas in which Lin Feng's activities took place.

This series of activities furnish us with sufficient information to understand that a maritime network, including China, Japan, the Philippines, and Southeast Asia, had been firmly established by the late sixteenth century. Here, I would like to address another interesting question. Why did Lin Feng (and other pirates) go to the Philippines? Juan Gonzalez de Mendoza wrote that Limahon set out to take the Philippines, and make himself lord and king. However, he first had to rid the archipelago of the Spanish, which he thought he could easily do because of their small number. In addition, because the Philippines stood far away from the continent, Lin believed the islands would provide a secure and friendly base where

Map 6.2 Areas of Lin Feng's Activities, 1571–89

he and his followers could live without fear of attack from the imperial Chinese fleet. It would be a perfect site for his piratical and trading operations in the greater China Seas region.

Whether these represent his true motivations or not, the Philippines apparently functioned as an alternative to the Chinese coastal islands, where Lin Feng and other pirate groups found it increasingly difficult to establish posts because of the Chinese navy's persistent military campaigns. Why did they choose the Philippines instead? The maritime route from Malacca to Japan went by way of the Chinese islands, usually via Macau.[42] Further, the Ming maritime bans prevented the setting up of trading bases except on the islands, though the anti-pirate campaigns also meant loss of these way-stations for the Japanese, the Portuguese, and the overseas Chinese. Therefore, the Philippines served as an accessible choice for traders and pirates operating in the greater China Seas region. Clearly, Spain also needed the Philippines as a center of their activities in the western Pacific Ocean instead of the Moluccas.[43] To put it simply, the Philippine Islands stood at the crossroads of global trade at that time, and pirates played a key role in their development.

Piracy and Trade

How did relations between the Philippines and Japan change during the sixteenth century? Here, I want to focus on this question not only from the perspective of Japanese history, but also from that of its impact on Philippine history. The maritime route linking the two countries appeared, in fact, crucial for the Philippines. However, to fully understand this, we need to consider the phenomena of both piracy and trade. Since the 1540s, the Philippines had harbored many non-native Asian pirates (not to mention native pirates), and had continued to do so until the end of the century and beyond. Trade steadily increased and went hand-in-hand with the development of piracy. First, I will take up the issue of piracy.

The example of Lin Feng clearly demonstrates that *wakō* activities continued into the late sixteenth century. In addition to Lin, evidence exists of other piratical activities in the Philippines. António de Morga wrote that around 1580–81, Juan Pablo de Carrion, with some ships, had driven off Japanese pirates who had occupied the port near Nueva Segovia (Vigan City today) and built a fort there.[44] Gonçalo Ronquillo de Peñalosa also reported *wakō* in this period, who had come to the islands and fought with native inhabitants, wounding many. In his account, dated June 16, 1582, he explained that Japanese pirates arrived in the Philippines with ten ships and that he had sent out a fleet of six ships to intercept them.[45]

Another interesting case occurred in 1582. We learn about it from an anonymous report based on correspondence between Juan Pablo de Carrion and an unnamed *wakō* chieftain. When Carrion disembarked at Cagayan Province in March 1582, he found a *wakō* fleet already anchored there. The pirate captain sent a letter to Carrion pointing out that, under the direct command of the Japanese "king," he and his fleet had reached the islands first; therefore, if Carrion wished him to leave, he would have to pay him a large sum of gold. Carrion replied that the Spanish intended to protect the natives and regain the gold that the *wakō* had plundered; if necessary, they would attack the pirates with six hundred armed men. Carrion intimidated the pirate leader by saying that the soldiers inside the fort would kill him. As a result, the Japanese left the area, apparently without a fight.[46]

An urgent sense of crisis seemed to have developed in the 1580s in the relations between Japan and the Philippines. In 1586, the Spanish governor, Santiago de Vera, wrote that many enemies, including the Japanese, surrounded the islands.[47] He particularly feared insurrections and invasions from natives, Chinese, English, Southeast Asian neighbors, and Japanese. He explained that the great numbers of natives required intense suppression, and the more than five thousand Chinese inhabitants required careful monitoring. He further mentioned that the English, who had settled nearby in the Moluccas, posed a threat; and the natives of those islands had made at least two incursions into the Philippines. Furthermore, the Japanese attacked the islands every year.[48] This dispatch notably pointed out not only the multinational relations of the Philippines, but also the possibility that some Japanese (perhaps pirates, perhaps traders) intended to colonize Luzon.

Though the information remains sparse, I must now address the issue of trade. As already noted, in a letter by Miguel Lopez de Legazpi, dated July 23, 1567, evidence shows that the Japanese began trading in the Philippines at a relatively early date. In the 1580s, despite pirate intrusions, Japanese merchants intended to conduct a more peaceful and secure trade in the Philippines. A letter by Santiago de Vera, the president of the *Audiencia*,[49] dated June 26, 1587, notes that a Japanese vessel carried letters from the "king" of Hirado, Matsura Takanobu, and Don Gaspar, his brother. They also brought merchandise and weapons to sell. Matsura and another Christian king, Konishi Yukinaga or Don Augustin, offered to send troops and people to the governor of the Philippines without asking anything in return. The proposal suggested a type of military alliance with the Spanish on the islands. At the same time, it also recommended opening a trading route from Japan to the Philippines, although nothing seemed to have come of this.[50]

Some information on the manner of Philippine–Japan trade in this period survives. Juan Pacheco Maldonado reported on the trading of great quantities of silver from Japan to the Philippines every year.[51] A Florentine merchant, Francesco Carletti, recorded the sea route from the Philippines to Japan, and described its activities in detail. According to the *Ragionamenti del Mio Viaggio Intorno al Mondo* (1701), he left the Philippines in May 1597 and arrived at Nagasaki the following month, with a ship laden with earthenware vases to trade in Japan, an item that the powerful hegemon, Toyotomi Hideyoshi, wanted to purchase entirely.[52]

Conclusion

In this chapter, I have attempted to delineate the clandestine trading system during the sixteenth century in the greater China Seas region, with particular emphasis on the Philippine Islands as an important international crossroads. I argue that both trade and piracy developed at the same time and even complemented one another. Both pirates and traders, often one and the same, helped open up and develop new maritime routes that crisscrossed the waters between Japan, China, and Southeast Asia. The arrival of the Spanish and Portuguese also added them to the mix. The Philippine Islands provided the crucial hub that connected all the diverse component parts.

In reconstructing this history, however, we have encountered several problems — not only those inherent in using a large variety of materials in many languages, but also the fact that we have few reliable sources. Another difficulty lies in dealing with the complexity of the trading network itself, and in analyzing the role that piracy played in the development of trade and its system. Pirates and smugglers, of course, left few records, and those that we do have suffer from subjectivity since their opponents wrote them.

Nevertheless, I have shown that China's relations with the Philippines had predated the Spanish occupation of Manila, and I have also suggested the strong possibility of Japan's relations with the Philippines in roughly the same period. In any case, by the 1560s, we have clear indications of well-established trade routes from the Philippines to other areas of the greater China Seas. Interestingly, pirates or *wakō* critically influenced the development of these routes.

Over the course of the sixteenth century, the Philippines came to play a key role in the growth of the whole region, a fact overlooked by most scholars. We need to pay more attention to the relations between the Philippines and Southeast Asia, as well as with China and Japan in this period. Otherwise, grasping the significance of the Philippines' location will become impossible. In conclusion, therefore, the Philippines evolved into a key international trans-shipment center replacing the Chinese islands (such as Shuangyu), which the military campaigns against the pirates rendered inaccessible. At the crossroads, the Philippines became the all-important way-station for the Japan-Malacca trade, as well as for the Mexico-Moluccas trade, and for the China-Japan-Moluccas trade. For a better understanding of the significance of the Philippine Islands in sixteenth-century international relations, we must consider the role of piracy in this period.

7
Piracy and Coastal Security in Southeastern China, 1600–1780

Paola Calanca

The years 1600 to 1780 were particularly important in Chinese history in general and in the history of piracy in particular. The first half of the seventeenth century marked a time of great chaos and anarchy highlighted by the Ming-Qing dynastic wars. Social disorders on both land and sea continued until 1683, when the Manchus conquered Taiwan. The island had survived as the last bastion of Ming loyalism and an important stronghold of the powerful Zheng family that controlled Chinese maritime trade from the 1630s. Once the Manchus had consolidated their authority over all of China, the empire witnessed a century of amazing stability, prosperity, and population growth, prompting some historians to call the hundred-year period from 1680 to 1780 the High Qing.

The region along the southeastern littoral most profoundly felt the great changes taking place in China. The years 1683–84 signified a watershed in the history of that area. In Fujian and Guangdong, destructive wars and repressive governmental policies continued for over forty years between the 1640s and 1683, greatly disturbing the region's socio-economic equilibrium. During those years countless numbers of people died from wars and famines, and many displaced survivors became wandering refugees. Some people fled overseas to Taiwan and Southeast Asia, while many others became beggars, bandits, and pirates. Once the wars ended, however, the new Qing rulers opened up maritime trade, and recovery came quickly. The southeastern coast experienced enormous commercial development, and the Qing Empire fully incorporated the island of Taiwan. As people returned to work, social disorders diminished.

Between the early seventeenth and late eighteenth centuries, the profession of piracy also changed dramatically in terms of its structures, stimuli, and objectives, as well as the people who practiced it. Pirates, like everyone else, had to adapt to the new circumstances as they evolved. Two important factors helped shape events: internationally, the transformation in Asian sea trade, and regionally, the management of the coast by the government through the power of certain influential local families. In this chapter, we will examine the changes in the nature of piracy in southeastern China, as well as the governmental responses to piracy (see Map 7.1). The discussion that follows is divided into three sections: first, the upsurge of merchant-pirates between 1600 and 1683, second, the petty piracy of the eighteenth century from 1684 to 1780, and third, an overview of Ming and Qing coastal security policies over this whole period.

Piracy from 1600 to 1683

The *wakō* disturbances and the intrusion of Westerners into eastern Asia, discussed in the preceding chapters, left a lasting mark on the Chinese collective memory. Events of the early seventeenth century comprised, in many respects, continuations of unresolved issues of the previous century. Although the Ming somewhat relaxed their earlier sea bans after 1567, they reenacted the prohibitions in 1572, 1592, 1626, 1628 and 1639, and, as a result, overseas trade continued to experience restrictions and obstructions. As in the past, merchants and seafarers, who lacked opportunities to trade legally, turned to piracy and smuggling. Given the turmoil and anarchy of

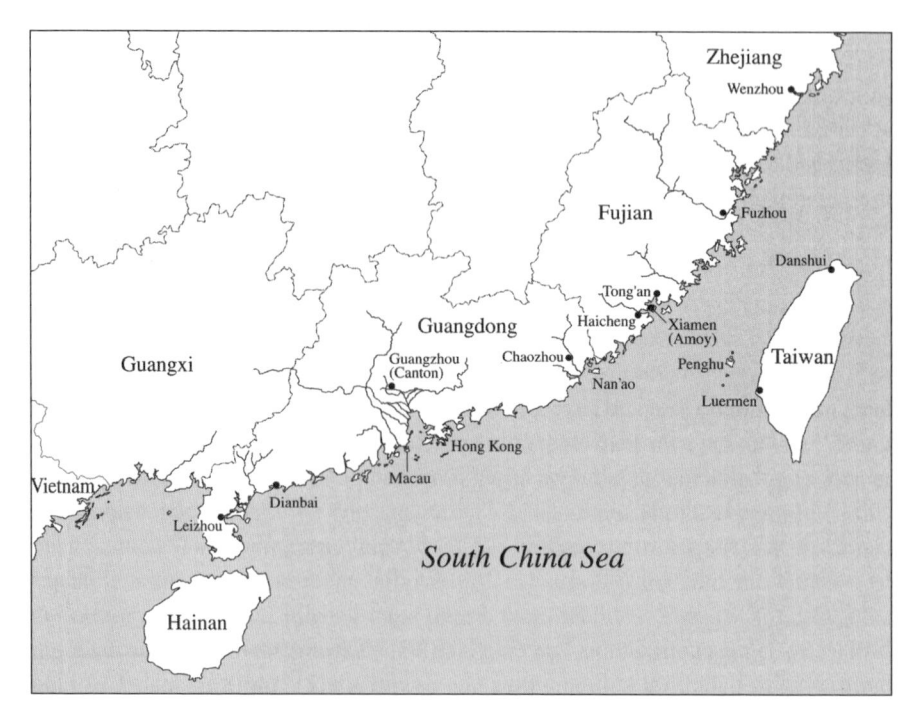

Map 7.1   The Southeast Coast of China in the Eighteenth Century

the Ming-Qing transition, hegemonic power-brokers of the Zheng family managed to take advantage of the circumstances to forge a maritime empire in the greater China Seas region. This marked the last time, however, that influential coastal families — most with close ties to the maritime trade — actively supported piracy in clear defiance of the government.

In the early seventeenth century, piracy noticeably surged in southeastern China. The most skillful pirates generally associated with smuggling syndicates or gangs that conducted trade with Japan, Manila, Macau, and elsewhere.[1] Between 1610 and 1630, for instance, over ten pirate-merchant fleets operated, competed, and coexisted in the waters of Fujian and eastern Guangdong. They alternated plundering one another and merchant ships with business ventures to Nan'ao, Penghu, Taiwan, Japan, and the Philippines. The Dutch settlements, first, on Penghu (1604 and 1622), and later, on Taiwan (1624), contributed further to destabilizing the coast, not only because they intercepted ships trading with China, Japan, and Southeast Asia, but also because they supplied weapons to pirates and fenced their booty. Therefore, the pirates never lacked the money, food, and arms necessary for pursuing their nefarious activities.[2]

Although these outlaws have often been described as merchant groups,[3] it would be more accurate to define them as fleets of adventurers given both to business and to piracy. This description equally applies to many Europeans who both intercepted junks navigating between China, Japan, and the Philippines, and who also waged vicious wars among themselves — a smaller-scale reflection of the sea wars then raging in Europe. In fact, English and Spanish records reveal that both countries felt that the struggles among Europeans in the eastern seas posed greater threats to security than the activities of Chinese merchant-pirates, whom they considered militarily inferior.[4]

The actors in Asiatic trade had always competed intensely for business, especially the Fujian sea merchants who played major roles in both trade and piracy. Foremost among them was Zheng Zhilong, a merchant-smuggler-pirate from southern Fujian, who displayed exceptional entrepreneurial and organizational skills.[5] Beginning in the 1620s, he slowly built up a vast network that included not only his fellow countrymen and relatives, but also European and Japanese merchants and officials. Eliminating his rivals one by one, he developed a huge piratical empire that controlled the sea lanes and trade throughout the China Seas region. He had become so powerful that by the end of the decade, as one official explained, "All merchant junks passing through the South China Sea had to have Zhilong's safe-conduct pass. Therefore, all of the outlaws and rabble in the whole region pledged allegiance to him and came under his control."[6]

Along with economic stimuli, ecological factors also pushed many people, for simple reasons of survival, to work on the ships of the smuggler and pirate fleets. Commencing with the 1590s, a series of natural calamities struck the Fujian and Guangdong coasts leaving innumerable people destitute. For several decades, earthquakes, droughts, and floods followed upon one another in rapid succession, and the reality or threat of famine hung heavily over the heads of the population. As the cost of food and other necessities skyrocketed, bandits and pirates appeared everywhere.[7] Given the terrible situation in Fujian, Zheng Zhilong showed his savvy by robbing the rich and helping the poor. On the one hand, in dealing with merchants, he favored a "pre-emptive tax on merchandise" (*baoshui*), a form of extortion that gave him the exclusive first right to purchase goods and, in all likelihood, to also set prices. On the other hand, he aided the poor and destitute by providing them with food and jobs, thereby acquiring a reputation as a beneficent man.[8] As the Grand Coordinator of Fujian, Zhu Yifeng, emphasized, this latter tactic proved undeniably effective and people flocked to his service: "The bandits kill soldiers, but not the people; they pillage the rich and give a small part [of the booty] to the poor. [Thus], their power spreads."[9]

The Ming military establishment, perpetually short of equipment, provisions, and men, also could do little to prevent the development and growth of piracy. Adding to the chaos of this period, as well as to the constant budgetary constraints, the imperial navy faced problems of corruption and, particularly, cowardice among its officers and men. Some commanders, as often reported, did not hesitate to flee or to cut deals with pirates in order to spare their own lives and those of their troops.[10] A shortage of officials also made it necessary to keep people on duty that should otherwise have been punished or relieved of their posts. The standard formula of "shoring up one's errors by acquiring merit" (*daizui ligong*) had now become "pay off one's errors while awaiting a successor" (*daizui houdai*).[11]

Zhu Yifeng, a newcomer in the region, who tried to judge the actions of military officers in Fujian objectively, sometimes showed signs of discouragement. In a memorial to the throne, he explained:

> The Fujian military allows the situation to deteriorate and does not know what it means to reprimand the [sea] bandits. For some ten days, your servant [i.e., Zhu] made plans … . [My writing] brush lost its bristles. But the officers have no desire to fight, and let themselves be tricked by the bandits, mistakenly believing that they will not come, but when they do [those same officers] are perplexed and lose their heads.

Still worse, he continued:

> The Fujian commanders fear [sea] bandits more than they do the law, [while] the people follow bandits more willingly than they do officials. This ailment is now fatal, [as if] someone were sound asleep and powerless to awaken.[12]

Furthermore, many of their fellow countrymen did not consider these pirates and smugglers outlaws, because they frequently worked in partnership with coastal inhabitants who served as fences, suppliers, and arms dealers.[13] The merchant-pirates and coastal residents often interacted cordially, at least, in the areas where the former came from and conducted trade, making it, in fact, easier for pirates to acquiesce and for local officials to "pacify the seas" (*pinghai* or *jinghai*). As a rule, pirates carried out reprisals only when refused the possibility of pardons.

In one particular case, in the late 1620s, when Zheng Zhilong — already in good repute in the region around Xiamen — made overtures to the Ming government to surrender, officials dared not treat his proposals lightly. At that time, he had the most powerful armed fleet on the seas and controlled a vast maritime empire based on trade and pillage. His armada, better equipped and larger than the imperial navy, stood as the only one capable of resisting European ships. Also with the Manchu armies rapidly advancing across the Liaodong Peninsula, it became crucial for the Ming court to bring peace to the southeastern coast. In other words, Zheng Zhilong appeared as the right man at the right time, owing to his military power, his local connections, and his knowledge of trade and of the Europeans. After his surrender in 1628, he "legitimately" controlled the whole Fujian economy, while his appointments, first, in 1633, as regional vice-commander (*fu zongbing*), and later, in 1640, as regional commander (*zongbing*), assured his authority over the military.

In 1646, Zheng Zhilong surrendered to the Manchu conquerors, but instead of rewarding him, they arrested, and eventually, executed him in 1661. Nevertheless, his son, Zheng Chenggong (known in Western literature as Koxinga), took advantage of the chaos to raise the banner of Ming loyalism, and continued to expand his father's maritime empire. For the next ten years, his fleets, like his father's before him, monopolized shipping in Fujian, Taiwan, Guangdong, the Philippines, and much of Southeast Asia. He financed his huge syndicate through commerce, robbery, and extortion. In 1661, after he failed to take Nanjing, he withdrew to Taiwan, where he drove the Dutch away. Although he died unexpectedly six months later, his heirs kept up resistance to the Manchus until their defeat in 1683.[14]

The sustained domination of the Zheng clan on the southeast coast had serious consequences for the dynastic transition between 1644 and 1683. The conflict among multiple adversaries devastated southeastern China. For four decades, southern Fujian, in particular, found itself at the center of fighting, pillaging, and destruction, its population effectively held hostage to the various antagonists: pirates, bandits, and soldiers. Dispossessed by one side, people did not have the time to recuperate before troops or brigands came back to raid again. Their distress mounted to the level that "there were no more boys or girls to be sold by their families."[15] (See Figure 7.1.) The testimony of Censor Wang Yingyuan, while on tour in Fujian, was particularly striking:

In the eighth and ninth lunar months [of 1652, in Haicheng County] the price of rice had risen to 150 taels per picul. The people had run out of grasses, roots, wood, and leaves, as well as mice, sparrows, water buffalos, and horses. In their desperate search for food, nothing was left but human flesh. Fathers and sons ate one another, and those who had not ended up in the stewpot died of diseases or hunger. [Others] drowned or hung themselves.... Everyday thousands died. The bodies piled up and the stink could be smelled for several *li* away.[16]

Beginning in 1652, in order to isolate the Zheng forces from their continental support, the Qing government issued a series of harsh sea bans. In rapid succession, imperial decrees commanded officials in coastal areas to burn all boats; to bar the construction of large ocean-going junks; and to ban the purchase of foreign-made ships and the sale of Chinese ships to foreigners. They prohibited Chinese merchants from Shandong to Guangdong from setting out to sea under pain of death. Then, in 1661, the government went even further by issuing an evacuation policy, requiring coastal residents in Fujian and Guangdong to resettle thirty to fifty *li* inland. It

Figure 7.1 Famine Victims Selling Their Children
(Source: *The Famine in China, Illustrations by a Native Artist*, London, 1878)

ordered the burning of all houses and buildings within the evacuation zone and the execution of anyone caught trying to return home. Testimony at the time portrayed the extreme distress to which the inhabitants were subject.[17]

Although the draconian policies brought great hardships to the coastal people, they did not put a stop to the Zheng forces. The edicts did, however, make communications with the continent quite difficult. In any case, the Zheng family held on to Taiwan, and continued to resist the Manchus until 1683. The Qing restrictions backfired by alienating large segments of the population, sometimes turning innocuous fishermen into rebels. Between 1663 and 1664, in the Canton region, for instance, Zhou Yu and Li Rong led bands of displaced fishermen in an uprising that shook the economic core of Guangdong Province.[18] Above all, the stringent Qing policies and fighting totally disrupted the flow of trade, which moved away from China to Taiwan, the foreign enclave at Macau, and to other trading ports in Asia.[19]

Piracy from 1684 to 1780

The years 1683–84 signaled a turning point. Once the Qing had eliminated the Ming loyalists and subdued Zheng's maritime empire, reconstruction began in the coastal region. Moreover, the Kangxi Emperor had finally realized that the peace and security of the southeastern provinces depended on their prosperity that based itself on maritime trade. Therefore, in quick succession, the court abrogated the rigid sea bans and began, in fact, to cautiously encourage trade. Afterwards, the government also started to enact laws to protect private property and to regulate sea traffic.[20] The new measures brought stability and prosperity to coastal South China. Piracy declined.

To say that piracy declined, however, did not mean that it had completely disappeared. For roughly one hundred years, from 1684 to 1780, petty piracy replaced the previous large-scale one. Now, most pirates came from common stock; and, in general, wealthy merchants and members of respectable families no longer turned to piracy as they had in the past. Many of the people who became pirates appeared to have belonged to marginalized groups that deliberately indulged in brigandage, as well as sailors and fishermen who took to crime on a part-time basis. Raiding continued according to age-old patterns, dating back to the Han dynasty, which followed the rhythms of the monsoons. Although piracy occurred year-round, it traditionally increased dramatically along China's coast between April and August, and then decreased between November and December. It was no coincidence that food prices in the densely populated coastal areas of Fujian and Guangdong reached their peak each year between April and July, and as one of the Qing literati noted, whenever food prices increased so too did piracy.[21]

The relative calm was shattered for a brief period between 1690 and 1726. During that short span, the risk of attack on the seas seemed to have been great. In 1708, for instance, officials reported that in spite of the protection of three naval vessels, pirates attacked a seventeen-boat fleet of a rich merchant from Shanghai, Zhang Xingke, who lost one of his vessels in the attack.[22] The necessity of naval escorts revealed the underlying climate of insecurity. At least two other large gangs, led by Zheng Jinxin and Chen Shangyi, were operating between 1699 and 1713. From the extant documents, unfortunately, we can not tell the relationship between the two groups; but we do know that both gangs haunted the same areas, sailing with several ships. Zheng Jinxin, who came from Fuzhou, was captured in April 1711, in the company of Cai Yuanliang from Zhejiang, Zhang Jinglong from Shandong, and some fifty other pirates. Although condemned to death, they were pardoned and sent to Heilongjiang to serve in the imperial navy.[23] Chen Shangyi surrendered in January 1713. According to his testimony, he did not attack European ships because of their superior firepower; instead, his victims chiefly consisted of Asian merchant junks laden with rice and other commodities.[24] These pirates, with bases in Fujian and Guangdong, seasonally plied the waters between Zhejiang and the Liaodong Peninsula.[25]

One of the most interesting cases of piracy occurred in 1726. During the late summer and early autumn, two fleets that appeared to have worked in conjunction with one another threatened the waters of Zhejiang and Fujian. The first group consisted of a small squadron of four ships that attacked a fishing boat and six trading junks between August 2 and September 3. Curiously, officials noted that when these pirates advanced, they raised banners on their ships with the slogan "rob the rich and succor the poor" (*jiefu jipin*). The pirate leaders, they further remarked, wore long red robes like Buddha's disciples (*luohan*), and they sat on great cushions of the same color. The whole crew dressed — *ninja*-like — in close-fitting red and green garments, armed with ten to twenty muskets. Judging from their accents (the reports said), they came from Fujian and Guangdong. This first group of pirates was captured sometime before November, when the second group, wearing similar clothing, was apprehended.[26]

The above-mentioned pirate gangs were generally well-equipped and well-organized. Official naval reports said the pirates made good use of artillery, especially, fire-ships, and, as a tactic, they often lured ships for surprise attacks.[27] Some of them also operated from bases on offshore islands and secluded bays, where they traded booty, purchased weapons as well as supplies, and launched raids. According to the testimony of a pirate, Chen Minglong, captured in 1711, the islands of Jinshan (in southern Jiangsu) and Yushan (in Zhejiang), and some unnamed islands off the coast of Danshui (in northern Taiwan), provided bases from which Zheng Jinxin and his gang launched their expeditions. These islands, situated on the major sea lane for grain shipments from Taiwan to Beijing and to provinces having rice shortages, held a highly strategic position for controlling the entire maritime traffic, including coastal and overseas trade. Furthermore, the volume of grain cargos pillaged suggested that the pirates had continental or foreign networks where they could sell their loot. They obviously operated in well structured groups.[28]

Beginning in 1711, the imperial court began issuing new regulations in an attempt to control the activities of Chinese fishermen and seafarers, the main perpetrators of piracy. One law aimed to restrain Fujian and Zhejiang fishermen from leaving their home provinces.[29] In 1712, a letter from Korean officials notified the Chinese authorities of the presence of bogus fishermen anchoring off their coast. In fact, they consisted of pirates who customarily took refuge in that area. The Qing Ministry of Rites decreed that it henceforth authorized the Korean government to combat the pirates and extradite prisoners back to China.[30] The situation, however, did not improve and, in 1722, the Qing emperor issued another edict stipulating that the Korean authorities should escort home Chinese subjects who stayed in Korea due to storms and held regular permits (see discussion on *aojia* below). If they did not have licenses, they were to be judged according to local law; however, Beijing requested the Korean government inform them of the port from which any outlaws had left China in order to punish the officials responsible for negligence.[31]

Despite repeated pronouncements, the Qing failed to solve the problem of fishermen and sailors engaging in occasional piracy. But for most officials, petty piracy created a nuisance and not a serious threat. Nevertheless, the few piratical incidents described in government documents only represented a tiny fraction of the total number of cases. In fact, many victims did not lodge complaints, either because they were themselves operating clandestinely or they preferred to avoid contact with the authorities, which could lead to extortion or an inspection that would tie them up too long.[32] Year-end reports like that of Gao Qizhuo, dated December 8, 1727, appear frequently. It begins:

> This year, from spring to the end of autumn, the Fujian sea was quiet everywhere. There were only small gangs of robbers, not in any way [comparable] to the large groups of several tens of individuals, allied in a fleet for plunder, who used to attack and carry off merchant ships.[33]

To summarize the archival evidence, most of the pirates between 1684 and 1780 hailed from southern Fujian and eastern Guangdong, and carried out raids as far away as Korea. Most of the pirates began as fishermen and sailors who considered piracy an occasional and seasonal occupation. They did not operate as career criminals, though a good many of them developed into what the records called "habitual pirates" (*jizei*). Officials classified pirates into different categories according to the number of attacks, use of force, type of arms, wounds inflicted on victims, resistance to government agents, and collusion with other outlaws. Pirates chose their main prey from merchant shipping, sailing alone or in concert, and killings seem to have been rare, at least in the known cases. Violence towards merchants and fishermen usually only occurred when they resisted their aggressors.[34] Most accounts depicted the piracy at this time as a survival strategy among marginal people who turned to crime to supplement honest but insufficient earnings.

Coastal Security, 1600–1780

In the Ming and early Qing periods, perhaps even more so than in previous dynasties, because of the rampant and widespread development of piracy, coastal security always remained a major concern of the state. An elaborate coastal defense system evolved from the fifteenth to the eighteenth centuries articulated around two axes: a military component that aimed to protect the coastline and a civilian one that sought to control its population. In order to insure security along the shore, Ming and Qing officials instituted a plethora of laws, regulations, and organizations concerning regular naval patrols; a network of military guard posts, batteries, watchtowers, and signaling stations; local militia and other community self-defense groups; and an elaborate "mutual responsibility system" (*baojia* and *aojia*). To work effectively and efficiently required not only coordination between the various agencies but also, and even more importantly, the cooperation of the inhabitants, especially the wealthy merchants and prominent families. We notice important changes not only in governmental policies but also in the attitudes of certain important members of the coastal communities toward the state precisely during the years covered in this study, from roughly 1600 to 1780.

By the late Ming, the military establishment had become impotent. Internally, corruption, factionalism, incompetence, and fiscal bankruptcy crippled the government. Externally, Manchu incursions on the northeastern frontier challenged Ming sovereignty, and forced the government to commit large amounts of money and soldiers to defend its northern borders, thereby weakening its military power on the coast. In the 1620s and 1630s, the quota of ships and troops stationed in forward naval outposts had decreased by two thirds, and, as a result, bands of pirates occupied, or at least frequented, islands and bays that the armed forces could no longer maintain.[35] Given the situation, the Ming court, understandably, "abandoned" the task of protecting the coast to the Zheng family, with their large fleets and well-trained crews.[36] The whole system collapsed, however, during the Ming-Qing dynastic wars, and, as we noted above, the new Manchu rulers, in a desperate effort to stop piracy, initiated a drastic coastal evacuation policy in the 1660s.

Once the Manchus consolidated their authority over all of China by 1684, and the Kangxi Emperor rescinded the maritime bans in favor of opening up trade, the central government quickly revamped the coastal security system. It established or re-established an interconnected network of customs offices, sub-county *yamens*, and military posts, all along the southern littoral. The civil officials and commanders who manned them had the specific assignments of regulating trade and controlling piracy and smuggling. As for the Qing soldiers, in particular, the government relied mainly on the Chinese troops of the so-called Army of the Green Standard (*lüying*) for coastal defense. Its system seemed to have worked fairly well at least until the late eighteenth century.[37]

In attempting to administer the always unruly southern coastal population, the Ming and Qing governments depended upon a variety of mechanisms, including one of the most important, the mutual responsibility system (*baojia* and *aojia*).[38] *Baojia* had ancient antecedents and Chinese governments had employed it on and off (and with mixed results) since the Song dynasty (960–1279). In the 1620s, in the face of military incompetence and rising piracy, the Ming court reinstated *baojia* agencies in several areas on the coast.[39] It organized fishermen and sailors into an equivalent system of "anchorage groups" (*aojia*), which dated back to at least the early Ming as a counter to the *wakō* disturbances. In 1616, for instance, Xiao Ji suggested using the *aojia* concept as a key to controlling the seafaring population on the southern coast.[40] Ten years later, *aojia* groups emerged in Tong'an County in Fujian, possibly instigated by Zheng Zhilong.[41] However, the government did not use the organization universally, as court and local officials continually called to have it reinstated.[42] Still, the success of the *baojia* and *aojia* structures depended on competent administrators and local cooperation. During most of the Ming, animus toward the sea bans held back popular support, and the effectiveness of both systems suffered.

The new Qing rulers maintained the earlier Ming policies of sea bans and mutual responsibility systems. As for the latter, Qin Shizhen, the governor of Zhejiang, established anchorage groups along the coast in 1654, but they would not have been in widespread use in the 1660s due to the evacuation policy.[43] In any case, in 1703, the Qing restored *aojia* in some ports, and in 1707, incorporated it in the dynastic statutes.[44] In 1729, Guangdong's Dan boat people, and in 1765, all other commercial and fishing boat operators came under the system. Boats also had to display, at least in theory, wooden licenses, equivalent to the door placards on homes on land. These permits, placed on the bow or stern, identified vessels as being either commercial or fishing boats, and included the name and age of the boat master, family members, and crew, as well as home port, registration number, and date of issue (see Figure 7.2).[45]

During the early eighteenth century, the *aojia* system apparently provided an effective tool for control and defense of the coast. It also served as an important bridge linking state and local society. Administrative correspondence reveals that, indeed, the coastguard and mutual responsibility units closely cooperated. The rapidity with which they identified and arrested petty pirates testified to the coordination between government and community representatives. This, however,

96　*Paola Calanca*

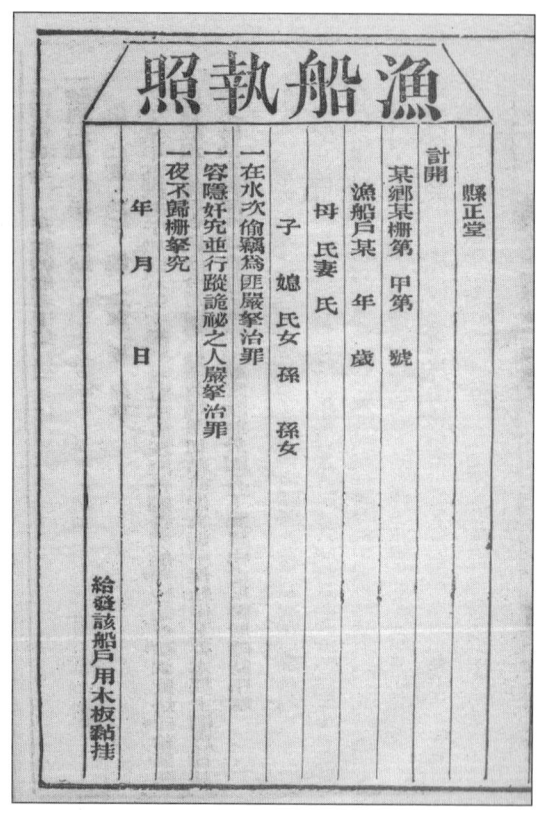

Figure 7.2　Qing Era License for Fishing Boats
(Source: *Baojiashu jiyao*. Shanghai, 1838)

does not mean that *aojia* had no problems, as numerous complaints about corrupt and incompetent officers as well as *aojia* personnel surfaced. In any case, in the 1770s, the whole structure began to break down.

The incorporation of native officiers into the imperial navy and coastal defense forces constituted the key to implementing Qing coastal security policies. We may interpret this choice as a desire of the government to accommodate inhabitants traumatized by a long period of war (1640s to 1680s), as well as to make use of the strong "nativistic" identity that the coastal population felt for their homes. This arrangement actually began in the early Qing period. In their struggle against the Zheng regime, the Manchu rulers came to depend on a Fukianese navy commanded by men who had come over from the Zheng camp. Furthermore, after 1684, Fukianese officers, whose connections with the trading world lent them legitimacy among the local population, proved indispensable to the new government in its efforts to establish a navy. Because of their mercantile connections, and knowledge of local customs and language, these officers supplied critical information for setting up a coastal defense system within the framework of re-opening maritime trade.[46]

In the early eighteenth century, these officers received support from the court in Beijing as well as from local notables to whom they were related. Open to discussion, they often counseled high-ranking civilian provincial officials on matters regarding coastal security and trade. In the same period, with regard to the struggle against piracy, a concrete, if not always infallible, collaboration existed between local authorities, members of the great families, influential merchants, and representatives of the population. These men, experienced in naval matters, also possessed socio-cultural backgrounds that facilitated understanding of the maritime world and the ways of controlling seafaring activities and coastal inhabitants. After the Ming-Qing dynastic conflicts, a number of these officers participated directly in discussions about reorganization of the coastal economy and the preparation of laws intended to govern maritime activity. It seems obvious that they did this while safeguarding their own and family interests.[47]

Conclusion

Between 1600 and 1780, two basic forms of piracy occurred along the southeastern coast of China: large-scale, well-organized fleets of merchant-pirates and small bands of oportunistic petty pirates. The former, active mainly in the first half of the seventeenth century, contributed directly to the rise of maritime commerce, especially the clandestine trade with Japan. As with the *wakō* of the mid-sixteenth century, these later merchant-pirates factored importantly in stimulating the overseas Chinese and Asian trade. But contrary to what had occurred during the earlier *wakō* crisis, these later pirates conducted fewer raids on coastal towns. Instead, they operated mainly on the seas, plundering ships and also developing protection rackets.

In contrast, most of the eighteenth century stayed relatively calm. Piracy remained a smaller problem for authorities to handle, and, in fact, they approached it in much the same manner as local banditry. The merchant-pirates disappeared after the Qing consolidation of power in 1680s. Chiefly, individuals on the margins of society, who were not professional pirates, but rather took to crime as temporary undertakings made up the vast majority of pirates during this later period. They mostly worked as sailors and fishermen, as well as laborers, coolies, and peddlers, who engaged in occasional piracy as a supplement to regular wages or when they were out of work.

The changes in the nature of piracy reflected the vicissitudes in society in general. The events that characterized the Ming-Qing dynastic transition also greatly affected both international trade and the socio-economic equilibrium of the southeastern littoral. Wars and anti-commercial policies of the Ming and early

Qing disrupted old trade patterns and helped create new ones. Bans on maritime commerce forced some merchants and coastal families to turn to piracy, either directly or indirectly, as a source of livelihood, but, perhaps, more in an attempt to maximize profits. The powerful Zheng family took advantage of the chaos to forge a huge maritime empire throughout the greater China Seas region. Beginning in the 1680s, with peace and stability, prosperity followed. It was no longer a time of adventure but of consolidation. With the new stability, piracy declined, but never disappeared. Documents of the period describe an optimistic climate in which even the *baojia* and *aojia* systems of population control seem to have succeeded, since they helped to eradicate large-scale piracy and brought petty piracy under control.

Besides ecological and economic conditions, we must also consider the role that governmental actions played in the changes in piracy. A near disappearance of the state on the southeastern coast characterized the era of the merchant-pirates, a time of dynamic increase in maritime activity throughout the greater China Seas. All governmental attempts to restrict trade backfired and instead furthered smuggling and piracy. Large numbers of coastal residents, including merchants and influential families, defiantly opposed imperial decrees and laws. By the turn of the eighteenth century, however, the new Qing government resolved to open up maritime trade, and to regain support from the coastal population in its war on piracy. To do this, the government made a concerted effort to recruit local Fukianese into the navy and coastal defense apparatus. Moreover, many of the new officers had family relations in the world of trade, while others had even begun their professional careers working aboard seagoing merchant junks. They probably stayed closely linked with the transoceanic ship owners, and maintained their best personal interest in keeping a careful watch over the coastal society and economy.

For several decades, until about the mid-eighteenth century, local elites cooperated with the government, taking charge of not only the coastal population, but also the regional economy, allowing no opportunity for large-scale, organized piracy, leaving behind only small-scale, petty piracy. The Qing court succeeded in reviving the coastal economy and maintaining security by leaving representatives of local society considerable room to maneuver, even if the government was deprived of *de facto* control of the inhabitants. This policy, however, had detrimental repercussions in the 1780s, when large-scale piracy reemerged, a topic taken up in the next chapter.

8
Piracy and the Shadow Economy in the South China Sea, 1780–1810

Robert J. Antony

In China, when pirates extorted money and goods from victims, they euphemistically referred to their actions as "levying duties on personal wealth" (*xishu caibo*).[1] Although they acted outside the law and the normal, licit trading system, pirates considered their activities a justifiable collection of tribute on private property. They attacked shipping not to destroy trade, but rather to gain a more equitable share in it. Theirs was a plunder-based political economy. Pirates and their complex of accomplices actually created an important shadow economy that operated alongside the regular economy and commercial system. Numerous black markets sprang up to deal specifically in stolen goods and to supply pirates with food, weapons, and other necessities. Pirates also needed safe harbors where they could careen and repair their vessels, and friendly ports where they could gather information and relax. Those who aided pirates became their partners in crime. By extending their operations on land, pirates entrenched themselves in local villages and made contacts with a wide cross-section of society. They built up a large underground network that included not only gangsters, smugglers, and Triads, but also fishermen, farmers, merchants, soldiers, gentry, and officials. Piracy, in fact, played an integral and pervasive role in the political economy of the South China Sea in the early modern period.

In recent years, a growing number of scholars have taken an interest in the shadow or informal economy, emphasizing its importance to the overall economy. They point out that to fully understand any economic system we need to go beyond the formal regulated and recorded economy to also examine the informal, unregulated, and illegal (or quasi-legal) one. Shadow economies develop organically, and provide job opportunities and incomes for millions of people around the world today. They include not only criminal activities such as smuggling, drug dealing, gambling, and prostitution, but also, illicit activities such as street hawking and the underreporting of income in legitimate businesses. These studies have discovered that in many contemporary societies, the shadow economy, although difficult to quantify, actually occupies a significant place in the "real economy." One economist, for example, estimated that in recent years the informal economy in Taiwan may be as large as fifty percent of the country's GNP.² Often too, with the predominantly illegitimate nature of the shadow economy, it has become closely tied to organized crime while its success depends on violence.³

Most studies have examined contemporary shadow economies without paying much attention to its predecessors in China. This chapter examines piracy in the light of what it can tell us about the socio-economic conditions and power structures of early modern China's maritime society. In particular, I seek to engage with the literature on piracy as an economic menace and to argue, instead, that it also had important positive economic consequences. This does not deny the negative impact of piracy on legitimate trade, but rather, explores a fresh, alternative approach to a well-traveled subject.⁴ The main focus of this chapter centers upon the shadow economy that piracy had fostered around the South China Sea, and in particular, along the Guangdong coast, in the early modern era.

Piracy in Context

In the South China Sea, the years from 1780 to 1810 proved a time of paradoxes. Tremendous population growth stimulated a commercial revolution that, in turn, created fabulous wealth that, unfortunately, was distributed unevenly. For some, this was a time of great opportunity, but, for others, of great distress. By the late eighteenth century, as unemployment, vagabondage, and poverty mounted, so did social unrest. A series of uprisings and rebellions stretched from Vietnam to southern and central China — the Tay Son Rebellion in Vietnam (1771–1802); the Lin Shuangwen Rebellion in Taiwan (1787–88); the Miao Uprising in Sichuan, Hubei, and Guizhou (1795); the White Lotus Rebellion in central China (1795–1804); and the Triad Uprising in Guangdong (1802–03). Banditry, armed feuds, and ethnic unrest were likewise on the rise. Throughout this whole period, South China also experienced an unusually large number of natural disasters — floods, typhoons, locusts, droughts, and earthquakes — that caused famines and added further to disorder and dislocation.⁵ Indeed, during these troubled years, the whole region suffered.

Piracy comprised yet another social disorder to plague the South China Sea during this period. After a century of relative calm (as discussed in the previous chapter), in the 1780s, large-scale piracy reappeared in the region when Tay Son rebels in Vietnam began to sanction raids into Chinese waters to bolster their revenues and increase their manpower with the addition of Chinese pirates. Although not the cause of the upsurge in piracy, the Tay Son Rebellion did significantly contribute to its expansion and organization. Soon afterwards, in the wake of the Lin Shuangwen Rebellion, many refugees fleeing Qing repression escaped to Fujian and Guangdong where they joined pirate gangs. Within twenty years, the number of pirates had grown to more than seventy thousand individuals as well as countless numbers of people on shore who aided them. Between 1802 and 1810, several large pirate leagues emerged to dominate the coastal area from Zhejiang to Vietnam. Cai Qian and Zhu Fen became the most powerful pirate chiefs in Zhejiang, Fujian, and Taiwan, while Wushi Er, Donghai Ba, Zheng Yi, and later, his widow, Zheng Yi Sao, and Zhang Bao, controlled the waters around Guangdong and Vietnam (see Map 8.1). Although by 1810, these pirate leagues had collapsed, nonetheless, petty piracy continued in the region.[6]

Piracy must be understood in the context of the vibrant commerce of this period. Once the Qing government lifted the sea bans in 1684, maritime trade not only recovered, but expanded tremendously. Beside the thriving foreign trade centered at Canton, an even more dynamic Chinese overseas and coastal junk trade also developed. For more than a century before the Opium War (1839–42), Chinese merchants and junks dominated commercial shipping in the South China Sea. All along China's coast, ports reopened and new ones appeared to handle the nascent commerce. The majority of them were relatively small in size and chiefly engaged in the coastal trade and indirectly in its overseas counterpart.[7] Visible wealth, in terms of the large amounts of goods and money transported by ships, provided greater

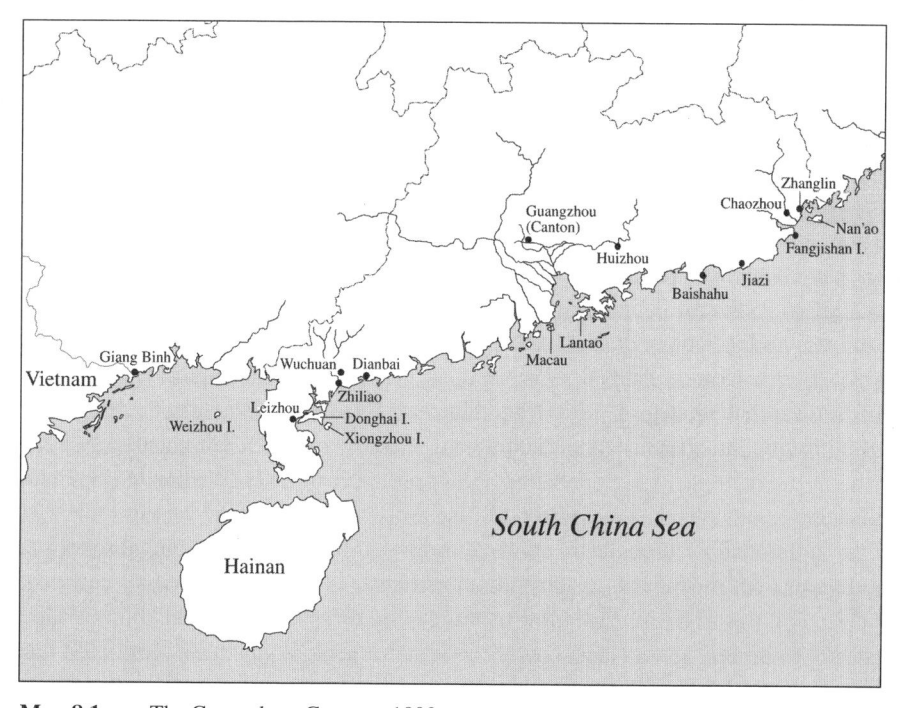

Map 8.1 The Guangdong Coast, c. 1800

opportunities and greater temptations for people to commit piracy, especially those living in poverty and with fewer chances for advancing their lives by legitimate means. Paradoxically, then, this age of prosperity also marked an age of poverty and piracy.[8]

Pirate Lairs and Friendly Ports

The shadow economy existed alongside and as an adjunct to the legitimate, regulated one. Pirates operated from lairs and strongholds located not only on secluded, out-of-the-way islands but also, quite significantly, in areas located near major commercial and political hubs. Repeatedly, Chinese and Western maps and charts clearly noted notorious pirate haunts, with some simply labeled "dangerous," while others had ominous names such as the Ladrones,[9] a group of small islands at the mouth of the busy Pearl River. Chinese officials also posted notices and warned travelers and merchants to stay clear of well-known "pirate bays." Most, however, stayed unmarked and went unrecorded. Often pirates shared anchorages with fishing boats, making them appear innocuous and anonymous. Table 8.1 lists the better known pirate bases, as well as sanctioned and unsanctioned ports with connections to piracy during this period.

Table 8.1   Sanctioned Ports, Unsanctioned Ports, and Pirate Lairs in Guangdong, 1780–1810

Region	Sanctioned Ports	Unsanctioned Ports	Pirate Lairs
West Guangdong	Wuchuan Dianbai Zhiliao Anpu	Giang Binh (Jiangping) Sanhewo Zhangshan	Weizhou Donghai Xiangzhou
Central Guangdong	Macau Canton Zhenkou Jiangmen Shanwei	Zhuo Jia Cun Jiu'ao Dayushan (Lantao) Changzhou Aotou	Ladrones (Wanshan) Taipa (Danzai) Coloane (Luhuan) Hengqing Dayushan (Lantao) Changzhou Liyumen Mirs Bay (Dapeng Wan) Bias Bay (Daya Wan)
East Guangdong	Jiazi Chaozhou Chenghai Zhanglin	Magong Baishahu	Nan'ao Fangjishan

Pirate lairs, situated everywhere along the coast and on offshore islands, functioned not only as safe havens but also as centers for clandestine trade. Bases provided everyday refuges and hideouts where pirates returned after raids to rest, refit ships, and sell booty. They exercised care in selecting lairs with protected harbors where they could careen their vessels and find shelter from storms. For example, several unnamed islands at the mouth of the Pearl River — perhaps the Ladrones — offered regular anchorages where pirates "hauled their vessels on shore, and cleaned their bottoms."[10] Bases also required abundant fresh water and firewood. Pirates favored relatively isolated areas yet within easy reach of friendly markets and well-traveled sea lanes.

Although some pirates used makeshift bases, others settled their families and built trading posts in fortified strongholds. Just east of the Leizhou Peninsula, on Donghai and Xiongzhou islands, they constructed shanties where they lived and conducted business. In 1805, officials reported that peasants from as far away as three hundred *li* would travel to Donghai to sell rice to the pirates because they paid above-market prices. On Weizhou, on the western side of Leizhou, approximately 500 pirates and their families shared the island with 150 illegal squatters. The island had an abundance of fresh water and firewood, and the inhabitants grew rice and vegetables, and raised pigs and chickens that they sold to the pirates. Merchants regularly came to the island to trade with pirates. Although somewhat isolated and remote, all these bases occupied positions along important trade routes.[11]

Pirate bases not only developed in distant areas such as Donghai, Xiongzhou, and Weizhou islands, but also around the bustling commercial hubs of Macau, Canton, and Chaozhou. The islands of Taipa (Danzai) and Coloane (Luhuan) near Macau, and Cheung Chau (Changzhou) and Lantao (Dayushan) near Hong Kong supported thriving populations of pirates, smugglers, and fishermen for many centuries.[12] In Hong Kong harbor at Liyumen, in 1753, the pirate, Zheng Lianchang, built an Empress of Heaven Temple (the patron deity for seafarers) and a stronghold in the hills behind it. From this vantage point, his gang commanded the entire region. Half a century later, this same area continued to serve as a base for Zheng Yi, Zhang Bao, and other pirates.[13] Further to the east, on the rugged Huizhou coast, Mirs Bay (Dapeng Wan) and Bias Bay (Daya Wan) remained well-known pirate haunts from the early fifteenth to late twentieth centuries. Somewhere along this coast (its exact location unknown), stood a San Po Temple, whose deity, Zhang Bao especially worshiped because of her efficacy in aiding pirates. The unnamed bay in front of the temple served as a regular pirate anchorage.[14] (See Map 8.2.)

Near the entrepôt of Chaozhou, in the far eastern corner of Guangdong, the island of Nan'ao had continually acted as an important pirate haven since at least the Tang dynasty. Zhu Fen and other pirates established bases on Fangjishan (Releasing Cocks Island), near the bustling ports of Chenghai and Zhanglin. The island boasted a famous Empress of Heaven Temple — a favorite stopover for sailors, traders, and

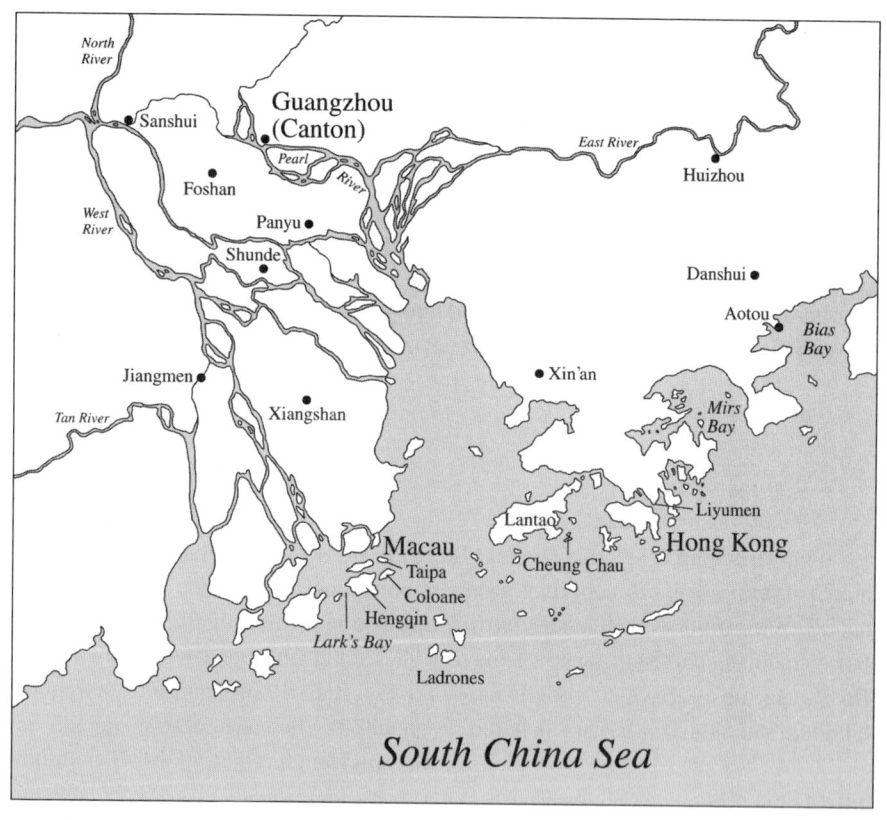

Map 8.2 The Pearl River Delta, c. 1800

pirates. Each year, during the southern monsoons, pirate fleets returned to the tiny island to refit their ships and handle business.[15]

From these locations, pirates conducted trade with a variety of black markets situated in both sanctioned and unsanctioned ports (see Figure 8.1). Sanctioned ports, which were officially recognized by the state, normally had a customs house, military post, or, at the least, some minor official stationed there. They included key entrepôts such as Macau, Canton, and Chaozhou, as well as hundreds of smaller harbors such as Zhiliao, Jiangmen, Jiazi, Chenghai, and Zhanglin. Important for promoting trade, these ports were normally situated along or near the mouths of navigable rivers, thereby linking the coast with the interior. Most participated in both the domestic coasting and overseas junk trade.[16]

At the entrance to the Han River delta, to give one example, Zhanglin functioned as a major commercial hub with direct links to domestic markets in Chaozhou, Canton, Amoy, Taiwan, and Shandong, as well as with those in Japan and Southeast

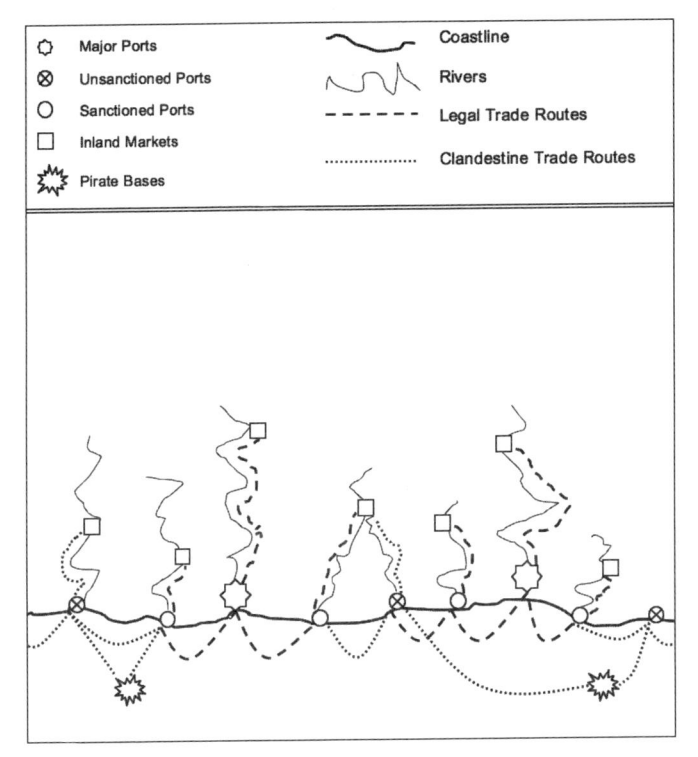

Piracy and the Shadow Economy in the South China Sea, 1780–1810 **105**

⟡	Major Ports	⌒ Coastline	
⊗	Unsanctioned Ports	⌇ Rivers	
○	Sanctioned Ports	− − − − − Legal Trade Routes	
☐	Inland Markets	⋯⋯⋯⋯ Clandestine Trade Routes	
✺	Pirate Bases		

Figure 8.1 Clandestine and Legal Trade Routes

Asia. It reached its economic peak in the last decades of the eighteenth century. At that time, hundreds of shops and warehouses, numerous merchant associations (*huiguan*), a maritime customs office, and several nearby military posts signaled Zhanglin's economic importance. In the 1790s, the Zhanglin customs office collected roughly one-fifth of the total revenue for the entire province. The port also contained a large Empress of Heaven Temple, built in 1787, financed and managed by local shopkeepers and sea merchants.[17] As we shall see below, Zhanglin was intimately connected with the shadow economy.

Unsanctioned ports were those that the state neither officially recognized nor regulated. They developed spontaneously and, because they received no government recognition, remained unlawful. Despite the opening of numerous new harbors during the eighteenth century, commerce outstripped the growth of legitimate markets. To meet demands, innumerable small unsanctioned ports sprang up and became deeply involved in the burgeoning clandestine trade with smugglers and pirates. Although sources failed to record most of them, occasionally, officials and other writers mentioned the names of friendly ports and villages where pirates congregated to do business, including Giang Binh, Sanhewo, Zhangshan, Zhuo Jia Cun, Aotou, Baishahu, and Magong (see Table 8.1).[18]

106 Robert J. Antony

Giang Binh (or Jiangping in Chinese) represented the most notorious clandestine port at this time. Situated on the ill-defined Sino-Vietnamese border, the town occupied part of Vietnam's An Quang Province until it reverted to China in 1885, as part of the settlement ending the Sino-French War. An important frontier town, it thrived on the pirate and smuggling trade from 1780 to 1802, when royalist troops fighting the Tay Son rebels razed it. Located near the mouth of a small unnavigable river, with almost impenetrable mountains at its back, and land too poor for agriculture, Giang Binh instinctively developed as a black market.[19] (See Figure 8.2.) By the end of the eighteenth century, it grew into a lively border town with hundreds of shops and roughly two thousand Vietnamese and Chinese households. It also held a large squatter population of mostly poor Vietnamese, settled on the sandy shoals at the entrance to the harbor. Many residents specialized in handling stolen goods and provisioning the pirates who frequented the port and lived on many of the nearby islands. Traders from Guangdong, Guangxi, Fujian, and Vietnam travelled to the port specifically to sell merchandise and to buy booty.[20]

Giang Binh served as an integral node in the vibrant shadow economy that crisscrossed the South China Sea, linking and forming an extensive network of licit and illicit trade. In its prime, Giang Binh stood as the hub of a vast network of black markets, pirate bases, and friendly ports that stretched northward up the Chinese

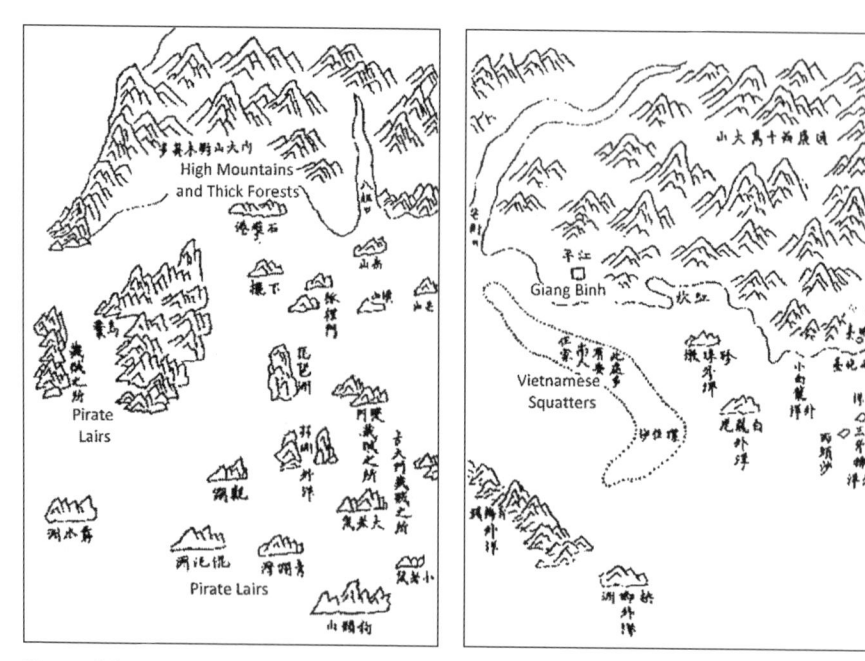

Figure 8.2 The Unsanctioned Port of Giang Binh
(Source: *Guangdong tongzhi*, Guangzhou, 1864)

coast from Hainan Island and Guangdong to Fujian, Taiwan, and Zhejiang, and southward along the Vietnamese coast to Da Nang, Hoi An, Saigon, and beyond.[21]

The island of Taipa (Danzai), just south of Macau and astride the busy shipping lanes linking Canton and the Pearl River delta, also became closely connected to pirates and the shadow economy. Actually, in the late eighteenth century, Taipa composed three interconnected islands and several small farming and fishing villages. Before 1847, the year that saw a fort constructed, virtually no official presence existed in the area. The earliest village, Zhuo Family Village (Zhuo Jia Cun), was established in the late seventeenth century in a well-protected inner channel between two of the islands. Sometime later, villagers built a temple dedicated to both the Empress of Heaven and Guandi (the god of war and wealth), indicative of the emerging community of fishermen, farmers, and merchants. By the start of the nineteenth century, shops appeared in Zhuo Family Village and elsewhere on Taipa, and the island became an important stopover for smugglers, pirates, and traders. In fact, not too far from Zhuo Family Village, near what is today the Puti Buddhist Monastery, stood a well-known pirate anchorage.[22] Taipa's convenient location allowed it to handle the transshipment of goods between nearby pirate bases and the surrounding islands, Macau, and Canton.

The city of Macau, though a "sanctioned" port itself, evolved into one of the most famous pirate and smuggler rendezvous. Somewhat similar to Giang Binh, the administration of Macau appeared ambiguous, as it operated under both Portuguese and Chinese jurisdictions. Soon after the Portuguese arrived, residents elected a governing body, the Senado da Camara, to rule the city and regulate trade. In the 1680s, the Qing government created a customs office for Macau, and sixty years later, established the fortified posts of subprefect (*tongzhi*) near the border at Qianshan and assistant magistrate (*xiancheng*) in the village of Wangxia, outside the city wall and Portuguese control, but on the Macau Peninsula. These two officials assumed responsibility for overseeing the burgeoning foreign trade and for keeping pirates and smugglers in check. However, neither the local Chinese nor Portuguese officials possessed much authority; instead, the Portuguese in Goa and the Chinese provincial government in Canton controlled the city from the outside. Throughout its history, inefficiency and corruption plagued Macau's government, and its dual jurisdiction became an incessant administrative nightmare.[23]

Once called the "the wickedest city in the Far East," early in its history, Macau acquired a reputation as a seedy, disreputable, and dangerous city. It became an international meeting place for desperados and misfits, and, for many people, a place of last resort. Like the Cape of Good Hope and Port Royal in Jamaica, Macau operated as one of a series of "refreshment ports" established along major shipping routes. It also constituted part of an intricate economic zone that comprised both legitimate and illegitimate trade on land and sea.[24] One foreign resident wrote of Macau in 1800, that "it is the fit resort only of vagabonds and outcasts."[25] Bazaars notorious for gambling, prostitution, drunken sailors, and street brawls dotted its Inner Harbor. As an area of uncertain jurisdiction, Macau proved the natural place for pirates to meet and socialize, to recruit gang members, and to conduct business. Not surprisingly, Zhang Bao made it the headquarters for his extortion operations. There, in Canton and several other towns along the coast, he established "tax bureaus" (*shuiju*) for collecting protection fees and ransom payments, as well as for procuring food, weapons, and other supplies. Full-time scribes and bookkeepers kept detailed, accurate records of all transactions. Agents, such as the doctor Zhou Feixiong, not only handled ransom payments and protection fees, but also acted as intermediaries with foreign merchants who traded with the pirates. The pirates had created a state within a state.[26]

The Han River delta also developed as a busy emporium with many licit and illicit ports that traded with pirates and smugglers. The ancient port of Zhelin had a long history of involvement in clandestine trade, and during the late eighteenth century, several of the city's merchants began doing business with pirates, both buying their loot and selling them weapons and food. Much of the stolen property was then resold in other nearby coastal marts, for example, Chenghai, Zhanglin, and in upland river markets.[27] Lin Wu and Lin Ban, local merchants, regularly collaborated with the pirates and gangsters operating in the Chaozhou region. Lin Wu, a wealthy ship-owner, purchased a minor degree in Chaozhou prefecture. To safeguard his merchant fleet, he acted as the agent for pirate bosses, such as Zhu Fen and Zheng Laodong, selling provisions and collecting "port fees." For instance, Lin charged his fellow merchant, Chen Guangsheng, two hundred to five hundred silver dollars (*yuan*) per ship for each safe-conduct pass. Lin Ban owned a shop in Zhanglin and merchant junks that traded with Vietnam and Siam. In 1803, after involvement in a homicide, he began to conduct business with local pirates. That year, he bought a hundred sacks of pepper from Fujian pirates for 520 dollars (*yuan*), and then quickly resold the goods; later, he sold five cannon to another gang of pirates. In both cases, he made large profits.[28]

As cosmopolitan centers, entrepôts such as Macau, Canton, Chenghai, and Zhanglin usually tolerated outsiders, even criminals, as long as their presence proved profitable. Many merchants never asked questions about the origins of the goods they purchased, and even local officials paid little attention to illegal enterprises providing they remained discrete and orderly. The merchants and traders who traveled to Giang Binh and other unsanctioned ports acquired stolen goods, which they then transshipped and resold in various sanctioned ports much in the same way they did other goods.[29] As Gonçal López Nadal has explained, it would be "difficult to describe these methods of economic activity in terms that are conceptually distinct from commerce in general."[30] Macau, Canton, Chaozhou, and Zhanglin became inescapably linked to the shadow economy of Giang Binh, Sanhewo, Lantao, and Zhuo Jia Cun, blurring distinctions between licit and illicit trade.

The Pirate Trade

Piracy fundamentally was a business enterprise that involved large amounts of buying and selling. Most people became or helped pirates to make money. Unlike merchants and smugglers, however, pirates traded in stolen goods obtained through predation and violence. Except for food, weapons, and other necessities, pirates sold or bartered most of their booty on the open market. Loot mostly consisted not of gold and silver, but rather of various amounts of copper cash (*wen*) and objects of daily life. Here is the inventory of one haul dated 1782:

> 63 strings of cash each having 600 [copper] coins; 3,000 dried betel nuts; 2 boxes of gilded auspicious paper ingots; 1 iron cooking wok; 1 basket for holding cooked rice; 15 pecks (*dou*) of rice; 7 catties (*jin*) of raw tobacco; 2 catties of fresh betel nuts; 2 hand towels; 3 paper fans; 20 writing brushes; 1 sickle; 1 cloth bundle holding four sets of clothing, a money purse, and an umbrella.

In the above case, after the heist, the pirates retired to Zhangshan, one of many unsanctioned ports, where they first divided up the cash among themselves, and afterwards took the loot ashore in small amounts to sell in the local market.[31] While small, ad hoc gangs typically split up the loot soon after heists, the larger, more permanent gangs usually put most of the spoils into a common fund, either kept aboard ship or stockpiled on shore in lairs. Gang members would later sell the loot and share the profits in equitable portions.[32]

The primary source of pirates' revenue came not from the sale of booty, but rather from the collection of ransom payments and protection fees. Table 8.2 gives some idea of the amounts of money pirates earned from ransoms. Gangs also sold "safe-conduct passes" to fishing and cargo vessels, and levied "port fees" on merchants and shopkeepers. Ship fees, paid annually or semi-annually, varied according to the size and value of the cargo. By 1805, pirates had become so powerful that they virtually controlled the state-monopolized salt trade in Guangdong. Officials reported that salt junks purchased passes from pirates at a standard rate of fifty dollars (*yuan*) for every one hundred sacks of salt. Even Western merchants paid protection money to the pirates to prevent attacks upon their ships.[33] Merchants, shopkeepers, and fishermen treated such payments as a form of insurance. For the pirates, the protection racket gave them financial stability and predictability. With cash, pirates purchased food, weapons, and other necessities.

As pirates increased in numbers and power, so too did their networks of accomplices. Between 1805 and 1809, at their strongest, pirates' supply networks extended for a thousand miles along South China's coast. According to Dian Murray, pirates obtained rice, wine, *tong* oil, and wood from agents in Dianbai, Donghai, Xiongzhou, and Xin'an, and iron, cannons, and ammunition from representatives

Table 8.2   Amounts of Ransoms Paid to Pirates, 1796–1809

Date	Victim	Amount of Ransom
1796	vessel and cargo	130 silver dollars
1797	three travelers	$107 and 30,000 cash
1800	vessel and cargo	350 silver dollars
1806	John Turner	$6000 in money and goods
1806	Chinese customs officer	2000 taels
1809	Richard Glasspoole	$7000 in money and goods
1809	1,140 villagers	15,000 taels
1809	250 women	$600 to $6000 each

Sources: GZD (1496) JQ 1.11.18, (3728), JQ 3.2.19; XKTB (78) JQ 6.11.9; Yuan Yonglun, 1830, 14; and Chinese Repository, June 1834, 3/69–70.

in Xiangshan, Haikang, Wuchuan, and Hainan.[34] Pirates even used prearranged rendezvous and signals. Along the Chaozhou coast, for example, pirates would fire their cannons when they wanted to trade with villagers and fishermen.[35] Piracy had become big business and a regular part of daily life for untold numbers of people living along South China's coast.

Despite harsh laws and periodic crackdowns against harborers and fences, pirates encountered little difficulty conducting trade. They sold booty at below-market prices, and bought goods and services at above-market prices. A few examples will suffice. In one case, in 1809, an unnamed man purchased stolen tobacco from pirates operating off the Huizhou coast for an unspecified amount of money, which he then sold in a local market in Baishahu harbor for seven hundred copper cash (*wen*) to a man named Zheng Afan, who then resold the same items in an inland market in Chekang for 1,140 cash.[36] In another case from 1805, a fisherman named Zeng Yasi had borrowed eight silver dollars (*yuan*), which he used to buy a pig, four large jugs of wine, and one and one-half piculs (*shi*) of rice at Yantian market. He then transported his supplies to a pirate named Huang Yasi, who paid him eleven dollars. Not too long afterwards, Zeng and a friend, Li Yunlian, took thirty dollars to Danshui market in Guishan County, where they bought ten piculs of rice and several other items. These, they sold to Huang Yasi, who paid the men forty-four dollars.[37] Also, on Nan'ao Island, soldiers reportedly sold their weapons to pirates for as much as ten times their normal costs.[38]

Pirates also promulgated codes that safeguarded their business interests. In 1805, seven of the most powerful pirate chieftains in Guangdong, including Zheng Yi, Wushi Er, and Donghai Ba, signed a pact that included a stipulation forbidding pirates from plundering or kidnapping merchants and villagers who aided them. Another rule guaranteed protection to vessels having safe-conduct passes. Two years later, Zheng Yi Sao and Zhang Bao adopted a similar practice.[39] Apparently, the pirates strictly abided by their regulations. Sources reported that when pirates attacked and robbed a fishing boat which had purchased a pass, the pirate chief not only made his men return the stolen property, but also compensate the victim with five hundred dollars for damages. Because pirates paid high prices and had a reputation for dealing fairly, they were "abundantly supplied" with all that they needed.[40]

Since the shadow economy operated outside the control of officials and government rules, it required self-regulation. As noted above, pirates developed a highly sophisticated protection racket and promulgated codes to protect their trade. They also relied on other informal mechanisms, particularly, personal relationships (*guanxi*) based on geographic and kinship ties. Pirate chiefs preferred to employ family members or subordinates and agents who came from their home areas. Wushi Er filled key positions in his organization with his older brother, Wushi Da, and younger cousin, Wushi San, as well as with several individuals from his native Haikang County.[41] Zheng Qi hired his nephew, Zhang Lianke, to report on the movements of merchant junks around the port of Leizhou. For each piece of information, Zhang received ten silver dollars.[42] Chiefs adopted subordinates as sons, another important strategy, as illustrated in the example of Zhang Bao, the foster son of Zheng Yi. In another case from 1795, Zheng Qi abducted a twelve-year-old boy, He Song, and raised him as his adopted son. Several years later, Zheng gave him a captive female as his bride and seven thousand taels of silver (*liang*) to return home to set up a store for the pirate trade. Later, Zheng bestowed command of three ships upon He Song.[43] Pirates, as well as smugglers and gangsters, also bonded together in fictive kinship relationships by swearing oaths of brotherhood.[44]

Clandestine Networks

By the late eighteenth century, the maritime economy of the South China Sea had become highly sophisticated and fully integrated. An intricate web of ports and markets connected the littoral with the interior, each supporting and complementing the other. The entrepôts of Macau, Canton, and Chaozhou linked to hundreds of smaller coastal ports and inland upriver markets, both sanctioned and unsanctioned (see Figure 8.1). The entire Pearl River delta, as Paul Van Dyke has shown, encompassed a single huge trading system that involved Western trade at Macau and Canton, as well as the coastal and Southeast Asian junk trade.[45] Chaozhou and the Han River delta formed another major trading system with connections to domestic coastal marts and Southeast Asia and Japan.[46] Significantly, too, the vast shadow economy of pirates, smugglers, and Triads had fully integrated into the regular legitimate economy.

Extensive smuggling networks had already become well-established in the whole region by the mid-eighteenth century. Because authorities tightly regulated and restricted the legal trade, the illicit one developed spontaneously. A number of merchants and captains preferred to unload cargo in ports where officials kept no records.[47] Smuggling involved officials, soldiers, *yamen* underlings, Chinese and foreign merchants, as well as local gangsters, Triads, and pirates. According to Suzuki Chusei, smuggling operations actually furthered the expansion of piracy in the South China Sea at this time.[48] Smugglers and pirates exploited clandestine commercial networks, as the case of Luo Yasan, a Chinese merchant, whose family had lived in Vietnam for several generations, vividly illustrated. In the summer of 1796, he participated in the lucrative smuggling trade at Giang Binh on the Sino-Vietnamese border, selling contraband rice to Chinese traders and supplying Tay Son rebels with medicine, cloth, and other goods. On one of his trips, however, pirates robbed him. To recoup his losses, Luo formed his own gang and plundered two junks.[49] Luo's case showed how easy someone could move back and forth in the nebulous world of smugglers, pirates, and merchants.

Opium and salt smuggling, of course, had already turned into big businesses. In the 1780s and 1790s, on the western side of Hengqin Island south of Macau, Lark's Bay served as an important anchorage where Western merchants warehoused opium for subsequent transshipment to other coastal and inland markets, often with the connivance of customs agents and outlaws.[50] In 1794, officials in Huizhou mentioned several unsolved cases involving a local gangster known only as Asan, who had links with pirates and transported opium from Hengqin to an unnamed harbor in Mirs Bay, an area with a long history as a pirate stronghold.[51] Further to the east, Bias Bay had prospered as a well-known smuggling and pirate area for hundreds of years. In the early nineteenth century, Triads already had firmly established themselves in the area's market towns and played an important role in salt smuggling and other illegal commerce. Pirate and smuggling ships unloaded their cargo at unsanctioned ports like Aotou, and Triads sent the merchandise to the market town of Danshui (also mentioned above in the Zeng Yasi case), a key distribution center for the East River and its tributaries.[52]

One of the most famous cases of the early nineteenth century involved a shady merchant, Li Chongyu, who came from the town of Jiazi, a bustling port with hundreds of shops and a customs office on the Lufeng coast. Li, who had purchased a *jiansheng* degree, had close ties to local officials and *yamen* staff, as well as to pirates, such as, Lin Yafa, Zhu Fen, and Wushi Er. Sometime around 1804, Li helped organize a Triad society with a bandit, Shi Chenglian, and also opened a rice shop in Jiazi that served as a front for buying and selling stolen goods. In addition, Li operated a brothel and gambling den. After his nefarious dealings came to light in 1805, he quickly surrendered to authorities in exchange for a pardon.[53] With their broad-based connections to officials and gangsters, the Triads functioned as the "perfect organizational tool" for smuggling, gambling, prostitution, and extortion rackets, as well as for pirates who needed help in selling and distributing their booty on shore.[54]

Conclusion

Whenever piracy flourished, so too did the shadow economy, providing tens of thousands of additional jobs to coastal residents. While it did detract from legitimate trade and profits, nonetheless, piracy also had important positive economic consequences. Not only did the growth of legal commerce promote the development of new ports, but so too did the pirates' illicit trade. Numerous harbors and black markets sprang up around the South China Sea designed just to handle the trade in stolen goods and to service pirate ships and their crews. Black markets operated as a shadow economy alongside legitimate trade centers. Pirates and smugglers performed important services by redistributing goods to areas where they otherwise would not have gone. They brought the prices of goods within the reach of a wider public while, at the same time, they expanded the distribution network. Piracy allowed marginalized fishermen, sailors, and petty entrepreneurs, otherwise excluded, to participate in the broader commercial economy.

Furthermore, this illegitimate trade also tended to perpetuate piracy. Once pirates generated supplies of goods for sale at discount prices, they attracted buyers to the black markets that arose to conduct business in stolen goods. Illegal businesses thrived. The establishment of markets specifically to handle stolen merchandise clearly indicated the weaknesses in the structure of normal, legal markets.

Many pirates made eager customers who paid above-market prices for goods and services. Pirates required food, clothing, and entertainment, and operated ships in need of regular provisioning and refitting. Although the scale of the pirate trade remains impossible to gauge, nevertheless, it must have pumped large amounts of money and goods into the local economies in exchange for necessities and services. Pirates contributed to the accumulation of local capital. Like the pirates themselves, most of the individuals whom they traded with worked as ordinary fishermen and sailors, as well as petty entrepreneurs who engaged in both licit and illicit trade as vital for their livelihoods. In many instances, the extra money gained from clandestine activities provided an important, even a major, part of their overall incomes. A rich trade in cash and commodities flowed in and out of black markets, all of which lay outside the control of the state and normal trading networks. Because large numbers of people on both sea and shore came to depend on piracy, either directly or indirectly, for their livings, it became a self-sustaining enterprise and a significant feature of the South China Sea in early modern times.

Moreover, pirates built strongholds not only on remote islands, but, more importantly, in and around key commercial and political hubs such as Macau, Canton, and Chaozhou. There, they defiantly set up their "tax bureaus" to collect tribute and ransom payments and to conspire with soldiers, *yamen* underlings, and officials on their payrolls. Protection rackets most directly and effectively allowed pirates to exercise hegemony over an area. In fact, piracy constituted a level of control over maritime communities that acted independently of that of officials and local elites. The close proximity of pirate lairs to economic and political centers clearly showed just how deeply piracy had penetrated South China's maritime society.

9
Poor but Not Pirates:
The Tsushima Domain and Foreign Relations in Early Modern Japan

Robert Hellyer

Over the past few decades, historians have demonstrated that, during the Edo period (1603–1868), Japan pursued foreign relations policies very much in tune with its Asian neighbors. For one, Arano Yasunori has illustrated how Japanese leaders restricted overseas trade and the movement of foreign merchants, took measures to stamp out Christianity, and established diplomatic protocols in ways that mirrored those of their counterparts throughout East and Southeast Asia.[1] Despite these similarities, by the early nineteenth century, Japan had in one respect become exceptional in Asia and, for that matter, in the world. It was free of maritime pirates, namely, individuals or groups who use violence or the threat of violence to commandeer shipping or to attack coastal settlements.

In the decades after 1800, pirates infested the Mediterranean, the Caribbean, and, as explored in other chapters in this volume, the coast of China to the Gulf of Tonkin, as well as the waters around Singapore. One would assume that maritime piracy would also have plagued Japan, a state with few coastal defenses and no navy. Yet, as I have noted elsewhere, official documents rarely mention piracy.[2] A report of an incident in Japan's Inland Sea in 1870, for example, provides the only direct reference to pirates in Japanese waters in the "Dai Nihon Ishin Shiryō Kōhon," the most comprehensive collection of central and local government records chronicling events from 1846 to 1872, the unsettled period surrounding the Meiji Restoration of 1868.[3] Others, such as *Tsūkō ichiran zokushū*, a five-volume compilation of all types of Japanese intercourse with foreigners in the first decades of the nineteenth century, also register no attacks by pirates in the nineteenth century on either coastal settlements or shipping.[4]

The absence of piracy is intriguing particularly given the long history of such activity in Japanese waters spanning the period from the fourteenth to the late sixteenth centuries. As the chapters by Peter Shapinsky and Maria Grazia Petrucci show, sea-based, marginal groups used violence as one tool to carve out political and economic power and authority in the Inland Sea. In addition, James Chin highlights the important role that Japanese merchants played in sixteenth-century transnational trading networks headed by Chinese who engaged in piracy and smuggling simultaneously. He notes that some of these "merchant-pirates," based in Kyushu, developed ties with, among others, traders-cum-pirates from Satsuma, a feudal domain in the southern part of the island. In the seventeenth century, however, Satsuma turned away from piracy. Like other Japanese coastal provinces, Satsuma did not return to it, even as political turmoil and increased trade in the first half of the nineteenth century created an environment where pirates conceivably could have prospered (see Map 9.1).

As I have argued elsewhere, Satsuma, instead, chose smuggling, establishing a broad network of domestic and overseas partners extending in the south from Ryukyu (present-day Okinawa prefecture), an island kingdom dominated by Satsuma during the Edo period, to Ezo (present-day Hokkaido), then the northern frontier of the Japanese state. Unlike pirates, who use violence to seize goods, smugglers try to circumvent established commercial channels, often with the help of others, thereby engaging in activities that violate state laws or restrictions, in this case, regulations imposed by Japan's central authority, the Tokugawa shogunate (*bakufu*). At ports on the Japan Sea coast, Satsuma ships illicitly traded Ryukyu sugar and Satsuma goods for marine products, primarily kelp, sea cucumbers, and abalone, harvested in Ezo. In clandestine exchanges with Chinese ships that arrived on domain shores, Satsuma used these products to obtain Chinese and Southeast Asian pharmacopeia, in high demand on the Japanese home market.[5]

In sum, Satsuma leaders anticipated piracy by reducing the opportunities for individuals to extract goods from coastal shipping and settlements by force. They also incorporated into their burgeoning commercial network domestic and foreign groups that might otherwise have organized fishermen or coastal merchants into pirate bands to raid the Japanese coastline. In a broader sense, the case of Satsuma reveals first, the vigor of a Japanese domestic market that produced a range of goods which buoyed maritime trade. Second, it demonstrates the viability of Japanese-Chinese trade in the early nineteenth century, particularly outside the long established trade center of Nagasaki in Kyushu.[6]

This chapter explores further the absence of piracy in late Edo period Japan by considering the situation of the Tsushima domain, a feudal fief on the island of the same name located in the straits between Kyushu and Korea. Tsushima provides, in many ways, an even more interesting case study. First, because of the domain's history: from the early fourteenth to the mid-sixteenth century, the island served, at varying levels of intensity, as a base for pirate bands which attacked especially the Korean coast (only fifty kilometers away, half the distance to the nearest Kyushu port of Hakata). Second, owing to its key role in smoothing relations between the shogunate and the Korean court, Tsushima enjoyed a high level of agency — the ability to exercise discretionary authority in trade, diplomacy, and defense — which

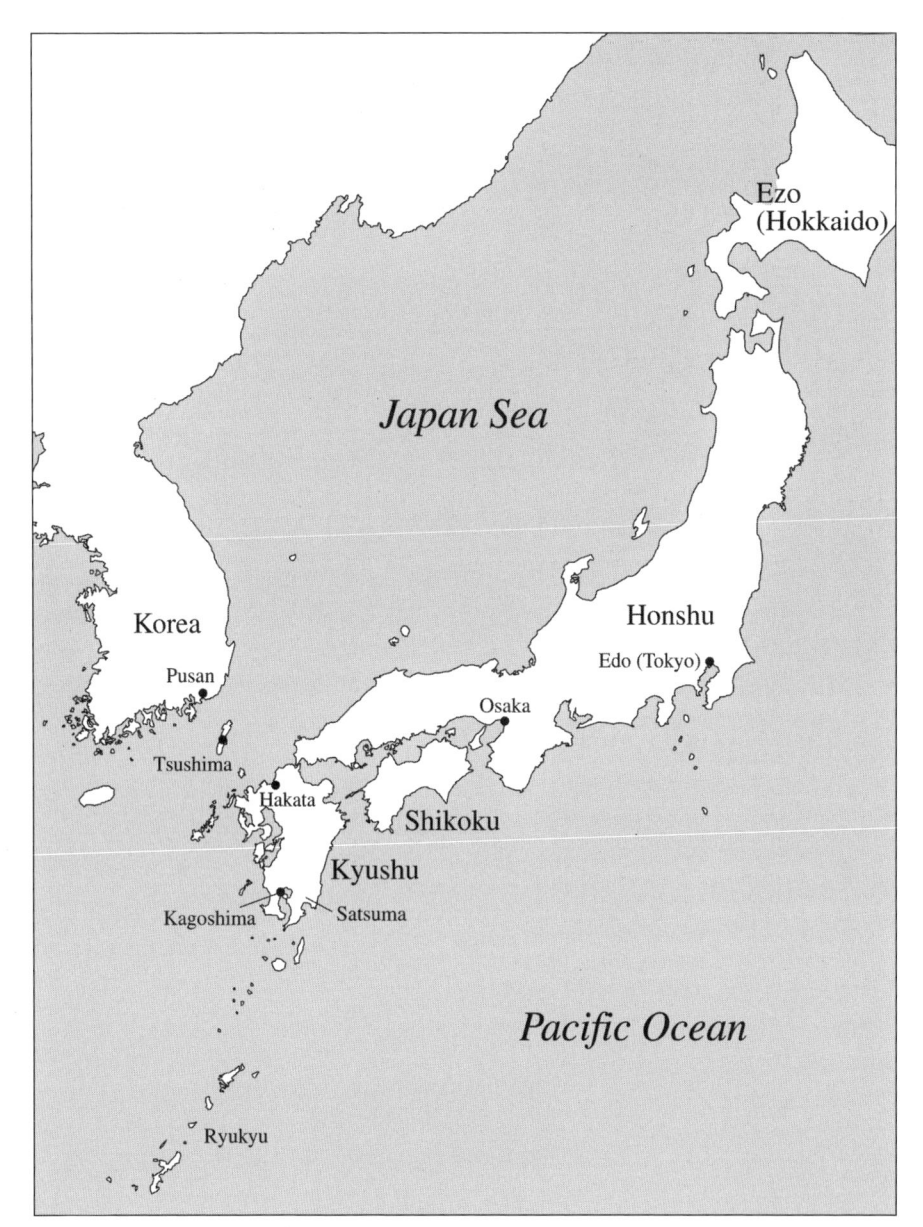

Map 9.1   Japan in the Early Nineteenth Century

offered a potential platform to facilitate piracy. Third, beginning in the second half of the eighteenth century, Tsushima leaders faced a crippled domain economy resulting chiefly from a decline in trade revenues, but also from poor agricultural production. This dire economic situation conceivably could have prompted Tsushima leaders to resort to piracy. Finally, they had numerous opportunities to undertake piracy in league with the Western merchants whose ships increasingly visited its shores after 1846.

Yet, despite all of these potential reasons, Tsushima leaders and the island's denizens did not choose the path of piracy. As this chapter outlines below, the domain's established relationships with Korea and the shogunate, particularly the financial grants offered by both authorities, made a move to piracy less appealing. Moreover, domain officials viewed the Westerners calling at its harbors more as possible enemies than as potential partners for piratical schemes. Indeed, as the visits of Western ships multiplied, domain leaders sought to abrogate the agency Tsushima enjoyed in relations with Korea and, instead, to enhance its place within the larger defensive system of the Japanese realm. Overall, Tsushima leaders aimed to incorporate their territory more into existing Japanese state structures than to chart an independent course in defense and trade.

Tsushima between Korea and the Shogunate

In the late medieval period, Tsushima became a pirate den first because of its position in the middle of sea lanes between the Korean Peninsula and western Japan. Second, the mountainous terrain of the island made agriculture more challenging, and led a significant amount of the population to engage in maritime trade and, by the beginning of the fifteenth century, to increasingly launch violent attacks on Korean merchant ships and coastal cities. Pirate activity had become so pervasive that in 1419 a frustrated Korean court dispatched a fleet of over two hundred ships to the island. Although the Korean force destroyed countless vessels and burned several villages, a few years later, pirates once again began to send out raids from the island. Searching for a more lasting solution, the Korean court encouraged clans on Tsushima, as well as in Kyushu, to codify regular ties with it.[7] The court bestowed titles and seals to allow specific clans to trade with Korea on the understanding that they would endeavor to eliminate piracy and prevent Japanese ships that traded at Korean ports from using forged documents or counterfeit seals. In 1443, Korea granted the Sō clan, the most prominent on Tsushima, the privilege of sponsoring fifty trading ships a year and provided a yearly stipend of rice. In return, it expected the Sō to verify the official sponsorship of Korea-bound Japanese ships. As an added bonus, Korea also allowed the Sō to levy transit duties on cargoes and collect other maritime fees.[8]

The Sō, therefore, became akin to the "sea lords" of Japan's Inland Sea that Shapinsky explores in his chapter, namely, the lord of a group who, owing to its dominance over a maritime area, forced land-based entities to recognize them as the legitimate authority over that region's maritime networks. The Sō differed, however, because the Korean court came to see the clan as indispensable in policing the waters between Japan and Korea. Several times, Korean leaders restored relations with the Sō despite its participation in pirate offensives against Korea. For example, in 1510, the clan's ships advanced upon an island off the southern Korean port of Pusan in support of Japanese traders and fishers who were there rioting in an attempt to gain trade concessions from Korean officials. Although aware of the Sō's involvement, Korean officials reinstated the clan's special privileges just two years later, believing that they needed it to help suppress even more potentially devastating pirate attacks that they feared might originate from western Japan.[9]

While sporadic pirate raids continued, Korea faced far more destructive Japanese assaults in the form of invasions launched between 1592 and 1598, under the orders of Toyotomi Hideyoshi. Korean forces, aided by the Ming, repelled both attacks, and Korean officials subsequently refused to establish diplomatic relations with the Tokugawa shogunate, which emerged as the definitive central authority of Japan in 1603. When Korea and the Tokugawa eventually formed ties in 1607, the Korean court again insisted that the Sō serve as the intermediary, dictating that all trade and diplomacy take place through the clan. Korean leaders calculated that they could use trade to manipulate the weaker Sō, and thereby maintain an upper hand in relations with the shogunate, as well as mitigate future Japanese aggression and a possible revival of piracy. Korean support certainly helped the head of the Sō continue his rule over Tsushima, now as a lord in the new Tokugawa-dominated state. In contrast, Hideyoshi and the first Tokugawa leaders forced the sea lords of the Inland Sea to move off their island outposts, effectively eliminating their role in the Edo period polity, as well as in piracy.[10]

Korean leaders made the Sō a vassal, and established a series of relationships intended to ensure that the clan would stay in line. The court granted its vassal a monopoly of Japanese trade with Korea, but expected the Sō to dispatch regular diplomatic missions to the Japan House, a walled compound in the Korean port of Pusan, which housed around five hundred Tsushima merchants and officials. Consistent with Chinese diplomatic practices, the Sō first participated in an "official" trade where they annually offered specific tribute items: tin, copper, and a variety of Southeast Asian goods obtained at Nagasaki — pepper, sappanwood (used as a red dye), water buffalo horns (used as military equipment), and alum (a sulfate used as an astringent and in the manufacture of dyes and paper). The Sō also received official seals that legitimized the clan's commercial monopoly.[11]

In return, the Korean court annually bestowed valuable gifts, initially a sizeable consignment of cotton, which, to the approval of Tsushima leaders, they changed to a substantial amount of rice in mid-seventeenth century. The domain came to depend upon the Korean rice shipments to supply the Japan House residents, to pay for the cost of envoys on missions traveling between Korea and Tsushima, and, most importantly, to feed a significant portion of its population. Researchers have estimated that, in 1700, of Tsushima's population of 32,000, roughly 18,000 people lived on rice and barley grown on the island, 7,000 on rice cultivated on Sō lands in Kyushu, with the remaining 7,000 dependent upon Korean rice. Tsushima leaders continued to follow the necessary diplomatic protocols not simply out of devotion to the Korean court, but also to maintain the vital rice shipments.[12] Korea also offered an even more valuable commercial reward by permitting the Sō to engage in a "private" trade, which involved Tsushima traders exchanging goods with officially licensed Korean merchants at a market near the Japan House. Korean officials restricted the overall volume of exchanges by limiting the number and size of ships that Tsushima could dispatch and by sanctioning only a handful of trading days per month. Despite these controls, the domain and its merchants enjoyed handsome profits as the middleman in the import of Chinese silk and Korean ginseng, both purchased with high quality Japanese silver ingots.

A recent study by James B. Lewis offers fresh insights on why the Korean court granted such generous concessions to Tsushima. He concludes that trade with Japan was critical to the economy of Kyŏngsang Province, the location of Japan House, calculating that tax revenues from trade amounted to just over fifty percent of all those collected in the province. Nonetheless, he believes that in the end, relations with Tsushima proved a burden because of the costs incurred by the reception of its envoys and to the supplying of the Japan House. In addition, the gifts presented as part of the official trade — particularly the annual one of rice — outweighed trade-related revenue. Lewis asserts that Korean leaders maintained ties because they believed that if they prohibited the people of Tsushima from trading, they would turn to piracy, as their ancestors did. In addition, the Korean court also took seriously the ideal that Korea, as a more civilized and advanced state, had an obligation to help the less fortunate denizens of Tsushima.[13]

Because of the Korean court's stance, the Tokugawa regime recognized the Sō's intermediary role and granted the clan a monopoly on Japanese-Korean trade. Although the shogunate controlled sales on the domestic market of goods Tsushima imported, the domain's independent relationship with Korea allowed its leaders a significant amount of agency. Domain merchants conducted trade with their Korean counterparts free of Tokugawa oversight, and its officials often concealed from the *bakufu* transgressions, such as smuggling, in its relations with Korea. The shogunate's prosecution in 1634 of the Sō's leading retainer, the Yanagawa clan, for forging diplomatic correspondence with Korea several decades earlier illustrated the strength of the Sō's position. Although the Sō clearly assisted in the crime, the Tokugawa leadership chose to punish only the Yanagawa, aware that removing the Sō would threaten relations with Korea.[14]

The shogunate protected the Sō's role first because the clan assisted in the *bakufu*'s reception of envoys from Korea. Ronald Toby has demonstrated that the Tokugawa regime used connections with Korea, the Ryukyu Kingdom, and to a lesser degree, the Dutch East India Company mission at Nagasaki, to craft a "Japan-centered world" of diplomacy based on Chinese models. He demonstrates that the Tokugawa shogunate, which had only recently gained military hegemony over the lords who ruled largely independent domains, viewed diplomatic relations with East Asian states as an opportunity to bolster the legitimacy of the new regime. As a key step, the *bakufu* leadership created elaborate receptions for the occasional Korean embassies that would travel to Edo to celebrate a shogunal succession. As an independent kingdom actively participating in the Chinese world order, the reception of Korea's embassies functioned as the cornerstone of the "Japan-centered world." Based upon their special relationship with the Korean court, the Sō negotiated important details related to the embassies — with Tsushima as the first to receive one, and domain officials accompanying the Koreans on the round-trip to and from Edo.[15]

Tsushima also facilitated the repatriation of Japanese castaways from Korea, as well as any Korean fishermen or merchants shipwrecked on Japanese shores. In addition, the Sō used their trade contacts with Korea to glean intelligence about events outside of Japan, particularly in China, which it forwarded to the shogunate. In the early eighteenth century, Amenomori Hōshū, a Confucian scholar serving the domain, emphasized that such activity made Tsushima a "primary strategic bulwark" that played a role in the overall defense of the realm by "gauging the relative importance of information gathered from foreign countries." He added that "this task contributes to the protection of all of Japan."[16] Amenomori's comments helped Tsushima protect its privileges against *bakufu* attempts to limit the domain's foreign trade. Until the early eighteenth century, it garnered tremendous profits acting as an intermediary in the flow of silver to Korea. Korean tribute missions would carry the silver to Beijing and exchange it for Chinese silk, which they in turn shipped to the Japanese market via Tsushima. The domain also profited as the sole purveyor of Korean ginseng, which many Japanese viewed as a vital medicine.[17]

Economic Distress

As illustrated above, a series of diplomatic and commercial contacts tied the Sō and the Tsushima domain to both Korea and the shogunate. By the mid-eighteenth century, however, strains began to appear, precipitated by Tokugawa decisions to limit silver outflows as well as to devalue currency, and especially by increased domestic production of silk and ginseng, which came to supply the Japanese market. As a result, Tsushima's trade slowed to a comparative trickle. Moreover, the domain's agricultural production remained languid, despite earlier attempts to augment it, specifically by eliminating the large population of deer, which ate and trampled crops, and wild boar that threatened the agriculturalists minding the fields.[18] As profits declined, Tsushima leaders received a series of loans from merchants in the cities of Osaka and Edo to keep the domain economy afloat. They attempted to restart business but the failure of direct trade with Korea to generate the financial rewards Tsushima enjoyed serving as the intermediary between the Japanese and Chinese markets stymied them. Sales of Korean cowhides as well as cow hooves and horns, cut to make combs and hair accessories, yielded modest returns but they never compared to the huge ones resulting from the silk-for-silver trade. By the 1770s, domain officials despaired that the most valuable private trade had, for all intents and purposes, reached a standstill, bringing the domain to the brink of economic collapse.[19]

At this point, Tsushima leaders, facing mounting debts and little potential to obtain profits from established trade links, might have considered turning to piracy. As their ancestors had done two centuries before, domain ships could have attacked the Korean coastline or even ventured further south, since no naval force that patrolled East Asian waters could stop them. In other words, domain leaders could have used Tsushima's agency as the intermediary in Japanese-Korean relations as a springboard to improve its position. Yet, they never had to take such a drastic step. After constant appeals, in 1776, the shogunate bestowed a regular stipend upon the domain, which allowed Tsushima leaders to stave off further and potentially catastrophic financial decline. Because trade remained languid in subsequent decades, the shogunate offered additional monetary grants to assuage the domain's lost revenues as well as new lands in Kyushu as a reward for duties performed in receiving a Korean embassy in 1811. Finally, the shogunate also showed its awareness of Tsushima's dependence on Korean rice shipments when it awarded a one-time allocation of ten thousand *koku* of rice (just under half of the domain's annual production) that offset the reduction in imports resulting from poor harvests in Korea.[20] As a consequence of the combined grants, Tsushima officials could feed the domain's population and also repay its obligations to Osaka and Edo merchants.[21]

Finding a New Defensive Role: Border Bulwark

While the Tokugawa stipends stabilized Tsushima, they treated merely the symptoms and not the larger malady affecting the domain — the lack of trade revenue. Leaders still faced a precarious situation in maintaining adequate food supplies, as well as financing the domain's debts. Into this challenging environment, a new factor emerged, beginning in the mid-1840s — an increasing number of Western visitors, in the form of merchantmen, whaling vessels, and warships, calling on Japanese shores. In late 1846, Tsushima officials voiced their concerns to the *bakufu*, stressing that because of its compromised financial status, the domain was in no position to repel a possible armed Western incursion. As they appealed for more aid to strengthen their coastal defenses, Tsushima leaders presented a new vision of the island's place in Japan's overall defensive network. Instead of contributing by collecting intelligence through trade, they emphasized that Tsushima now served as a physical border bulwark, which, if fortified through Tokugawa assistance, would help protect the entire Japanese state. Despite this stance, *bakufu* leaders rejected the domain's request.

A handful of Western ships detected off the Tsushima coast in 1847 confirmed the fears of domain leaders. The following spring, the territory reported to the *bakufu* that in a two-day span, they had sighted ten foreign ships offshore.[22] While the vessels did not appear hostile, the domain leadership worried that their increasing numbers foretold a future incursion, and moved to strengthen coastal defenses. In petitions to the *bakufu* for financial support, Tsushima officials lamented their domain's dependence upon Korean rice and complained that the slowdown in the once prosperous trade with Korea had emptied their coffers. With the arrival of foreign ships, Tsushima leaders began to assert that the domain's unique defensive needs — particularly its position far from other parts of Japan — made more aid necessary. After two years of appeals, *bakufu* leaders eventually granted a sizeable loan they would award in installments over the next two years.[23]

Yet, Tsushima officials could not rest as more Western ships visited the island. In separate incidents, in 1849, two American whalers put men ashore, prompting domain leaders to further reinforce coastal positions.[24] Later in the same year, they began to report an incredible increase in the number of vessels. For example, they averred that in a twelve-day interval during the fourth month of 1849, they had spotted thirty-three foreign ships. Moreover, the domain stated that in the following month, lookouts had recorded the comings and goings of an additional thirty-two ships during just a five-day period.[25] Perhaps, domain outlooks were counting the same ship twice or three times as it sailed up and down the coast. Domain officials at the Japan House in Pusan might have made the same miscalculation, declaring that fifty-four foreign ships had passed near the Korean coast in recent months.[26] In any case, domain leaders became clearly concerned about a possible invasion and especially about the burden of spending additional funds to bolster coastal defenses. They therefore asked that the shogunate extend the loan granted the previous year for two additional years. In their request, domain officials asserted them that Western pressure had become relentless, stating that during that spring alone, they had sighted a staggering 180 ships in the waters around Tsushima.[27] *Bakufu* leaders unquestionably doubted Tsushima's allegations and denied the appeal for further assistance. Their only support came two years later in the form of deferral of payments of the loans Tsushima had received from the shogunate over the past decades.[28]

All the while, Western ships continued to arrive. In the second month of 1850, the domain reported that in a nine-day period from the twenty-fourth day of the first month to the second day of the second month, they had detected twelve ships off the domain's coast. Next, domain officials claimed that in a ten-day span in the second month, fifteen additional ships had appeared off Tsushima, with four more seen off the Korean coast.[29] In early 1851, the domain noted that numerous ships had resurfaced along its coastline.[30] Domain officials once again petitioned the *bakufu* for relief to absorb costs related to defense. This time, Sō Yoshiyori, the lord of Tsushima, took a new tack contending that recent Western pressure on Korea threatened agricultural production there. Yoshiyori maintained that because lower agricultural production had also recently plagued Korea (circumstances for which the *bakufu* had previously helped Tsushima financially), the increased Western presence in Korean waters could force the Koreans to spend more on defense and, in turn, jeopardize Korean rice shipments to Tsushima. The lord thus appealed for seven thousand *koku* of rice, a request that *bakufu* leaders denied.[31]

Coming in the wake of a nearly continuous stream of Western ships visiting its shores, the Tokugawa rejection, coupled with the disapproval of earlier aid petitions, might have impelled Tsushima leaders to embark on a radically different course. Exploiting the leverage that Tsushima enjoyed as an intermediary in Korean-Japanese relations, domain leaders could have pursued ad hoc exchanges or long term alliances with the Westerners arriving there, perhaps, even forming, as their ancestors had done, pirate bands to attack the Korean coast. It is reasonable to speculate about such possibilities as leaders of the Satsuma domain, while not resorting to piracy, did establish numerous official and unofficial commercial relations with Westerners in the late 1850s and 1860s. For example, Satsuma officials supported a treaty that the Ryukyu Kingdom (then still politically dominated by Satsuma) signed with France, which they anticipated would also bring trade revenues to their domain. It also developed less formal ties with a prominent British merchant.[32] In Tsushima, domain officials had no particular desire to maintain the status quo with Korea, illustrated by a proposal, just a decade later, to commence an invasion of Korea which would allow Japan to gain new trade opportunities on the peninsula and with China.[33]

Yet, the Tsushima leadership did not choose such a path; in its place, they decided to appeal anew for Tokugawa support. In so doing, the domain continued to move to abrogate its position as intermediary between Korea and the shogunate, instead emphasizing that Tsushima played a vital defensive role as a physical border bulwark for the Japanese realm. A memorial that Sō Yoshiyori presented to the *bakufu* in 1853 evidences the approach. In a well-known tactic, Abe Masahiro, a senior *bakufu* official, requested that the roughly 250 lords of the Japanese state provide opinions concerning US President Millard Fillmore's letter to Japanese leaders. Delivered by several warships under the command of Commodore Matthew Perry in 1853, the letter requested the opening of diplomatic and commercial ties.

In his memorial, Sō Yoshiyori, who had ruled Tsushima since 1843, echoed some of the same themes developed by other lords. He stressed the need to increase studies of Western gunnery and to use negotiations to buy time to improve the overall defensive posture of the realm. Yet, he also urged the *bakufu* to take note of Western pressure on *his* domain. To make his point, Sō Yoshiyori attached an additional memorial that detailed how "small and weak" Tsushima was, bearing an inordinate brunt of Western advances. Reflecting some of the same grievances presented in earlier memorials, he complained,

> As I stated many times before, the Tsushima domain is a bulwark against foreign states. Our domain, however, is an isolated island separated from the rest of the realm. As we are surrounded on four sides by the ocean, we have a coastline that is over one hundred *ri* (approximately 392 kilometers). We cannot defend all of that area alone. Additionally, we must consider how the recent unrest in China [i.e., the Taiping Rebellion] will affect defense. The domain is also troubled because there is little hope of restoring trade with Korea to past levels.[34]

Sō Yoshiyori clearly enunciated his main point: in this time of crisis, with coastal defense a vital issue, Tsushima constituted an important sector in the defense of the realm which required extra funds to allow it to repulse a possible foreign attack. Unfortunately, for Tsushima, Yoshiyori's appeal did not bring additional financial assistance.

Nonetheless, he and his leadership circle continued to press Tokugawa leaders for aid, and, following two additional Western incursions, for them to take a more direct role in defending the domain. In 1859, a British warship surveyed Tsushima's coastline for several weeks, and even more seriously, for six months in 1861, three Russian naval vessels established a temporary naval station on the island.[35] While the Russians eventually withdrew, domain leaders believed that it was only a matter of time before another Western nation would send more vessels, possibly to seize the island outright. They therefore requested, without success, for the shogunate to directly administer the domain and relations with Korea. Throughout the 1860s, domain leaders continued to implore the shogunate, and after it fell in the Meiji Restoration of 1868, the subsequent Meiji government, to take a commanding role in the domain's interactions with Korea.

After 1868, the reluctance of Korean officials to revise the existing relationship hampered the domain's effort. The officials hoped to maintain the upper hand they believed they held in negotiations with Japanese central authorities that resulted from conducting business through the Sō. In addition, Korean officials resented Japanese attempts to establish titular superiority over Korea in diplomatic dispatches and worried that the new Meiji government was scheming with Westerners to plan a military attack there.[36] As a result, despite the willingness of Tsushima's officials to abrogate the Sō's diplomatic and commercial roles in the Meiji government, the clan remained an intermediary until 1874. Subsequent Japanese-Korean agreements, often prompted by Japanese gunboat diplomacy, helped establish direct state-to-state ties based upon Western methods of diplomacy, a process completed with the signing of the Treaty of Kanghwa in 1876.

Conclusion

By considering the reasons the people of Tsushima did not choose piracy, we gain valuable insights on the workings of the system that guided relations between Korea and Japan from the early seventeenth to the late nineteenth centuries. Because Korean leaders so concerned themselves with the denizens of Tsushima taking up piracy, they created enticements and restrictions that made it an unappealing option. Although not as focused on potential piracy, the shogunate similarly used financial aid to stabilize Tsushima, thereby also helping to mitigate a possible turn to piracy, especially in the late eighteenth and early nineteenth centuries. Together, the actions of Korean and Tokugawa leaders kept peace in the seas between Japan and Korea until Westerners arrived in force, beginning in the 1840s.

Western merchantmen and warships, eagerly seeking to establish trade and diplomatic ties, undeniably injected a new dynamic into Japanese foreign relations in the middle of the nineteenth century. Historians of Japan have usually concluded that the rising tide of Western visitors forced Japanese leaders to make an either-or choice: to maintain a long-standing closed country policy or open Japan to the West and "modernity."[37] According to this perspective, Japan's traditional commercial and diplomatic relationships, as for example, those with Korea, were irrelevant as they only constituted some of the conventions that Japanese leaders could chose to maintain or to abandon. By asking why piracy did not develop in Tsushima, we see that actors had more nuanced options — including the domain's new self-definition as border bulwark — made possible both by the opportunities and the restrictions inherent in the established system of foreign relations. Tsushima leaders enjoyed a reasonable level of agency which they opted to forego because of the combined challenges of the dearth of trade with Korea, domain debt, and the steady stream of Western visitors, and not simply because of a desire to adopt "modern" Western practices.

10

The Business of Violence:
Piracy around Riau, Lingga, and Singapore, 1820–40

Ota Atsushi

In the early nineteenth century, Dutch and British authorities knew well that an increasing number of piratical attacks around Riau, Lingga, and Singapore were seriously damaging trade.[1] To manage this problem, both colonial governments ordered their officials to collect detailed information on the pirates. Numerous reports, both published and unpublished, resulted. Writings from the colonial period, often authored by high-ranking administrators, focused on chronicling European efforts to combat pirates, paying only scant attention to their motives, goals, and networks.[2] Scholars seeking to understand the developments of piracy in Southeast Asia in this period, however, have never fully utilized these valuable documents.

Based on British and Dutch colonial records, this chapter explores how indigenous pirates developed their activities; how they organized military and commercial networks; and how local states and European administrators dealt with piracy. Economic aspects will receive greater scrutiny because available sources clearly indicate that economic gain constituted the primary consideration of the pirates. Here, I also want to argue that piracy, fundamentally a local strategy, both reacted to changing conditions in the region and triggered the formation of colonial states. I examine piracy based on Riau, Lingga, and Singapore because they comprised the most important pirate strongholds around the Malacca Strait where the piratical activities intricately connected with each other.[3] I confine my discussion to the pirates residing in these islands because they had a far greater impact on the policies of local and European leaders than other groups temporarily visiting there from bases in other places. I focus on the twenty-year period from 1820 to 1840, when the Dutch and British indirectly controlled Riau, Lingga, and Singapore (see Map 10.1). Indigenous piracy and European countermeasures profoundly affected the history of those years as well as those of the following decades.

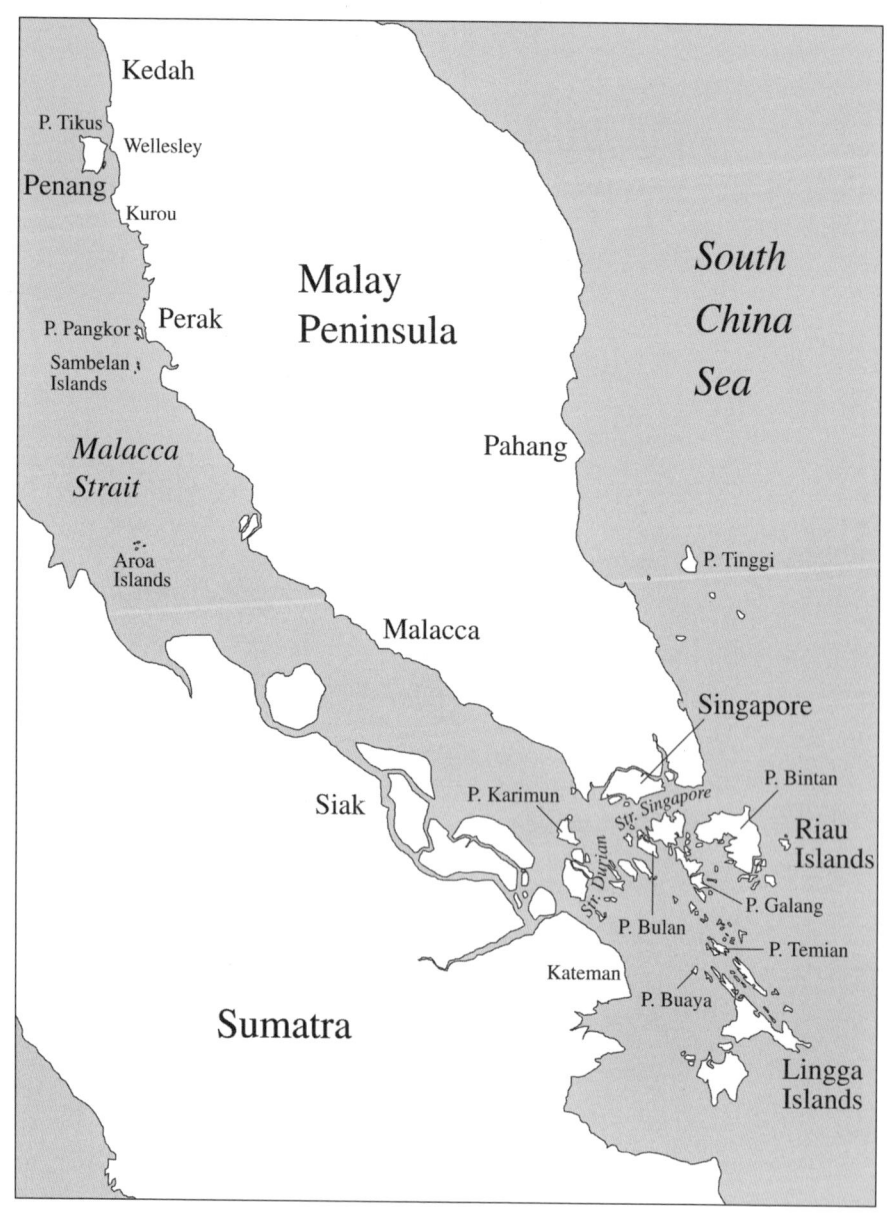

Map 10.1   Riau, Lingga, Singapore, and the Malacca Strait, c. 1840

Preliminary Concepts

Our views of Southeast Asian piracy have changed in recent years. Colonial authors attributed the causes of piracy to the uncivilized character of native Asian and Muslim rulers, their ineffective maritime controls, or to the Dutch East India Company's monopolistic trading practices.[4] Most academic studies before 1980 sought to either confirm the old colonial stereotypes or to reinterpret piracy as a form of anti-colonial resistance.[5] Since the late 1970s, scholars have moved to "normalize" piracy, and have tended to explain the goals and motives of pirates from economic perspectives.[6]

"Pirates" and "piracy" represent arguably negative and Eurocentric terms, as Anthony Reid has suggested in his chapter. Nonetheless, nowadays, individuals often overlook the pirates' victimization of native populations, who certainly viewed them adversely, as shown in their accounts. For local and European victims, the use of violence and the lack of fair compensation distinguished piracy from normal economic activities. In this chapter, we will examine pirates and piracy from the vantage point of the victims, and treat both terms, respectively, as persons who and actions that forcefully seized property and/or people under threat or use of violence without equitable exchange on the seas or in coastal areas. Those who used maritime violence justified their behavior, labeling them reprisals, a defense of sovereignty, or maritime security. Here, we will focus more on the economic and practical aspects of maritime violence rather than the political implications claimed by raiders, local rulers, and European authorities.

Malay States and European Powers

Although Riau and Lingga, the core regions of the sultanate of Johor, were well-known for piracy in the ancient past, after the 1780s, the problem became particularly distressing to shippers and governments. In the 1760s, Johor emerged as a powerful state in the region, when joint rule by the Malay royal family and the hereditary Bugis viceroys became stabilized after decades of conflicts. Its capital on Pulau Bintan in the Riau Islands prospered as an entrepôt for long-distance and interregional trade.[7] In 1784, however, the Dutch, irritated by the "piratical" manner of the Bugis traders, conquered Riau. They forced Sultan Mahmud to accept their occupation of Bintan and the expulsion of the Bugis (see Figure 10.1).

The Dutch subjugation of Riau in 1784, nonetheless, triggered an increase in piracy in the Malacca Strait. In 1787, the sultan invited the Iranun, previously active in the surrounding waters, and, with their military assistance, successfully expelled the Dutch from Riau.[8] But the Iranun soon left Riau, and Sultan Mahmud departed for Lingga with his followers, fearful of a Dutch reprisal. He organized raiding fleets there, consisting of Malay, Bugis, Iranun, and Orang Laut marauders,

Figure 10.1 Bugis Warriors
(Source: Johannes Nieuhof, *Johan Nieufofs Gedenkweerdige Brasiliaense zee-en lantreize*, Amsterdam, 1682)

who attacked shipping and coastal villages.[9] Mahmud, finding himself encircled by the new leaders of the Malay faction, moved the capital back to Riau, and made a valiant effort to gather Malay and Bugis forces. Nevertheless, Engku Muda, from an influential Malay family became the dominant force at Riau from 1795 to 1805. Mahmud returned to Lingga in 1795, and Engku Muda governed Riau and Johor from his base on Bulan in Riau. In 1805, Engku Abdul Rahman succeeded his uncle Engku Muda, and took the traditional title of Temenggong or prime minister. After this succession and Engku Muda's death in the following year, however, the sultanate split among several powerful elites who struggled with each other.[10]

In 1818, the British came to Riau in search of a new foothold in the region. They attempted to negotiate a commercial treaty with Raja Ja'afar, the sixth Bugis viceroy, based in Riau. Yet, a few months later when the Dutch approached him, he decided, instead, to cooperate and allowed them to reoccupy a part of Riau.

Disappointed, Temenggong Abdul Rachman retired to Singapore. On this island, he received Thomas Stamford Raffles, who now chose Singapore as the site of the new British settlement. In 1819, Raffles, the Temenggong, and the newly installed Sultan Husain (the son of late Sultan Mahmud, and the brother of Sultan Abdul Rachman at Lingga [not to be confused with Temenggong Abdul Rachman], who succeeded his father in 1812) agreed upon a treaty, which admitted the sovereignty of the English East India Company in Singapore in return for British pensions.[11] In such a manner, in 1818–19, a new political structure involving European powers emerged in the region. On the one hand, the Dutch had partial control over Riau and the British dominated Singapore; on the other hand, Sultan Abdul Rachman at Lingga claimed nominal authority while the viceroy Raja Ja'afar at Riau held the real power of the sultanate.

Both the Dutch and British administrators soon found their new footholds infested by Malay, Bugis, Iranun, and Orang Laut marauders. As Europeans believed that pirate attacks related to Malay rulers, they drew up treaties with local leaders stipulating their obligation to suppress pirates.[12] The Dutch and British governments also decreed in Article V of the London Treaty of 1824, that both countries should endeavor to stop Malay states from granting asylums and business opportunities to pirates.[13] Nonetheless, with the limited capacity of the local and European officials, these agreements had little effect.

Plunder, Sales of Spoils, and Networks

Pirates based in Lingga soon drew the attention of Dutch administrators who had just returned to Riau. The government ordered the Dutch Commissioner at Palembang and Bangka, Herman W. Muntinghe, to investigate pirates in the surrounding waters. He reported in 1818 that two chiefs directed piratical forces in Lingga: the two brothers styled Orang Kaya Lingga (Datu Panghulu and Datu Muda), both residing in Pulau Mapar, and Ungku Temonggong in Pulau Buaya (or Pulau Lima) in the northeast corner of the Lingga Islands. The former controlled eighteen vessels with four hundred men, while the latter commanded twenty-four ships with one thousand men.[14] According to a report by the Dutch Resident, Christiaan van Angelbeek, at Riau in 1825, one of the brothers resided in Mapar and led the Orang Laut on raids in Lingga waters. Both shared authority over the Orang Laut.[15] No map shows the location of Mapar, but from descriptions, clearly, it constitutes one of the tiny islands in the vicinity of Lingga.

Van Angelbeek stated that these piratical leaders based on Lingga were Malays, and attracted Orang Laut chiefs by providing them with ships, warships, and other necessities. The Orang Laut in Lingga were not professional pirates but fishermen, who usually collected agar-agar and tripang around Bangka and Bilitung, and only occasionally participated in plundering.[16] Sales of these maritime products to Chinese traders (known as Wankang) residing in Kwala Dai in Lingga furnished their primary means of living.[17]

Piracy by the Orang Laut correlated with the changing trade patterns at Lingga. Van Angelbeek explained that the conflict between Sultan Husain at Singapore and Sultan Abdul Rachman at Lingga caused a decline in trade at Lingga. Probably, in order to compensate for the drop in income, Selewatang, the prime minister, levied six Spanish *mats* for the issuance of passes for foreign traders coming to Lingga, which, however, resulted in the hampering of commerce.[18] Van Angelbeek stated that foreign traders, especially Thai and Chinese, avoided visiting Lingga because of the policy. Consequently, a number of Chinese residents left Lingga for Riau and Singapore, in all likelihood, in search of better business opportunities, thus, forcing people in Lingga to obtain necessities from Java.[19] Since the coastal parts of Java constituted an important part of the target areas for the Lingga pirates, they must have attacked these regions in order to acquire the goods that had become harder to find back home.[20]

After 1825, the pirates of Lingga seemed to have operated actively outside the islands' waters, often cooperating with other groups. British sources inform us that they also went on plundering expeditions to the northern part of the Malacca Strait and even further. A Malay shipmaster who barely escaped a pirate raid off the Perak coast in April 1826, reported that the attackers came from Lingga or the eastern part of the Strait, according to the appearance of their *prahus*.[21] A pirate fleet, allegedly manned with mixed groups from Galang, Temian (in Lingga), Pahang, and Teluk Blanga (in Singapore), assaulted a trading ship off Pulau Tinggi in September 1832.[22] Another flotilla, reported as composed of non-Muslim Orang Laut from Lingga, Siak, Galang, and other places near Singapore, plundered Wellesley Province and trading boats passing nearby in November 1833. They made regular visits to the northern part of the Strait and the Mergi Islands in quest of birds' nests and slaves.[23]

In such a manner, the Orang Laut in Lingga widened their piratical activities to both sides of the Malay Peninsula and, even north, to the Malacca Strait, organizing fleets together with raiders from Riau, the vicinity of Singapore, and other places. Two concomitant factors accelerated and expanded their activities: one, the decline in trade in Lingga, which worsened unemployment; and two, the development of British-driven trade in the Strait, which increased the flow of goods. Poverty and opportunity went hand-in-hand.

In Riau, the Dutch had rights only to a small part of Pulau Bintan, restricted to the control of trade and land lease, as well as jurisdiction over Chinese and other Asians. The Malay and the Orang Laut remained under the sway of the sultan and the viceroy. Van Angelbeek reported in 1825 on the two most notable pirate chiefs in the region, Pengulu Hamba Raja in Mapar and Raja Lang in Bulan. The latter, an elected leader possessed authority over the pirates in Bulan and adjacent Galang in the Riau Islands.[24] Nonetheless, his power did not seem to extend very far over others, as we see the names of many other pirate leaders based on Riau in British sources.

The piracy the Riau raiders conducted closely related to the slave trade. Bugis natives made up the most prominent among those operating in Singapore. They imported slaves under the name of "slave-debtors," and sold them to the Chinese, who, in many cases, took them to Malacca to resell.[25] As the British increasingly tightened their regulations on slaving, which they finally prohibited in 1830, Singapore ceased to be a good business center for the Bugis. As a result, 260 to 270 Bugis merchants in Singapore migrated to Riau from 1824 to 1825. The Dutch Resident Lodewijk Carel van Ranzow welcomed them. After some negotiations, the Bugis leader, Prince Aru Belawa, decided to submit to Dutch rule in return for a monthly pension of five hundred guilders. His Bugis followers were organized under three traders, called *nachoda*, and engaged in the purchase of opium, linen, Chinese goods, as well as weapons in Singapore; and in the export of these commodities and Riau gambir to Sulawesi and Java. This business, however, did not generate as much profit as the slave trade.[26]

Whether the Bugis migrant traders in Riau involved themselves in the maritime raids to capture people for slaves remains unclear, although, without doubt, the pirates based on Galang became the main players in it. Among them, Panglima Tarah was the most renowned leader.[27] We know nothing about his background, though, allegedly, his followers consisted of Malays.[28] During 1826, he supposedly participated in three separate piratical attacks against two Malay trading vessels and one Malay fishing ship, off the coasts of Kedah, Penang, and Pangkor. Each time, he tried to seize as many people as possible, whom he transported to Kurou on the west coast of the Malay Peninsula afterwards. Once, he locked up forty to fifty people in his *prahus* anchored there, and, at another time, he held a group of twenty-five Chulia, Chinese, and Malay men and women, all from Penang, in Kurou. He carried most of them further to different places for sale as slaves, while forcing a few of them to work on piratical *prahus* in Galang. In one transaction, for instance, the pirates took approximately twenty detainees to the northern parts of Malacca, where they sold three of them to the raja for three *krisses* (decorated daggers). (See Figure 10.2 for the various types of weapons in use at this time in Sumatra). Then, they proceeded to Galang, where they sold about half of the remaining captives.[29]

Besides Panglima Tarah, many other pirate leaders also used Galang as a base, among them, Panglima Humong and Panglima Limbang, who jointly raided a Malay trading ship off Pulau Bunting in November 1827. They took their captives to Pangkor, another important hub for the slave trade.[30] In November 1832, the leaders based at Temian Island in Lingga and those from Galang in Riau jointly organized another pirate fleet, and attacked a trading ship near Pulau Tinggi. Interestingly,

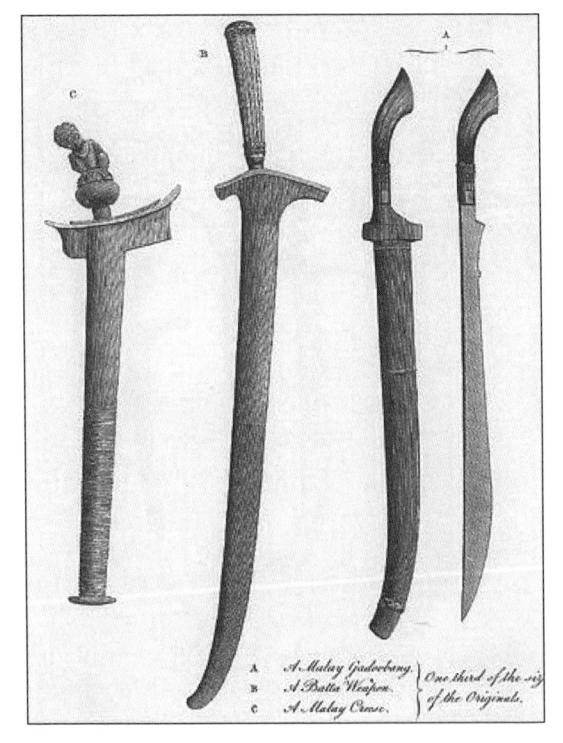

Figure 10.2 Sumatran Weapons
(Source: William Marsden, *The History of Sumatra*, London, 1811)

Malay traders on the victimized ship recognized two of the pirate leaders as Chinese who used to reside in Riau, although at the time, they professed the Islamic faith and wore Malay clothing.[31]

Galang served as an important piratical base deeply involved in slave raids and the slave trade. Local pirates sold captives not only in Galang, but also in other places including Kurou, Pangkor, Karimun, and the northern parts of Malacca. The location of the last place remains unclear, but the sales of slaves near Malacca demonstrated a similarity to the Bugis slave trade once conducted in Singapore before the British prohibition. In Malacca, under British control, the European, Malay, Chinese, and Indian populations owned considerable numbers of domestic slaves in the 1820s, in spite of British regulations. Possessing slaves reflected the owners' status and prestige. Foreign owners sometimes integrated female slaves into their family through marriage, making up for the small number of females. Slaves in Malacca came from various places such as Kedah, Borneo, Bali, Makassar, other islands of the Indonesian Archipelago, and from as far away as Mozambique and the Indian coasts.[32] Those whom Galang pirates supplied comprised mostly Malay,

Chinese, and Indian residents, or traders who passed by in the Malacca Strait and the neighboring waters. It seems possible that the slaving of the Galang pirates replaced a part of the previous one Bugis carried out in Singapore. They continued the century-long practice even after the British regulations came into effect in the 1820s.

According to the testimony of a Malay trader detained in Galang for several months, pirates lived there on their *prahus* with their wives and families.[33] However, other reports show that they actually settled on land there. A British army officer, Peter James Begbie, speculated that in 1823, six hundred men, four hundred women, and three hundred children lived in Galang; he further claimed that the male population consisted entirely of pirates, while the women fished and prepared tripang and agar-agar.[34] A British expedition to Galang in June 1836, took note of three large villages with an estimated three to four thousand residents, and that another six hundred men fled from their ships onto the shore or into the jungle when the British attacked. The British captain also reported that the sites showed no signs of cultivation or industry, strongly suggesting that Galang raiders operated as full-time pirates as Begbie said.[35] If both British observers have correctly assessed the number of inhabitants there, Galang experienced a considerable demographic increase over a ten-year period.

Galang also served as a marketing center for the pirate trade. A Malay trader who had been detained there described piratical fleets that carried back considerable prizes after their plundering trips. On one occasion, he noted spoils including cloths, salt, arms, and other items apart from captives, and at another time, booty consisting of piece goods, rice, ebony, and other stock, as well as thirty-eight captives. They sold the captives to Chinese merchants residing in Galang.[36] Traders trafficked not only in stolen merchandise, but, also, in necessities to the pirates, including armaments. In their 1836 expedition, the British found in the villages a great number of cannons and other weapons, as well as an immense quantity of ammunition, including several hundred barrels of English and coarse types of gunpowder. The British destroyed thirty large piratical *prahus* and forty to fifty small boats, also heavily armed.[37]

Although pirates used many locations for the sales of their spoils, they most frequently visited Kurou. Panglima Padi, a well-known pirate leader based on Kurou and active around Perak, brought his captives to Kurou and sold them to a man named Che Abbas for thirteen silver dollars each in April 1826.[38] Pirates, who assaulted Chinese and Acehnese traders near Pulau Barela in September 1826, also carried the captives to Kurou as well as to the Sambelan Islands and Pangkor.[39] One of the slave buyers in Kurou was a follower of Raja Ja'afar of Riau, which implies Riau's involvement in piracy and slaving.[40]

In Kurou, pirate settlements dotted the Kurow River. According to a Penang-based Bengali trader detained there, Panglima Sudin, one of the pirate chiefs, governed the area around the river's mouth. Pangulu (also known as Panglima or Nachoda) Udin, the most influential piratical leader, and uncle of Panglima Sudin, lived upstream. He had a wife in Penang, where he collected intelligence (perhaps on departing ships) and commodities such as opium and ammunition. Minor pirate leaders from downstream often presented Pangulu Udin with tribute and received booty. Pangulu Udin also had agents among the Chinese dealers and traders in Penang and Wellesley Province, who provided him with whatever he requested.[41] Pangulu Udin established his authority through his capacity to gather supplies and information. Kurou functioned as a key pirate settlement with intimate commercial connections to Penang.

The Kurou pirates also engaged in the "kidnapping business," holding captives for ransom. In December 1826, the pirates who seized fishermen off Pulau Tikus and detained them in Kurou sent one to Penang. In order to rescue his fellow crew members, the pirates ordered him to obtain a ransom of 110 silver dollars in cash, and collect a *colak* of opium, two bottles of arack, a bottle of oil, and clothing. On another occasion, fifteen silver dollars was paid for the release of each captive.[42]

Unfortunately, the backgrounds of Kurou pirates remain unclear, although Panglima Padi and other leaders seemed to be Orang Selat, deriving from around the Straits of Singapore and Durian.[43] The same report described their followers as Malays, but another witness said that Kurou pirates came from Lingga or the eastern part of the Strait.[44] Apparently, they originated from different places, but the information still indicates a close tie to Riau, Lingga, and Singapore.

In Singapore, the British authorities initially considered (or pretended to believe) that islands south of the Strait of Singapore, within the political boundaries of the Dutch, comprised the principal piratical strongholds.[45] In September 1826, however, the Dutch resident, Van Ranzow, at Riau, strongly protested the involvement of Sultan Husain of Singapore in piracy to the British authorities. Van Ranzow pointed out that Panglima Assar, a subject of Husain, attacked a trading *prahu* from Penang laden with pepper, and transported the hijacked vessel to Kateman on the east coast of Sumatra. In order to admonish Raja Ondut of Kateman, who allowed the pirates to anchor the pirate *prahu* in his domain, the Dutch dispatched a schooner. In response, Husain sent five heavily-armed craft to the Raja of Kateman and commanded him to guard the *prahu* from anyone who attempted to retake it. Van Ranzow emphasized that this demonstrated that the sultan not only protected but also supported piracy, and he insisted that the British had an obligation to take action against him, according to Article V of the London Treaty of 1824.[46]

Acting Resident Presgrave at Singapore shrugged off this Dutch protest. He replied that local pirates tended to implicate Sultan Husain, but it was impossible to prove anything. Although a large portion of the population in the region called themselves the subjects of Husain, actually he possessed no real authority over them. Presgrave politely rejected the proposed cooperation with the Dutch anti-piracy policing cruise, only promising to convey Van Ranzow's message to higher authorities.[47]

As a matter of fact, Sultan Husain did not completely control most of the pirates in the Malacca Strait. Moreover, the British authorities indeed recognized the connection between the sultan and some piratical practices conducted in the region. At the same council in which the British top administrators discussed Van Ranzow's protest, they received reports that among the pirates who attacked and captured a local trade ship near Malacca, four lived in Singapore, one Si Kooi, a confidant of Husain.[48] The British authorities, however, kept this information secret.

Throughout the period in question, trading ships heading for, or departing from, Singapore and, to a lesser extent, Penang constituted the main targets of the pirates from Riau, Lingga, and Singapore. Besides human cargoes, pirates preferred to seize certain types of commodities: local products including pepper, rattan, salt, and rice from the ships destined for the two British ports; and high-value imported ones such as Chinese raw silk, Indian textiles, and especially Bengali opium from the ships departing from those locales. Of the local goods, the Chinese demanded pepper and rattan; therefore, pirates could profit by selling their prizes to traders departing for China. Southeast Asia, where some places suffered from chronic shortages, valued salt and rice, and imported merchandise, such as Chinese and Indian textiles and Bengali opium. In particular, since the late nineteenth century, the demand for opium was increasing in many places throughout Southeast Asia, as for example, Kedah, Sumatra, Java, Borneo, Sulawesi, and Moluccas, among others.[49] Pirates themselves seemed to have consumed opium as they purchased it or obtained it as a ransom for captives, together with other necessities such as ammunition and food in Penang.[50] These targets and prizes indicated that piracy strongly correlated with the rapid development of intra-Asian trade centered on the British harbors, and the concomitant growth of inter-regional trade within Southeast Asia.

Pirates attacked almost all trading vessels passing the Malacca Strait, including Malays, Chinese, and Indians, but Cochin-Chinese ships comprised the most common victims because of the relatively light armaments of their ships. Even heavily-armed Bugis ships suffered assaults just after departing Singapore. In the 1830s, pirates also plundered European vessels near Singapore.

European Measures against Piracy

How did the Dutch and British colonial governments deal with indigenous piracy? Initially, the Dutch authorities attempted a "soft policy" to manage pirates. Unlike the earlier report by Commissioner Muntinghe, who proposed rather unrealistic measures to repress the pirates, Resident Van Angelbeek, the man on the spot in Riau, criticized forceful means. He suggested in 1825 that the Dutch should provide the Orang Laut in Lingga with an alternative source of income, such as engaging them in the collection of tripang and agar-agar under the supervision of the local chiefs. In fact, he reached an agreement with Raja Ja'afar and Pengulu Hamba Raja to put this idea into practice.[51] There is no record, however, that shows this action brought sufficient results.

Next, the Dutch colonial government, on the basis of existing treaties, believed that the local officials should take responsibility for moving effectively against pirates. In 1830, for instance, in all likelihood, under pressure from the Dutch, the Sultan at Lingga ordered Raja Ja'afar to send his son on an offensive against pirates on Pulau Buaya in Lingga.[52]

In 1833, however, the Dutch initiated a "high-handed" policy against pirates because local authorities had failed to solve the problem. In that year, the Dutch conducted a full-scale raid against pirates in Lingga. Up to fifty pirates in Pulau Sikana reportedly fled inland at the approach of the Dutch, and later died for want of food. The Dutch burned the pirate base in Pulau Temian to the ground. The sultan cooperated with them by sending eleven *prahus* in search of pirate leaders.[53] In the same year, the Dutch also started to use steamships to police the waters.[54]

However, to their disappointment, the Dutch authorities soon found the effect of the 1833 campaign ephemeral. Seeing the increase in piratical activity, in 1835, they sternly accused the sultan of Lingga. He explained that he lacked the ability to suppress pirates,[55] although, in fact, he had allied himself with them. In the next year, Captain Chad, who led a British anti-pirate force, reported that one of the captured pirates came from Lingga, and that the sultan had sent him and his comrades to engage in piracy near the Aroa Islands.[56] The sultan played a dangerous two-faced game.

The British reluctantly started their anti-piracy operations rather late in 1836. They feared that Singaporeans would oppose the increase in customs duties, which they needed to finance the military operations.[57] The lack of admiralty jurisdiction in Singapore, which necessitated that they send suspects to Calcutta for trials, offered another explanation for Singapore authorities' great hesitation in taking strong actions against pirates.[58]

Finally, in 1836, afraid of penetration of the Dutch influence in the Riau-Lingga waters as a result of their anti-piracy campaigns, the British started their own large-scale offensive, with the support of the Singapore and Calcutta governments.[59] After careful negotiations with the Dutch, the British fleets attacked Galang with steamships and patrolled Riau, Lingga, and elsewhere.[60] In Riau, the sultan at Lingga and other principal officials of the sultanate professed a desire to cultivate alliances with the English, and agreed to do all that they could to suppress piracy.[61]

After the British expedition of 1836, the Dutch strengthened their commitment against piracy, in all likelihood, in order to reestablish their ascendancy where the British had improved relationships with the local rulers. The Dutch officials decided to build a military station in Lingga.[62] Although they finally abandoned this plan because of a firm pledge from the sultan,[63] they continued their energetic measures to combat piracy in the years that followed, including a mission around Lingga in 1839.[64] The British feared that the Dutch would extend their influence to other Malay states, which would hamper British trade with Singapore. Governor Bonham suggested that the Calcutta administrators should request assurances from the Dutch at Batavia that they would not interfere with the trade in Lingga and other adjacent areas.[65]

The anti-piracy measures of the Dutch and the British affected the way they established policies regarding local rulers, who, in turn, tried to exploit the rivalry between the Dutch and the British in order to improve their relationships with the Europeans.

In Singapore, by the mid-1830s, piratical groups came under the control of Temenggong Daing Ibrahim, who succeeded his father at his death in 1825. Taking advantage of his location near Singapore, he provided pirates with information on ships — their cargo, dates of departure, and armaments. As their patron, the Temenggong subsequently expanded his authority over the leaders in the Strait region. A number of pirate-related Malay chiefs, among them those based on Galang, moved to Singapore seeking his protection.[66] Seeing the increasing power of the Temenggong, in 1836, Governor Bonham decided to cooperate with him in suppressing piracy. As a result, Ibrahim could now play an important role in contacts between the Singapore government and regional Malay leaders.[67]

In fact, British officials assisted pirate-related chiefs in neighboring islands in settling down in Singapore. Bonham reported to the Calcutta government:

> [O]ur young Native Chief [Ibrahim] informed me that if the government would receive them, 270 small boats containing families, who had heretofore more or less depended on Piracy for a livelihood, would resort to Singapore and reside there under his control ... I shall endeavour to make proper arrangement for their location ... locating them some where out of our jurisdiction but in the Territories of the Temenggong, our Native Chief, so immediately in our vicinity as to be under my strict surveillance would be preferable to having them on the Island.[68]

In this fashion, Bonham crucially affected the relocation of the pirate-related chiefs. It remains unclear whether his plan to keep them outside the island succeeded or not, but he gave similar aid on other occasions. In June 1837, Bonham promised to grant asylum in Singapore to former pirate leaders and their followers who left Galang.[69] Although the Dutch requested Singapore repatriate the Galang immigrants into their hands,[70] no record shows the British heeding the request.

In these ways, Bonham helped the Temenggong consolidate his power over the neighboring chiefs because he believed that an effective way to reduce piratical damage lay in, apart from military expeditions, placing pirates under the control of local leaders whom they held responsible.[71] It seems that he considered mastering pirates under the Temenggong's authority to be easier than controlling those under the sultan, upon whom the Dutch exerted strong influence.

Carl Trocki has suggested that Bonham's policy and the subsequent transfer of the Temenggong to Johor significantly affected the termination of piracy around Singapore, although the discovery of gutta-percha in his new domain constituted a more important reason for the disappearance of pirates because its procurement provided a different source of income.[72] Nonetheless, the lengthy works of J. L. Logan and a more recent study by Eric Tagliacozzo both discuss piracy and clandestine trade in later periods.[73] Piratical attacks on trading and fishing vessels, sales of piratical booty and captives, and European efforts to strengthen border security continued for the decades that followed.

Conclusion

Both Dutch and British sources indicate an intensification of piracy around Riau, Lingga, and Singapore in the early nineteenth century that stemmed from a combination of factors. Worsening conditions, such as Lingga's commercial decline and the British prohibition of slaving, drove some local traders and fishermen into plundering that represented a local attempt to take advantage of the new opportunities. As a result of commercial growth in the Malacca Strait, large concentrated amounts of exports and high-value imports were now exchanged in the area, making piracy much more profitable. For those excluded from the flourishing trade in the British ports, piracy offered a logical alternative. For some slave raiders and traders, the ongoing strong demand for slaves under the British regulations must have presented a good business prospect, where they expected high returns.

Major pirate leaders comprised petty chiefs based in a number of strongholds scattered in inlets, jungles, and small islands in the region, many of them labeled Malays, but also including converted Chinese and other ethnic groups. Pirate leaders made up their fleets mainly of Malays or Orang Lauts from various locations, although ethnic divisions and places of origin did not significantly factor in organizing them. Little mention of the Bugis exists, but we may take into consideration their relatively good relationships with European authorities in this period. Colonial officials tended not to describe their collaborators as pirates.[74]

The pirate leaders established their networks with merchants, informants, and dignitaries such as more important local elites or European administrators. Those who could better provide these links, which promised greater economic gain and safety, acquired more power. They undertook enterprises that used violence as a part of their business.

It is not clear whether piracy constituted an integral part of the functioning of a state in the period under examination, although contemporary Europeans strongly suspected it. As Presgrave suggested, it seems that the ties between sultans and pirates remained symbolic, and that pirates used such to justify their activities. The sources describe the involvements of the sultans in piracy as indirect and unsystematic. Neither functioned as power-holders or power-seekers in a real sense at this time, when the European authorities and petty piratical chiefs operated beyond their control. The strong influence of Temenggong Daing Ibrahim over pirate chiefs in the area proved exceptional, and at least partly a result of his extraordinarily good relationship with the British officials in Singapore.

Dutch and British anti-piracy measures generally failed to end piracy in the 1820s and 1830s. Because both sides feared the other would penetrate their territories in the guise of pirate suppression, the colonial governments strengthened their controls along the borders of their respective spheres of influence, contributing to the formation of their colonial empires in Southeast Asia. Under these circumstances, Bonham chose to cooperate with the local elites who had been involved in piracy — an attempt to incorporate the existing piratical networks within the colonial order, rather than choosing unrealistic methods of repression.

11
Smuggling in the South China Sea:
Alternate Histories of a Nonstate Space in the Late Nineteenth and Late Twentieth Centuries

Eric Tagliacozzo

The South China Sea presents researchers with an embarrassment of riches. Historically, it served as an important crossroads, funneling trade, migration, and the flow of ideas between East and Southeast Asia for at least two thousand years. Today, it still fulfills all of these functions, but also has taken on renewed geopolitical significance in the contest for resources and power between independent nation-states. The South China Sea touches upon many different polities, and it both connects and fragments at least a dozen countries in Asia, as well as the shipping of other nations whose vessels transect its open waters. Few bodies of water loom as large in considerations of environmental, strategic, and economic calculations; it is not an exaggeration at all to say that this constitutes one of the most "watched" spaces on the planet, both by academics and by those who formulate government policies.[1]

This chapter looks at both historical and contemporary dimensions of the South China Sea through the lens of smuggling. In the first half of this study, I show how contrabanding in this arena has been intimately linked to the development and evolution of regional maritime worlds in the nineteenth century. I then catalogue the place of Chinese smugglers in these activities, before examining the illegal "swirl of commodities" passing through this space in the last two centuries. The second half of the chapter, based on fieldwork, interviews, and documentary research completed in the late 1990s, analyzes the current scope of smuggling in the South China Sea. I examine the forces that both forge and fragment authority in the region, before studying the passage of illegal inanimate objects and the trafficking of humans in the last part of the chapter. I argue that both perspectives — historical and contemporary — can assist in piecing together the importance of this vast body of water to Asian societies over the past two hundred years. Several ongoing patterns make themselves evident in such a comparison, although significant disjunctures occur through the passage of time as well.

Smuggling in the Historical Period

Very few sectors on the planet have experienced as immense a growth in shipping and sea-traffic as the South China Sea did in the late nineteenth century. Seamen's guides to navigation of the waterways of the area were published often, outlining the winds, storms, and currents of the region for the merchantmen of many nations. Selling nautical charts became a large publishing industry on its own, with maps available on an ever-smaller scale, resulting in an overall shipping milieu with Asians and Europeans highly involved in area commerce.[2] Vessels ran west to Suez and the Indian Ocean, north to China and Japan, and even south to the expanding ports of British Australia. The South China Sea became a kind of *mare librum* without parallel, perhaps, since the time of the ancient Mediterranean.

Yet, the huge burgeoning of trade and of even very small-scale shipping in the South China Sea exposed two paradoxical phenomena.[3] Not only could states use shipping as an engine of growth and coercion, but those who wished to trade outside of the state's vision could also employ it. By the 1880s and 1890s, therefore, colonial nations made an effort to try to control these processes, and to bend maritime growth toward their own ends. In the Dutch East Indies, the Dutch Colonial Packet Service or KPM (*Koninklijke Paketvaart Maatschappij*) received its inaugural contract in 1891, with orders from Batavia to expand shipping links to the rest of the archipelago.[4] The Dutch used the KPM, and a series of exclusionary shipping rules, to try to monopolize trade and shipping patterns throughout their maritime empire in Southeast Asia. Yet, even as the marine transport arm of the colonial state developed, British, French, Chinese, and indigenous Southeast Asian shipping continued to ply the Indonesian islands. These craft connected ports across area frontiers, and still managed to carry large quantities of commodities of nearly all descriptions.[5]

Some of these trade items circulated outside of "official" channels, troubling colonial states a great deal. The control of sea-based trade and movement, therefore, became a serious policy concern for the Dutch, especially so in regard to merchant shipping emanating from the neighboring British possessions. By the turn of the twentieth century, the maritime expansion of the two colonial states had reached the entire width of what we today call Malaysia and Indonesia. The need to tabulate, understand, and define these marine spaces of the lower reaches of the South China Sea had become crucial, especially for Batavia. Steam-shipping outweighed sail in Singapore's port statistics only two years after the Suez Canal opened in 1869, yet the rising volume of *prahu* and junk traffic also meant that the South China Sea bustled with a wide variety of ships.[6]

Who was involved in smuggling commodities in this vast maritime domain of the South China Sea? One such community comprised European "country traders" who commissioned specialized ships, some of them small and fleet-winged to better smuggle opium.[7] A thriving business sprouted around Batavia for Chinese opium runners looking to purchase the illegal commodity. Country traders entered the shallow harbor, and paid the requisite bribe to crooked Dutch officials, who then told them where to pick up contraband cargoes of ocean produce amid the inlets frequented by the junks.[8] In this way, valuable local products found their way up to Canton. The country traders could thus continue their coasting trade in Southeast Asia, picking up more commodities while their original loads sped north on consignment. W. H. Coates has even published a letter of a Parsee ship-owner to his captain, instructing him on how to avoid customs patrols and war junks cruising around Whampoa.[9]

In addition to European country traders, many junks sailed south from coastal China into the South China Sea. Chinese shipping, a complicated endeavor, required a large cast of actors and their concomitant skills — merchants, capitalists, seamen, and navigators all came together to share in the enterprise. Syndicates called *bang* were set up in Guangdong, Zhejiang, and Fujian to defray costs and share in the risks, as construction fees on the junks alone often reached into the tens of thousands of gold in cash.[10] John Crawfurd noted the state of affairs in the 1820s by observing that "the cargo of Chinese junks is not the property of an individual but of many — the proprietors merely have their own compartments in the vessel."[11] Many people stood ready to invest despite the dangers involved. The profit margin on junks sailing across the South China Sea to Sulu in the Southern Philippines ranged between thirty and three hundred percent, with certain marine products commanding one hundred percent profits back home, and mother-of-pearl three times that amount.[12] Amoy in Fujian served as the main base for the fleets, although ships departed from as far north as Shanghai and as far south as Hainan. Most left China during the beginning of the northeast monsoon, arriving in Southeast Asia in January and early February.[13]

The very trying circumstances surrounding such endeavors made this penchant for tightly-coordinated cooperation vital. Overseas trade was continually restricted on an on-again/off-again basis while bankruptcy in such a dangerous business as transoceanic shipping loomed only as far away as the nearest pirate or squall. Yet, by far, the degree of official "propitiation" needed to oil the machine presented the most difficult hurdle in making them a success. Sarasin Viraphol estimates that traders earmarked twenty to forty percent of total costs during this period toward the local *yamens* to serve as "protection."[14] Chinese viceroys and customs officials did not necessarily oppose such journeys. They merely wanted their cut. Such graft and inefficiency, however, did take its toll. Official outlets for overseas goods were quickly ignored by many junk captains, who preferred to put into Chinese ports where such exactions could be minimized. There they could make separate deals with local coastal authorities, and if the price turned out unacceptable, the captain could simply move on.

As Western imperial power grew in the southern most reaches of the South China Sea, the illicit and unrecorded business of many Chinese networks, in particular, worried these regimes, as a large number of Chinese traded a broad range of products outside the vision and grasp of these states. Officials eventually designated several of them as illegal, such as unfarmed opium and firearms. A single Dutch report from Bangka in 1879 demonstrates some of these dimensions very well. A study-tour of these remote coasts yielded an unwelcome shock to Batavia: Chinese vessels were shuttling goods literally everywhere along these shores, from Pahid and Rangam to Roemah Batoe and Tandjong Nioer. Tandjoeng Tedoeng, seemingly the epicenter, funneled opium and textiles across the Bangka Straits by way of a string of ethnic Chinese villages along the shore. The report noted the absurd ease by which voyages of this type could originate from the majority of these villages, as the state exercised almost no supervision in the area, not to mention the strong business ties the smugglers had to Singapore, in particular.[15]

By the years leading up to the *fin de siècle*, the question of how to deal with Chinese in the South China Sea and their illegal trades exasperated both the Dutch and the British. This, however, presented a policy problem that they could never fully solve. All along the South China Sea basin, these patterns of "illegality" continued unabated, with Chinese merchants figuring out ways to sidestep the growing proscriptions of the state. Such activities happened in peripheral, outlying areas, away from the coercive "eye" and control of the center.[16] Yet, these transactions also happened right in the laps of colonial cities, as Chinese used the expanding size of these centers to lose themselves in the chaos and complexity of colonial capitals.[17] The movements, feints, and connections of overseas Chinese in Southeast Asia, thus, leapfrogged all crystallizing boundaries. This omnipresent aura of Chinese "illegality," so easy to see yet so difficult to control, frustrated both colonial states well after the turn of the century.

By the early decades of the twentieth century, the newly-established colonial governments in the region severely tested the mobility of Chinese smugglers in the lower latitudes of the South China Sea. Everywhere, attempts were being made to eradicate any transgressive powers that such smugglers might have, especially those which they could use to compete with the coercive abilities of the state. Java was experimenting with anthropometric identity-proofs, with an eye toward documenting all "Foreign Asians" (*Vreemde Oosterlingen*) in the Indies a few years later.[18] Dutch and British governments also tightened restrictions on Chinese "secret societies" (*hui*). One legal amendment, for instance, introduced flogging as a punishment for secret society participation. Colonial governments seemed to have been sending a message to the *hui* that the gloves were now coming off against any and all illicit activities such as smuggling.[19]

What kinds of commodities moved across the sweep of the South China Sea during this period? Although a huge spectrum of items might merit examination, the shadowy trade in spirits and narcotics provide an instructive window. From as early as the 1850s, ports such as Labuan, off the western coast of Borneo, farmed out licenses to sell liquor in order to raise revenues for the colony's exchequer. Almost as quickly, smuggling syndicates sprang up to challenge official monopolies, necessitating constant changes in the laws to fight these attacks on securing government profits.[20] Liquor was also contrabanded elsewhere in the British possessions, such as on the Malay Peninsula, while Malay-language newspapers from the 1890s made clear that even the seat of English power (Singapore) never stayed fully immune to these problems.[21] Spirits such as gin, brandy, whiskey, and even homemade arrack all poured across the border and into the Dutch Indies as well.[22] In places such as West Borneo smugglers brought European liquor in small batches at a time, to circumvent the regulations of the local monopoly.[23] Attempts to ban the transit of alcohol altogether as part of a moral crusade were doomed to failure because of the huge profits traders reaped by these sales. Only at the turn of the twentieth century were larger, more systemic efforts made to staunch these commodity flows, especially in such places as Sulu where the Dutch could count on cooperation.[24]

No item was smuggled more than opium. By the nineteenth century, it had been circulating in the South China Sea for a very long time. Though notices of opium use reach back far into the distant past, only in the seventeenth century did detailed records start to document its production and passage. Dutch merchants used Southeast Asia as a conduit to ferry small amounts of opium to Taiwan; from there, they traded it to the vast interior economy of China, often on the sly. Though traded freely in much of Southeast Asia, many local rulers tried to forbid or inhibit the sale of opium because of the drug's adverse effects on its populations. European traders and many Chinese, Armenian, and other merchant groups gradually subsumed under European power sold the opium anyway. Other local rulers saw the economic benefits from participating in this business themselves, as opium had a high resale value, especially in its retail form known as *chandu*. As European trading companies and indigenous Southeast Asian state-making projects evolved during the nineteenth century, however, different actors attempted to corner the market in drugs for their own long-term profits. States and private speculators competed, therefore, in selling opium over large expanses of the South China Sea, which would remain a functional pattern of this commerce into the twentieth century.[25]

Narcotics smuggling in the late nineteenth century South China Sea region, as a result, became very complicated. Colonial states took measures to directly control the opium trade, yet with only ambiguous results vis-à-vis smuggling. High-ranking European officials acknowledged as much in reports back to the colonial metropoles.[26] Smuggling seems to have risen by the turn of the twentieth century, partially because governments raised prices on legalized *chandu*, and partially because the farmers (now out of work) often used their specialized knowledge of smuggling mechanisms to practice it themselves.[27] In Insular Southeast Asia, the vast labyrinth of narcotics legislation and its uneven application to various territories and people also ensured continuity in smuggling. In the years in and around 1910, Britain promulgated separate rules for its various dependencies in the area while each polity wrote its own internal regulations. In the Federated Malay States (FMS), for example, legislation drew distinctions regarding the acceptability of narcotics use by race, occupation, and even by coastal or interior habitation.[28] The sheer complexity of the system, and the colonial state's inability to enforce it across all of its dominions, guaranteed that narcotics contrabanding in this region survived well into the early twentieth century. The Japanese eventually also took it up, as they began their own chapter of expanding power in this part of the world.[29]

Smuggling in the Contemporary Period

How do these historical smuggling patterns of the South China Sea look in our own contemporary world? How much will China be able to influence these patterns based on its own complicated history of interactions with the sea in this region, and the challenges to China's unity that often appear to arise from this proximity? Getting a sense of the political economy of the South China coast seems crucial in helping to answer these questions. In an interview conducted several years ago, the former Dean of the School of Journalism at the University of California, Berkeley, and prominent China-watcher, Orville Schell, mentioned that essentially three separate Chinas existed: the Communist North, a *laissez-faire* South, and an Islamic West, increasingly looking across the border to the Central Asian republics.[30] These de facto "polities" are nothing new, Schell said; they have persisted in uneasy juxtaposition under the same rubric of Chinese Empire for many centuries. Yet, for how long, he contemplated, is geopolitical unity possible under vastly changed present conditions? The Tang dynasty's An Lu Shan Rebellion or the Boxer Uprising of the *fin de siecle* around 1900 never included a global battle cry for democracy and the right to determine one's own individual economic destiny.[31] China has known many periods of fragmentation in its four millennia of recorded history, and one might conceivably imagine the formal, delineated rupture of the People's Republic sometime in the future, with certain and serious implications for the study of smuggling in the South China Sea.

Schell's musings are interesting, yet, a more believable, intermediate step might posit a less seismic change of events, although one with essentially many of the same characteristics. Guangdong and Fujian, fueled by Special Economic Zones such as Shenzen and Zhuhai and linkages to capital from Hong Kong and Taiwan, are now widening the gulf between mainland rich and poor by continuing their campaigns of frenetic modernization. Guangdong alone often receives up to half of all foreign investment entering into the People's Republic from abroad. Because of a fear of aggression from the United States and Taiwan in the two decades immediately following the 1949 Revolution, Chinese Central Planning located the majority of the nation's heavy industry *away* from these southern coasts. This policy currently reaps rewards for southern populations, who now have much less of a vestigial legacy of enormous state-owned inefficiency to bear. It also means that these places trade — and trade illegally — with actors across the South China Sea far more easily than other parts of China can hope to do so.

An entity which seems very close in some ways to a traditional polity may now be developing in Southeastern China, one with its own customs and bylaws and whose ways of exchange blatantly oppose a distant authority center one thousand miles to the north. The linkages within it — linguistic, cultural, and now increasingly monetary — are real and also part of a larger historical continuum predating even Marco Polo's descriptions of "Zaitun" (the contemporary Quanzhou).[32] Critics say that if Beijing does not figure out a way to either bring the rest of the country up to this same standard of living, or extinguish this brand of hyper-capitalism before it spins out of control, further revolutions could conceivably await in the wings. And yet, little evidence exists that the state wants to curb rampant growth.

The resultant southern polities abutting the South China Sea would develop into strong, mercantilist-minded dynamos, while their northern counterparts would have a much more difficult time competing for reasons as much historical as economic. What we may be witnessing today is the germination of a centuries-old evolution of fragmentation, yet, one (aided by technology and virtual communication) that potentially has more of a chance to succeed now than at any other point in history. Despite pledges of fifty-year grace periods in respecting contemporary economic systems, the first decades of the twenty-first century after 1997 should provide a useful litmus test in determining how Beijing will appraise the situation, and then set its own policies. In either scenario, Hong Kong seems to be evolving into the defacto cosmopolis of a new regional entity, servicing and being served by the cities of the northernmost part of the South China Sea.[33]

In the lower latitudes of the South China Sea region, Southeast Asia has a very open cadence to its trade which has distinguished this part of the world for many centuries. Because the modern territorial conception of borders was alien here and introduced only forcibly by Europeans, it should not surprise us that goods continue to flow across these demarcations, often without the blessing of the state.[34] Globalization, regional economic blocs, and the growth of sub-regional economic development "triangles" have only accelerated this trend in recent years, providing new avenues and an impetus to a range of traders (acting legally and illegally) to move their cargoes across national boundaries. The establishment of localized, multi-country growth areas has particularly aided this process, with combinations such as the BIMP-EAGA development triangle (centered on the Sulu Sea between

Malaysia, Indonesia, and the Philippines) proving especially profitable and problematic in this sense.[35]

The explosion of boundary discussions and commercial flows has led to a very large number of new infrastructural projects designed to better connect borders in the South China Sea region. In the above-mentioned BIMP-EAGA development sphere, for example, expanded postal routes now link northern Indonesia and the southern Philippines. Malaysia and Singapore have added a second causeway link between them; already the volume of traffic crossing the original road-bridge exceeded the ability of customs officials on either side to check all moving vehicles for contraband. Plans have even been announced for the construction of a huge bridge connecting Malaysia and Indonesia across the Malacca Strait, as well. Although the agreement has not specified the exact location of the structure's endpoints, it calls for railway, gas pipes, and power cables on the bridge, as well as a main connecting section of road.[36] The enormous opening of border facilities and connections along the South China Sea's margins, however, has come at a price. Alongside increased legitimate trade revenues across boundaries, have also flowed goods and problems of another kind. Contraband and security as it relates to border traffic, generally, have become major issues now in Southeast Asian geopolitics.

The salient openness of frontiers in the region has also spurred Southeast Asian administrations into taking firm steps to lessen the effects of smuggling that the boundary liberalization process includes. These efforts have manifested themselves in different forms, one of which has been to encourage co-operation of law enforcement agencies across frontiers: the police forces of Singapore and Malaysia have been particularly adept at this, while Vietnam and Cambodia recently signed a similar accord.[37] Another way has been to map out coasts and land with a greater degree of efficiency, both by increasing interdiction units in these areas and also by producing more accurate charts of difficult terrain. The Philippines has recently added more ships and Malaysia more coastal radar stations along these lines, while Laos is using Global Positioning Systems (GPS) to better chart its boundaries. Indonesia is closing down old markets and opening new ones along its frontiers, trying to influence the terms of regional trade more directly.[38] Finally, governments are attempting better "tagging" on human beings who frequently cross borders; so that they may keep a more watchful eye on these peoples' activities. Indonesia has now differentiated the passports which many of its citizens use to travel abroad illegally (sometimes, under the guise of undertaking the pilgrimage to Mecca, which requires different documentation than those not making the Hajj), while Kuala Lumpur has introduced electronic security features into Malaysian passports to prevent forgeries. Governments took all of these steps in the region in the hope that they will make the increasing porosity of Southeast Asia's boundaries profitable to national exchequers, while limiting the abilities of citizens who may wish to take advantage of the new openness in illegal ways.

Consumer goods, broadly defined, exemplified an important category of goods that can be examined in an analysis of contrabanding and boundaries in the South China Sea region. They epitomize a broad spectrum of illegally transited commodities: cigarettes, automobiles, compact discs, pornography, even antique sculpture and religious items. In terms of the sheer number of cases, this sub-branch of contrabanding is probably the most important in the region. "We can't catch the real smugglers," said one Southeast Asian official to the *Far Eastern Economic Review*, citing the traffickers' mobile phones and faster boats, which frequently render them far better equipped than border guards.[39] Yet, regional administrations have tried to combat smuggling syndicates, using measures as diverse as stiff fines and newly-computerized customs services. With disappointing results, from the state's viewpoint, smuggling of consumer goods still thrives in the South China Sea arena. The passage of contraband has spread so widely in the region, especially in the case of consumer goods, that singling out certain borders or spheres as being more problematic than others tends to be difficult.

Nevertheless, a glimpse at a few of these spaces can provide an idea of how systemic this trafficking has really become, and what goods it handles. The Sino-Vietnamese border is a high-volume transit area for contraband. Here, garments, electric fans, and bicycles are "hot" items, mostly because Hanoi restricts these goods in an effort to protect domestic production. Maritime spaces adjoining the South China Sea should also be mentioned in the Southeast Asian context, as there is no shortage of consumer-good smuggling in this realm. From interviews conducted with Indonesian sailors on Jakarta's docks, one gains the impression that they could easily arrange the passage of goods outside local waters to the country's neighbors. Meanwhile, Indonesian workers interviewed in Singapore said that almost anything could be ordered from nearby Riau, if one knew how.[40] In the Philippines, with a similar archipelagic geography, long coastlines and corrupt maritime patrols make for easy on- and off-loading, the opportunities stretching literally for thousands of miles.[41]

As we have noted in the historical section above, few inanimate objects travel as quickly or lucratively as narcotics. Over the course of the last century, the drug trade in Southeast Asia has evolved and showed certain remarkable continuities with the patterns of an earlier age. Though the early decades of the twentieth century saw a concerted effort by colonial administrations to streamline and gain from this commerce, international pressures — mainly from "opium suppression societies" based in the West — also challenged the status quo. Narcotics trading in Asia became increasingly criminalized, and global conferences (such as the Hague Convention in 1912) brought public opinion to bear on the colonial management of drug trafficking. Prices on opium in Southeast Asia were raised until it became difficult for local peoples to buy the drug legally on a regular, addictive basis.[42] Decolonization changed this dynamic to a degree, as the new independent states of the region strove to rid themselves of drug addiction, often attributed to the evils of imperial domination. Yet, the rigors of state-building allowed many segments of society, especially elites and minority frontier populations, to continue profiting from narcotics against the dictates of indigenous states. Graft, pre-existing networks of ethnic dispersion, and the evolution of long-range communications oiled these gears considerably. The prosecution of the Vietnam War spread drugs to new landscapes; the United States presence in the region acted as both a help (through GI's) and at least, nominally a hindrance (through the CIA) to these trades.[43]

A trade that began mainly as a transit in imported opium became, by the late twentieth century, a commerce in illegal substances far larger and more diverse than it had been in the past. The South China Sea region now imports *and* exports drugs. The notorious "Golden Triangle" has made narcotics trafficking in the region famous, but, in recent years, the trade has seeped into nearly every corner of ASEAN, and into all socio-economic classes. In Southeast Asia, countries outside of the Golden Triangle such as Indonesia and the Philippines are starting to admit that they no longer simply operate as transit nations, but also as consuming "end-destinations."[44] Norodom Ranariddh of Cambodia has warned that his country would soon be paralyzed by international drug-trafficking barons unless it received substantial outside assistance.[45] Even tiny Brunei, staunchly Muslim and easily patrolled, has acknowledged the onset of a serious drug problem.[46] All of these vectors point to serious concerns in the region, for local governments, health organizations, and international bodies (such as the United Nations) interested in stability in the area.

Exactly who can we blame for all of this smuggling? With the broad spectrum of narcotics and geography involved, it should not surprise us that these patterns also entailed a diverse net of people — politicians, merchants, professional criminals, and even "ordinary folk," all taking part in this commerce. One trend that stands out is that narcotics trafficking in the South China Sea region, as in the nineteenth century with Chinese and Armenian trade networks, often still seem to be accomplished along predominantly ethnic lines. For example, Pakistani groups have been caught selling heroin into Indonesia, while Indonesians are regularly arrested for contrabanding drugs north into Malaysia. This is perhaps because religious, linguistic, and cultural similarities, all historically-based, have facilitated kinship connections and trust. Chinese networks supply the Southeast Asian drug smuggling nexus by land and by sea including two Triad groups that have participated in these activities for a long time, the 14K and Bamboo Gangs, among others operating out of southern China, Macau, and Hong Kong.[47] These syndicates present contemporary manifestations of much older Chinese organizations, discussed in Robert Antony's chapter, which historically transited narcotics and other contraband between East and Southeast Asia.[48]

Life forms comprise another contraband trade that compellingly assist in drawing a genealogy of historical and contemporary patterns of smuggling in the region. Human trafficking makes up the majority of this commerce. The movement of people across boundaries in the South China Sea, both legally and illegally, also has a long history. Migration theorists have noted a fundamental, world-wide shift in the nature of population flows in the last two centuries: in the nineteenth century, the majority of migrants relocated from rich to poor countries, while in the twentieth century the direction has clearly reversed.[49] The brokered transit of human beings is clearly rising globally, and especially so in the South China Sea region. This human tide of trafficking constitutes a major dimension of contemporary smuggling networks in the region, one that also has strong links to the past.

As in previous ages, today, large numbers of workers move across national boundaries, very often illegally, in search of stable livelihoods. In the late 1990s, for example, over 700,000 foreign laborers lived in Thailand by official figures, 1.2 million in Malaysia, while over four million Filipinos were employed abroad.[50] Trafficked workers, governments argue, pose a threat and put themselves at risk at the same time. They are often accused of bringing crime and disease with them (including AIDS), but they remain concomitantly at the mercy of gangs who distribute them for the highest price. Receiving countries, however, often desperately need the migrants, whatever the means used to get them there.[51]

The transit of undocumented labor is not the only manifestation of human trafficking prevalent in the region. Prostitution has also been a magnet for the circulation of women through the South China Sea, as the poor of various countries have often had few alternatives but to sell their own bodies to make ends meet. In colonial times, the forces that drove prostitution-trafficking often started from outside the region: tales of Southeast Asia's burgeoning ports sometimes lured indigent country girls from China and Japan, reacting to famine and underdevelopment in their own countrysides.[52] Others were traded unwittingly, or even knowingly chose to sail south because they had few other options. These broad, systemic movements also took place from rural Asian landscapes into the new cities of empire, as well as into colonial barracks, plantations, and mines.[53] The contemporary scene has witnessed an elaboration and expansion of this dynamic, pushing women and children in new directions. The profits of successfully transporting women across long distances and into lives of prostitution have become simply enormous.[54]

Within Southeast Asia itself, prostitutes are moved to the great cities, and also to outlying areas in the region. In urban centers, a syndicate was exposed some years ago that brought Filipina prostitutes into Singapore, secreting them day and night through customs at Changi Airport. Officials ultimately arrested thirty-nine women, partially because the traffickers were also importing drugs in the same "shipments," and had thus aroused the attention of police. In Malaysia, Chinese networks out of Thailand and South China have run prostitutes into the country; many of the women have been lied to, and told that they have jobs in factories, so that they would readily make the journey.[55] The trade siphons women off even into rural geographies, however, so long as it is felt that there are profits to be made. The "resort island" of Batam off Singapore illustrates one example of this phenomenon, while women are also brought even to Indonesian New Guinea (West Papua), where Thai fishermen spend weeks at a time, far from their own homes.[56] Even religiously-conservative Brunei has seen this kind of trafficking: seven women were arrested in 1997 who had been trafficked to the sultanate, simply because the strength of the Brunei dollar made the risks worthwhile (the women included three Malaysians, three Indonesians, and a Filipina, all from poorer surrounding countries.)[57]

Conclusion

I stated earlier in this chapter that the South China Sea both binds and fragments the societies that ring it over several thousand kilometers. The littoral states of this body of water have traded, raided, and negotiated with each other for at least two thousand years. In the past several centuries, the vernacular languages of the region, as well as the documents and ledgers of European sources have written of many of these interactions. The activities of smugglers, also vital in these binding processes, left far fewer traces but nevertheless, remained important in forging this common world. Contrabandists helped cement a unity to this maritime field, and their voyages connected diasporas to ports and peoples even if their watery tracks no longer mark the evidentiary record. Occasionally, however, these journeys do survive in the archives. If their echo does not seem that strange to us as contemporary humans, it is because so many of these voyages are still being undertaken, along the entire width and breadth of the South China Sea.

The economic ramifications of this continuity remain obvious. Such movements affect national economies, and the official reporting of trade flows will never take into account the crucial importance that such journeys play in the economic development of local societies. Politically, too, the role of smuggling in the South China Sea retains great importance, as the transit of a variety of commodities — including weapons, drugs, and trafficked human beings — makes clear immediately, just by mentioning the categories of the transited goods. The passage of contraband certainly deserves a place in any serious discussion about the nature and evolution of the South China Sea as an integrated region, simply because of its great significance in both historical and contemporary epochs as a medium of human exchange. These patterns show every sign of continuing into the future as well, serving to delineate this region's coherence — or dissonance — as a unified maritime world.

Notes

Chapter 1: Introduction

1. See Van Dyke 2005, 124–5, 132, 141.
2. Among the important exceptions, of course, are the seminal sea-centered studies on Southeast Asia by Jacob van Leur and Georges Coedès, which are discussed in Sutherland 2003.
3. Bentley 1999, 217.
4. Wigen 2007, 15.
5. See Tagliacozzo 2005, and Reid 1996.
6. Matsuda 2006, 769.
7. Braudel 1972; also see Sutherland 2003.
8. Antony 2003, 139–40, and Shapinsky in this volume.
9. See, in particular, the chapters by Igawa, Ota, and Tagliacozzo.
10. Blussé 1999, 112.
11. See Reid 1997, Blussé 1999, Tagliacozzo 2005, and Chin, Igawa, Antony, and Ota in this volume.
12. See Chin and Calanca in this volume.
13. See Ng Wai-ming 2004, and the chapters by Shapinsky, Petrucci, and Igawa.
14. Blussé 1999, 116.
15. See, for example, Warren 1981 and 2003.
16. Reid 1997, 71.
17. Zheng Guangnan 1999, 3–7, and Matsuura 2003, 75; for a broader, cross-cultural perspective on piracy see Risso 2001.
18. See, in particular, the discussions in the chapters by Reid and Shapinsky.
19. Gould 2007, 105–6.
20. See Shapinsky's chapter.
21. Antony 2007, 44–45, and Reid's chapter.
22. *Chouhai tubian* (1562), cited in Elisonas 1991, 259.
23. Hellyer 2005, and his chapter in this book.
24. See, for example, the chapters by Reid and Ota in this volume.
25. Warren 1981 and 2002.
26. Besides Calanca, also see Antony in this book.

156 *Notes to pp. 9–23*

27. Van Dyke 2005, 120–37, and Tagliacozzo in this volume.
28. Leirissa 1994, 112.
29. In particular, see Shapinsky, Chin, Petrucci, and Antony in this volume.
30. See Ota's chapter.
31. See Ng Chin-keong 1983.
32. See Shapinsky's chapter.

Chapter 2: Violence at Sea

1. See Map 1.1 (p. 4) for the places discussed in this chapter.
2. Brunsson (1989) developed this concept, and Krasner (2001) applied it to the East Asian "system".
3. The so-called "Chinese world order" of tribute has an extensive literature, most recently discussed in Reid and Zheng 2009.
4. Cited in Warren 2003, 24.
5. See Henty 1905, Dalton 1972, and the 1935 Hollywood classic, *The China Seas*, which features "Malay Pirates" as a rich stereotype.
6. As made clear below, the *wokou* or *wakō* in reality comprised people who would today be considered Chinese, Japanese, Southeast Asians, as well as even Europeans and Africans.
7. I thank Fang Xiaoping for looking through relevant Chinese sources for me and for making a certain sense of the usage of these terms.
8. After 1684, the Qing government gradually abandoned this policy and licensed Chinese shippers, though retaining great caution about foreign ships. See Calanca's chapter in this book; also see Ng Chin-Keong 1983.
9. *Chouhai tubian* (1562), cited in Wang Tai Peng 1994, 39n.
10. Iioka Naoko, forthcoming.
11. Ma Huan as translated by Mills 1970, 10–11.
12. Kobata and Matsuda 1969, 179–80, and Chin, forthcoming.
13. Cited in So 1975, 26.
14. See, for example, the discussion by Calanca in this book.
15. Dian Murray 1987, and Antony 2003.
16. Van Vliet 1910, 93, describing trade missions from Siam in the seventeenth century. Houtman 1970, 14–32, narrated in more colorful and multilingual detail the way Asian trading ships were received in Aceh when they brought letters from their king.
17. Crawfurd 1856, 353.
18. Wilkinson 1959, 2:980.
19. Cited (without attribution) in Andaya and Andaya 1982, 130.
20. Trocki 1979, 56.
21. Starkey 2007, 3:381–84.
22. Reid 1969, 11.
23. See also the chapters by Ota and Tagliacozzo in this volume.
24. See Bassett 1980, 19–32.
25. Cited in D.G.E. Hall 1968, 528.
26. "The Battle of Qualah Battoo," broadsheet published in Portland, Maine, on the return of the *Potomac* from her punitive mission in 1832, reproduced in Putnam 1924, 93.
27. Andaya and Andaya 1982, 131.

28. Trocki 1979, 205–6.
29. Warren 1981, 285–87.
30. Majul 1973, 283–316.
31. Reid 1969, 87–88.
32. Twang 1998.
33. The issue of smuggling is taken up in Tagliacozzo's chapter in this volume.
34. Warren 2003, and Xu 2008.

Chapter 3: From Sea Bandits to Sea Lords

1. The author is grateful for helpful comments from David Bertaina and Erik Freas at the University of Illinois, Springfield.
2. I am here borrowing an argument by the Japanese scholar Tanaka Takeo (1997, 1–2) about the multiethnic bands of pirates in premodern East Asia known as *wakō*.
3. Historians generally translate two words signifying "pirate" in the context of premodern Japan. The term *wakō* is the Japanese pronunciation of a word that only appears in Chinese and Korean historical sources (Chinese *wokou*, Korean *waegu*), meaning Japanese pirates, whereas *kaizoku* is one Japanese historical sources use. Although some overlap exists in the populations represented by the terms *waegu, wokou*, and *kaizoku*, I will be focusing on the case of seafarers labeled as *kaizoku* because of the significant corpus of documents written by them.
4. This combination of external recognition and internal control draws on a model of sovereignty laid out in Thomson 1994, chap. 1. Shoguns were warrior hegemons who ruled in Japan in the name of the emperor between the fourteenth and mid-nineteenth centuries; *daimyo* were local warlords, who possessed a domain and also often exercised extensive power. In the period under discussion in this chapter, Japan was almost constantly in a state of civil war, and the power and authority of many *daimyo* rivaled those of emperors and shoguns.
5. On these changes, see Toyoda and Sugiyama 1977, 129–44, and Farris 2006.
6. Udagawa (1981) exemplifies this Marxist historiographical trend, but Japanese scholarship continues to use the term that can be translated as naval vassal (*suigun*).
7. Murai 1993, 39. For *wakō*, see note 2 above and Igawa Kenji's chapter in this volume.
8. Thomson 1994, 3–4.
9. Thomson 1994, especially chap. 3.
10. Conlan 2003, 149–50.
11. White 1995, 172.
12. In order to explore alternatives to understanding discourse as a unitary force, here I engage with Mikhail Bakhtin's (1981) ideas of the "dialogical."
13. For different ways in which seas are socially and culturally constructed over time, see Steinberg 2001.
14. Amino 1984, 30–31.
15. For estates as a "system," see Keirstead 1992; for the maritime dimension, see Hotate 1981.
16. See Kawai 1977, and EKS 1983, doc. 2179.
17. Murai 1988, 109–10, Batten 2003, 37, and Farris 1985, 53–55.
18. Ki 1957, 36.

19. Ennin 1955, 2, 6, 94, 125, and EKS 1983, doc. 1527.
20. Batten 2003, 118–19; Amino (1984) has argued that the term *ama* can encompass the identities of fisher folk, pirates, salt makers, and others, but no evidence exists of any seafarer self-identifying as a "sea-person."
21. Sōgi 1990, 411.
22. The *Kojiki* (712 CE) lists "sea people" as one of the groups owing tribute to the Yamato court. The eroticized, othered aspect of women of the sea can be found throughout classical Japanese literature (Goodwin 2007).
23. Quoted in Shinjō 1995, 500.
24. Matsubara 1999, 14–16, and *Ruijusandaikyaku* 1973, 614.
25. Satō Shin'ichi 1955, vol. 1, Kobayashi 1978, and Katsumata 1981.
26. EKS 1983, doc. 747.
27. Manzai, Eikyō 6 (1434) 1/19, and Eikyō 6 (1434) 1/30.
28. EKS 1983, doc. 1417.
29. For the Hosokawa, see EKS 1983, doc. 1663; and for the Kōno, see EKS 1983, doc. 2448.
30. See EKS 1983, docs. 1151, 1379, and Hashizume 2000, 207.
31. See *Jūroku-jūshichi seiki Iezusukai Nihon hōkokushū* 1994, 7:140–41, and EKS 1983, docs. 2102, 2433.
32. *Hagi-han batsuetsuroku* 1967, 4:174 doc. 10, and EKS 1983, doc. 1713.
33. Kishida 2001, 198.
34. EKS 1983, doc. 2302.
35. EKS 1983, doc. 1596.
36. Yamauchi 2005, 155–59.
37. Dening 1980, 157–58.
38. See EKS 1983, doc. 1340, Amino 1984, and John Hall 1966.
39. See EKS 1983, docs. 1733, 1901, Udagawa 1984, 440–41, and Kariyama 1989, 50–57.
40. EKS 1983, doc. 1900.
41. Ki 1957, 38.
42. See the selections from the *Chosŏn wangjo sillok* [Veritable Records of the Chosŏn Court], cited in Murai 1993, 36-39.
43. Song 1987, no. 162. For further discussions on the relations between Tsushima and Korea see Hellyer's chapter in this volume.
44. Amino (1984) is the germinal work on non-agricultural cultures in medieval Japan.
45. Amino 1984; *Hagi-han batsuetsuroku*, 4:175, doc. 13, Kawai 1981, 6–7, and Hayashiya 1981.
46. Yamauchi 2005, 22–23, and Batten 2003, 22–42.
47. Imagawa 1994, 406.
48. Tonomura 1992, 98–101, and Usami 1999, 20–21.
49. Sakurai 1994, 116–19, and Katsumata 1996, 279–84.
50. *Mineaiki* 1989, 64–65. According to Amino (1986, 96–111), the phrase *irui igyō* shifted its meaning in the late medieval period from a positively perceived "holiness" to a negatively perceived inhumanity, possibly because outlaws and other violent bands appropriated the symbolic markers of holiness, especially clothing, to demonstrate their power.
51. See, for example, EKS 1983, docs. 1051, 1903, 1904, *Kumano Nachi Taisha monjo*, vol. 3, doc. 1048, Manzai 1928, Eikyō 6 (1434) 1/19, Eikyō 6 (1434) 1/30, and Okuno 1969, hoi doc. 21.

52. Yamauchi 1997, 169, and Bairin 1996, 471.
53. Cited in Sakurai 1994, 123.
54. For this understanding of sea tenure, see Kalland 1995, 2–3, 146; also see Cordell 1989, 12.
55. Steinberg 2001, 26–30.
56. See Shapinsky 2007.
57. Song 1987, no. 162.
58. Quoted in Kishida 2001, 198.
59. Shapinsky 2007, 233.
60. Shapinsky 2007, 232.
61. Thomson 1994, 13.
62. EKS 1983, doc. 1733, Bairin 1996, 471, EKS 1983, doc. 1519, and EKS 1983, doc. 747.
63. *Jūroku-jūshichi seiki Iezusukai Nihon hōkokushū*, 7/141.
64. Thomson 1994, 27.
65. EKS 1983, doc. 1730.
66. Hashimoto 1998, 13, EKS 1983, doc. 1770, and *Daiganji monjo*, doc. 65.
67. Suzuki 2000, 86–89. Petrucci and Antony, in their chapters in this volume, also discuss piracy in the context of the developments of new ports.
68. *Daiganji monjo* 1978, doc. 68.
69. EKS 1983, docs. 1834, 2070.
70. EKS 1983, docs. 2075, 2103, 2176, and Udagawa 1981, 58.
71. EKS 1983, docs. 2116, 2119.
72. Conlan 2003, chaps. 4–5.
73. Kishida 2001, 171, 198.
74. EKS 1983, doc. 1838, Fujiki 1995, 16–32, 134, and *Hagi-han batsuetsuroku* 1967, 3:176–77, docs. 22, 23.
75. Fujiki 1995.
76. Song 1987, no. 85.
77. Song 1987, no. 154.
78. Yamauchi 2005, chap. 6, and Kawai 1981, 11–13.

Chapter 4: Merchants, Smugglers, and Pirates

1. See, for example, Zhou Jinglian 1936, 40–47, Zhang Weihua 1982, 1–56, Wang Muming 2000, and Fan Zhongyi and Tong Xigang 2004.
2. For a discussion on the commercialization of the Ming economy, see Brook 1998; and on piracy and the shadow economy in the mid-Qing period, see Antony's chapter in this book.
3. Deng Zhong 1592, 10/48a–b. Hokkiens refer to people of southern Fujian.
4. Zheng Shungong 1566, 6/2b.
5. Yu Dayou 1565, 7/20a.
6. Zheng Ruozeng 1562, 8b/569.
7. Zheng Shungong 1566, 6/2b.
8. Zhu Wan 1590, 4/2b–14b.
9. Zhu Wan 1590, 4/2b–14b, and Zheng Shungong 1566, 6/2b.
10. Zheng Ruozeng 1562, 11a/671–75. Similarly in the late eighteenth century, the black market town of Giang Binh, discussed in Antony's chapter, served as a clandestine trading hub.

11. Zhu Wan 1590, 4/2b–14b.
12. Zheng Ruozeng 1562, 8/571–74.
13. Zheng Shungong 1566, 6/1a–5b.
14. The Chinese people traditionally addressed each other in accordance with their family ranking, though they did have their own personal names. As a result, Chinese names, especially those from the lower social stratum, recorded in the Ming documents often appeared as Xu Yi (the eldest brother of the Xu family) or Xu Er (the second brother of the Xu family), instead of the actual names. With the development of their business, gradually people forgot their given names, but simply called them by their nicknames or adopted names derived from their standing in the family.
15. Zheng Shungong 1566, 6/8b–9a, and Zheng Ruozeng 1562, 8b/569–96.
16. See, for example, Xie Jie 1595, Book 2.
17. Zheng Shungong 1566, 6/9a.
18. Historians studying the history of *wakō* inevitably touch on the topic of Wang Zhi, but few of them have paid attention to his relations with the Portuguese. John E. Wills, Jr. (1979), and Rodirich Ptak (1998) have written the best studies on Wang Zhi in English.
19. See, for example, *Ningbo fuzhi*, vol. 22, entry of "Haifang."
20. On the contraband saltpeter trade, see Petrucci's chapter in this volume.
21. See Zheng Zhenduo 1947.
22. Wills 1979, 212. Professor Wills was basically correct but made a minor mistake by claiming that Zhu Wan killed Xu Dong on Shuangyu Island. Actually, Xu fled overseas.
23. For detailed accounts about Xu Hai's activities, see Zheng Ruozeng 1562, 5/320–47, Xie Jie 1595, and Gu Yanwu 1680, 90.
24. *Haicheng xianzhi* 1762, 18.
25. *Haicheng xianzhi* 1762, 14; see also Antony 2007, 111.
26. Zhang Xie 1618, 6/113–15, and *Haicheng xianzhi* 1762, 24.
27. *Zhangzhou fuzhi*, 1/31.
28. Zheng Shungong 1566, 6/11a.
29. Zhu Wan 1590, 4/7b.
30. See Chin forthcoming.
31. Zhu Wan 1590, 4/5a–9b.
32. See Xu Fuyuan and Chen Zilong 1640, 205.
33. Xu Fuyuan and Chen Zilong 1640, 267.
34. Zheng Ruozeng 1562, 4/275–84.
35. See Yin Guangren and Zhang Rulin, 1751.
36. See Teixeira 1994, 207–15.
37. See *Teppōki*, in Kunitomo, *Nanbo bunshu*, 18th cent. ed., 7–9.
38. Lin Xiyuan 1555, 5/30.
39. Lin Xiyuan 1555, 5/30.
40. See, for example, Huang Qinghua 2006, 1/136–37. In line with conventional Communist historiography, Huang fiercely condemns Lin Xiyuan's defense of the Portuguese as quoted above.
41. On the shadow economy, see, for example, Thomas 1992, Schneider and Enste 2002, and Williams 2006.

Chapter 5: Pirates, Gunpowder, and Christianity in Late Sixteenth-Century Japan

1. Sakurai 1996, 23, 386.
2. Shapinsky 2007, and his chapter in this volume.
3. Also see the discussion on Wang Zhi in the previous chapter by James Chin.
4. Zheng Ruozeng 1562, 3/6–8; also see Sakurai 1996, 386, 23. For the location of Shuangyu, consult Map 4.1 (p. 45).
5. Zheng Ruozeng 1562, 3/1–6.
6. Zheng Ruozeng 1562, 3/1–6.
7. Antony (2003, 27–28) explains how piracy actually decreased for a time after 1574, when the Jiajing Emperor allowed restricted international trade. Pirates once again became legitimate merchants.
8. Tanaka Takeo 1986, 240, and Matsuura 2003, 90. Although Tanaka seems to have attributed Sukezaemon's home to Hakata, other reliable sources depict Sukezaemon as a merchant of the wealthy Naya of Sakai. The Naya, a group of wholesale merchants, owned and rented warehouses throughout Japan for the transportation and storage of goods from province to province. However, it remains possible that this Sukezaemon from Sakai may have been a different person, though born in the same year, 1544. Sukezaemon traded not only with Wang in China, but also in Thailand and in the Philippines.
9. Tanaka Takeo 1986, 135.
10. Needham 1954, 5.7:453.
11. Ōta 2002, 329.
12. Sakuma 1979, 8.
13. Arimizu 1994, 145–53.
14. Ōta 2002, 312.
15. Ōta 2002, 383.
16. Udagawa, et al. 2005, 157, and Mote and Twitchett 1988, 976.
17. Needham 1985, 117–18.
18. Kage 2006, 261.
19. Kage 2006, 243.
20. Goodrich and Fang 1976, 631–38.
21. Kage 2006, 259.
22. Boxer 1963, 361.
23. Boxer 1963, 317–18. One picul equaled 133 and 1/3 of a lb avoirdupois; three piculs were about 400 lbs. One hundred taels corresponded to one *kan* or 3.75 kg (8.27 lb) of copper coins.
24. Kishida, et al. 1995, 116.
25. Reimon, 1562.
26. See *Cartas que os Padres e Irmaos de la Companhia de Jesus, que andão nos regnos de Japão escreverão – des annos 1549–1566.*
27. Udagawa 2002, 158/ 260, and Organtino, et al. 1597, 58. One *koku* measured mainly grain and rice. It corresponded to 180 liters or 47.654 US gallons.
28. Sanagi 1972, 103.
29. *Buke Mandaiki* 1644, 32.
30. Udagawa 2002, 111.
31. Udagawa 2002, 117.

32. *Buke Mandaiki*, 33.
33. ARSI, 46b/15.
34. Matsuda 1967, 657.
35. ARSI, 46b/155.
36. ARSI, 46b/657.
37. Organtino, et al. 1597, 58, 115.
38. Yamauchi 2005, 128.
39. Tanaka 1986, 134.
40. Yamauchi 2004, 75–82.

Chapter 6: At the Crossroads

1. See the recent studies, for example, by Shimizu 2005, Matoba 2007, and Nakajima 2007.
2. Cortesão 1944, 376–77.
3. Retana 1910, 16–17.
4. Varela 1983, 24, 58–61, 110.
5. Varela 1983, 120, 136.
6. Wicki 1948, 471–75.
7. Galvão 1987, 107.
8. Retana 1910, 16.
9. Galvão 1987, 16, 107, 155, 166–67.
10. Galvão 1987, 169.
11. Jacobs 1974, 1/202.
12. Retana 1910, 17.
13. Jacobs, 1974, 1/240.
14. There is some mention of *wakō* relating to the "Ningbo Incident" of 1523, but no further record of them in the 1530s. By and large, the *wakō* of the Mongol and Ming periods differed considerably. In the former period, Japanese constituted the majority of *wakō*, and they mostly raided Korea; in the latter period, a more multinational group made up *wakō*, and they mostly plundered China.
15. Zheng Ruozeng 1562, 8/24, 9/24. On the activities of Wang Zhi, also see the chapters by Chin and Petrucci.
16. See Igawa 2007.
17. Zheng Ruozeng 1562, 2/18.
18. MSLSZ, 298/6–7.
19. Zheng Ruozeng 1562, 8/24.
20. Also see the discussion by Chin in this book, and in Murai 1997.
21. See Igawa 2007, 201.
22. Zheng Ruozeng 1562, 5/19, 8/14.
23. Schurhammer 1996, 57.
24. Zheng Ruozeng 1562, 8/14, and Zheng Shungong 1566, 6/3; also see the discussion in Chin's chapter.
25. Zheng Liangsheng 1995, 365.
26. AGI, Filipinas 6-1-7, ff.1v.-2r.
27. AGI, Patronato 24-17, f.6r.
28. For a discussion on this topic, see Zheng Liangsheng 1995, 422.

29. Tomaru 1942, 54.
30. Gu Yanwu 1680, 26/8.
31. Yu Dayou 1565, 1/30.
32. MSLSZ, 8/1.
33. Lin Renchuan 1987, 108–10.
34. *Chaozhou fuzhi*, 7/31.
35. Gu Yanwu 1680, 28/63.
36. Staunton 1856, 2/11.
37. Pastells 1926, xxv–xxvi, xxxviii.
38. Staunton 1856, 2/302–03.
39. Retana 1910, 21; and Staunton 1856, 2/59.
40. *Guangdong tongzhi* 1864, 70/64.
41. See Zheng Guangnan 1999, 236–238.
42. Strictly speaking, Macau began to function after 1557; before that date, the nearby island, known as Lampacau, had served the same purpose.
43. Even after Spain abandoned her dominion over the Moluccas in the Treaty of Zaragoza in 1529, the Philippines continued close relations with them. For instance, in 1582, the Spanish governor agreed to send troops to quell disturbances in the Moluccas, and several years later, repeated the maneuver.
44. Retana 1910, 24.
45. AGI, Filipinas 6-4-49, f.2r.
46. Blair and Robertson 1903–09, 34/384–85.
47. Blair and Robertson 1903–09, 6/178.
48. Blair and Robertson 1903–09, 6/182–83.
49. In the Spanish empire, *Audiencias* had judicial, legislative, and executive functions, and therefore represented the king in his role as law-maker and dispenser of justice.
50. AGI, Filipinas 18A-5-31, f.3v, f.4r.
51. AGI, Filipinas 24-14, f.1v.
52. Biblioteca Angelica, MS.1331, ff.73v.-74r.

Chapter 7: Piracy and Coastal Security in Southeastern China, 1600–1780

1. MSLSZ, 117/476.
2. On this subject, see Giraud 1990.
3. See for example, Lin Renchuan 1987, who uses the phrase *siren haishang maoyi jituan* to describe these groups as private sea merchants.
4. See, for example, the discussion in Calanca 2008.
5. Carioti 1995, 30–39, and 1992, 72–73.
6. Comments of Shao Tingcai, cited in Antony 2007, 113–14.
7. Between 1589 and 1612, for example, twelve years of earthquakes hit the Fujian coast, mainly affecting the prefectures of Xinghua, Quanzhou and Zhangzhou — 1589 (Funing, Fuzhou, and Xinghua); 1591 (Fuzhou, Xinghua, and Zhangzhou); 1594 (Quanzhou); 1596 (Hui'an); 1600 (Tong'an, Anxi, Zhao'an, and Nan'ao); 1602 (Fujian and Guangdong); 1603 (Xinghua, Hui'an, and Zhao'an); 1604 (Xinghua, Quanzhou, and Zhangzhou, among others); 1605 (Fujian, Guangdong, and other provinces); 1607 (Quanzhou); 1609 (Xinghua and Quanzhou); 1612 (Zhao'an). During the same period, other disasters struck some areas:

in 1591 and 1594, drought and famine affected Fuzhou; in 1596, a typhoon hit Hui'an; in 1600, the prefecture of Quanzhou suffered an earthquake and floods; and then in 1603, a typhoon smashed into its coast. In 1602, Zhao'an experienced drought and famine, as did Xinghua in 1605. Also see Antony 2003, 30.

8. Cao Lütai 1959, 4, and *Chongzhen Changbian*, 11/ 41.
9. MDTX, 4.
10. See for example, the case of Mao Zongxian in his struggle against Zheng Zhilong (Calanca 2008, chap. 3, part 2).
11. MDTX, 3.
12. MDTX, 3–4
13. See the discussions by Chin and Antony in this volume.
14. On the Zhengs, see Blussé 1990, 245–64, and Carioti 1995.
15. Zhu Kejian, 2/5a.
16. Quoted in Cao Shuji 2000–02, 36. There were similar reports of famine and cannibalism from Guangdong; see Antony 2003, 30–31. One *li* equaled to 510 meters.
17. QSLSZ, 4/4/84, 4/7/127, and *Lianjiang xianzhi* 1927, 3/47a.
18. Zheng Guangnan 1999, 286–87.
19. We know that during this period of conflict, the Zheng greatly contributed, for example, to the development of ceramics production in Japan and its commercialization, especially from the 1650s. See Ho 1994, 35–70.
20. On legislation protecting private property, see Buoye 2000, 220; and see the discussion below on Qing measures to regulate sea traffic.
21. Antony 2003, 19–20.
22. KXZPZZ, 2/283–84.
23. QSLSR, 6/245/ 435 (KX 50.3.7), and 6/246/442–43 (KX 50.5.21).
24. QSLSR, 6/252/500 (KX 51.12.17), and 6/253/505 (KX 52.2.3).
25. QSLSR, 6/213/9 (KX 42.9.15), 6/246/442–43 (KX 50.7.21), and KXZPZZ, 3/191–94.
26. GZDYZ, 6/684–86 (YZ 4.10.2), 6/741–43 (YZ 4.10.13).
27. QSLSR, 6/253/502–03 (KX 52.1.23); also see KXZPZZ, 4/247–52, 313, 380–81.
28. KXZPZZ, 3/221.
29. DQHDSL, 629/1b.
30. QSLSR, 6/250/483 (KX 51.8.27).
31. DQHDSL, 629/1b–2a.
32. ZPZZ (*junwu fangwu*), QL 8.6.7.
33. GZDYZ, 9/185 (YZ 5.10.26).
34. The palace memorials provide some of the elements that enable us to determine the nature of these offenders, such as in ZPZZ (*junwu fangwu*), QL 8.6.7.
35. Chen 1630, 75/1986–87.
36. See Calanca 2007.
37. On maritime customs, see Huang Guosheng 2000; on sub-county officials, see Antony 2002; and on the Qing military, see Calanca 2007 and 2008.
38. On the *baojia* system, see *Baojiashu jiyao* 1838, as well as Hua 1988, 87–121, and Dutton 1992, 55–93.
39. Cao Lütai 1959, 4/63–66.
40. Zhang Xie 1618, 7/135–40, and *Ming shilu leizuan, Fujian-Taiwan juan* 1993, 549.
41. Cao Lütai 1959, 4/67–68, 71–76.

42. Cited by Ouyang Zongshu 1998, 243.
43. *Qingshi gao*, 32:240/9543-9544.
44. *Fujian shengli* 1873, 23/616–18.
45. *Yuedong shengli* 1846, 6/3a–b, and *Baojiashu jiyao* 1838, 1/4a–b, 2/31a–b.
46. Zhu Kejian, 4/2a.
47. See the discussion in Calanca 2007.

Chapter 8: Piracy and the Shadow Economy in the South China Sea, 1780–1810

1. Yuan Yonglun 1830, 10.
2. Cited in Winn 1994, 183.
3. See, for example, Winn 1994, and Bourgois 2002.
4. For a discussion of the negative economic impact of piracy see Anderson 1995.
5. For example, between 1775 and 1810, the coastal areas of Guangdong and Fujian suffered twenty-nine years of famines; during the height of the pirate disturbances in Guangdong between 1802 and 1810, the Pearl River Delta experienced food shortages in every year except 1807. See Antony 2003, 38, and Table 3, p. 40.
6. On Chinese piracy in this period, see Dian Murray 1987, and Antony 2003.
7. See Matsuura Akira 1983, 615–27, and Huang Qichen 1986, 155–56.
8. This topic is treated at length in Antony 2003, 54–81.
9. The word Ladrones derives from the Portuguese for bandit or pirate.
10. Turner 1814, 18.
11. Yuan Yonglun 1830, 10, 16, NYC, 12/90b–92a, 13/1b, and GZD (11082) JQ 13.r5.25.
12. Turner 1814, 7, 18, and Zheng Weiming 1987, 104b–105a.
13. XSXZ, 8/56b.
14. Yuan Yonglun 1830, 16. Incidentally, followers of the cult of San Po, a deity said to be the third sister of Mazu (Tianhou), practiced unorthodox exorcistic rituals and spirit possession.
15. GDHF, 1/1a–8a, and Zhang Weixiang and Xue Changqing 2006, 52–60.
16. Ye 1989, 159, and Antony 2003, 61–63.
17. Ye Xianen 1989, 160, 224–25, and Zhang Weixiang and Xue Changqing 2006, 63–69.
18. GZDQL (QL 21.6.17), 14/644, MQSLWB, 508a, WCXZ, 4/91b–92a, and Zheng Weiming 1987, 393a.
19. Suzuki Chusei 1975, 480–81, and Toyooka Yasufumi 2006, 50–51.
20. GZD (2368) JQ 2.4.24, and GDHF, 26/1a–2b.
21. GZD (1372) JQ 1.11.1, (2845) JQ 2.7.6, (3459) JQ 2.12.1, (3611) JQ 3.1.13, and (4602) JQ 4.5.29.
22. Turner 1814, 7, Zheng Weiming 1987, 105a–107b, 392b–395a, and He Weijie 2007, 63–64.
23. Yin Guangren and Zhang Rulin 1751, 78–80, 165, and Porter 1996, 77, 80.
24. See the insightful discussion on the Cape of Good Hope in Ward 2007.
25. Supercargoes to the Portuguese Governor of Macau, 1800, in the Oriental and India Office Records, British Library, G/1/19, fols. 209–11. Thanks to Prof. Rogerio Puga for bringing this document to my attention.
26. ZPZZ (1058) (*nongmin yundong*), JQ 10.11.22, Turner 1814, 32, *Chinese Repository* 1834, 3/82–83, and Zheng Weiming 1987, 109a.
27. XKTB (128) JQ 12.5.9, and Zhang Weixiang and Xue Changqing 2006, 53–54.

166 *Notes to pp. 108–119*

28. ZPZZ (1133) JQ 10.6.26, (1135) JQ 11.5.6, SCSX, 79/10a, and NYC, 12/15a–b.
29. GZD (1047) JQ 1.8.19, (2010) JQ 2.2.14, and (2845) JQ 2.7.6.
30. López Nadal 2001, 125–36 (quote on 127).
31. XKTB (102) 11.10.48. In this case, however, officials arrested the pirates before they sold much of the loot.
32. Yuan Yonglun 1830, 10.
33. NYC, 11/42a–b, 12/31b–32a, GZD (13513) JQ 14.3.5, (15187) JQ 14.8.23, and DGXZ, 33/22b.
34. Dian Murray 2004, 53.
35. SCSX, 38/1a–2b.
36. XKTB (189) JQ 16.5.21.
37. ZPZZ (1133) (*nongmin yundong*), JQ 10.9.5.
38. Katsuta Hiroko 1967, 40.
39. ZPZZ (1058) (*nongmin yundong*), JQ 10.11.22, NYC, 11/36b, and Yuan Yonglun 1830, 10.
40. Turner 1814, 32, 37.
41. ZPZZ (1121) (*nongmin yundong*), JQ 15.7.12.
42. GZD (6211 attachment) JQ6.9.23, and (6793) JQ 6.11.28.
43. GZD (5050) JQ 7.5.12.
44. *Chinese Repository* 1834, 3/72, 81.
45. Van Dyke 2005, 143.
46. Matsuura Akira 1983, 627, and Ye Xianen 1989, 186–87, 213–14.
47. Suzuki Chusei 1967, 102–103, Dian Murray 1987, 29–30, and Van Dyke 2005, 48.
48. Suzuki Chusei 1967, 103–104.
49. GZD (1643 attachment) JQ 1.12.7, (2010) JQ 2.2.14, and Dian Murray 1987, 187 n.39.
50. Van Dyke 2005, 126.
51. XKTB (84) JQ 1.9.23.
52. LFZZ (2684) JQ 8.1.3; on Triad involvement in salt smuggling in Huizhou, see Hsieh 1972, 155–60.
53. Antony 2003, 136–37.
54. Wakeman 1972, 30.

Chapter 9: Poor but Not Pirates

1. Arano 1988, i–ix.
2. Hellyer 2005, 1–3.
3. Descriptions of the incident can be found in three documents, in DNISK, ME 191–0009: 1870/06/19, 1870/06/19, and 1870/06/19. All dates follow the Japanese calendar with year/lunar month/day (Japan did not adopt the Gregorian calendar until 1873).
4. Yanai 1967–73.
5. For further discussions of the clandestine trade in Southeast Asia during this and later times, see the following chapters by Ota and Tagliacozzo.
6. Hellyer 2005.
7. See Osa 1965.
8. Elisonas 1991, 239–55.
9. Elisonas 1991, 247–49.

10. See Shapinsky in this book.
11. Tashiro 1981, 58–71.
12. Tsuruta 2006, 56, 65, 79.
13. James Lewis 2003, 107–45.
14. Arano 1988, 191–210.
15. Toby 1991, 53–109.
16. Quoted in Tashiro 1981, 337.
17. Tashiro 1976.
18. Izuhara Chōshi Henshū Iinkai, 763–66.
19. Tashiro 2001, 174–82.
20. *Koku*, a unit of measure, approximated five bushels or 180 liters, for rice and other grains. Because it comprised the staple crop, in the sixteenth century, the Japanese had begun to calculate taxes in rice. By the early seventeenth century, they calculated the wealth of domains in *koku*.
21. Arano 1988, 234–35.
22. DNISK, KA 002–0348: 1848/03/16.
23. DNISK, KA 005–0508: 1848/08/12.
24. DNISK, KA 010–0234: 1849/02/27; KA 011–0853: 1849/04/18; and KA 010–0234: 1849/02/21.
25. DNISK, KA 010–0234: 1849/04/09; and KA 010–0234: 1849/04[intercalary]/01.
26. DNISK, KA 010–1081: 1849/04[intercalary]/05.
27. DNISK, KA 010–1081: 1849/04 [intercalary]/09.
28. DNISK, KA 029–1134: 1851/11/24 and 1851/04/26.
29. DNISK KA 017–0620: 1850/02/03, 1850/02/28, and 1850/03/15.
30. DNISK KA 025–0452: 1851/02/23; DNISK KA 026-0083: 1851/04/03.
31. DNISK KA 039–0627: 1853/06/03.
32. DNISK, AN 110–0747: 1858/07/26, and Sugiyama 1984.
33. Ōshima Tomonojō, a domain official, presented a plan to invade Korea in 1864. The complete text of his proposal can be found in Tanaka Akira 1991, 108–17.
34. DNISK, KA 052–0942: 1853/09/04.
35. For domain and *bakufu* records concerning the visits of British and Russian vessels from 1859–61, see Hino 1968.
36. Kim 1980, 123.
37. Mitani 2006, xiv–xv.

Chapter 10: The Business of Violence

1. In this study, Riau (also Rhio, Riow, Riouw, and Rio) and Lingga (also Linga) respectively refer to the Riau Islands and the Lingga Islands, both located south of Singapore.
2. Chronicles of European anti-piracy measures include Logan 1849–51, Buckley 1902, 276–82, Cornets de Groot 1846–47, and Kniphorst 1876–81.
3. In 1824, an anonymous writer (assumed to be John Crawfurd) stated that "the most confirmed pirates are the Malay in the Straits of Malacca and Karimata," and their "most noted stations are in Lingga and Riau, and also Singapore." Anonymous 1825, 243.

4. Raffles 1817, 1/232–34, Anonymous 1825, Newbold 1839, 1:36–39, Logan 1849–51, and Cornets de Groot 1846–47.
5. For the former studies, see Tarling 1963, and Turnbull 1972; and for the latter, see Resink 1968, Lapian 1974, and a recent work by Algadri 1994.
6. See the studies by Trocki 1979, Warren 1981, Warren 2002, Leirissa 1994, Anderson 1997, and Teitler 2002; for the historiography of Southeast Asian piracy, see Campo 2003.
7. Bugis designates a few ethnic groups that originated in south Sulawesi. After the conquest by the Dutch East India Company of their places of origin in the 1660s, large numbers of them took refuge in many places in insular Southeast Asia. See Andaya 1995.
8. The Iranun (also Ilanun, Illanun, and Lanun) is an ethnic group that originated in central Mindanao. After relocating to the Sulu Islands in the late 1760s, they conducted regular piratical raids covering almost the entire Malay Archipelago. I adopt the spelling used by Warren 1981, 149.
9. The Orang Laut, or "Sea Peoples," generally describes the heterogeneous groups dwelling on boats in the southern Malacca Strait; see Barnard 2007.
10. Dianne Lewis 1995, 85–96, Vos 1993, 121–25, Ali Haji Ibn Ahmad 1982, 211–14, 221–22, and Trocki 1979, 22–30, 33–36.
11. Trocki 1979, 37–38.
12. See, for example, Anonymous 1825, and Logan 1849, 3:586.
13. The London Treaty, drawn up by the Dutch and British governments in March 1824, stipulated a division of the spheres of both countries' influence along the border in the middle of the Malacca Strait.
14. Logan 1849, 3:585, and Campo 2005, 31.
15. ADR 71/3 (1825): 31–32.
16. Agar-agar is a type of seaweed from which gelatin was made. Tripang (or sea cucumber) is an echinoderm that has a thick, wormlike body. Both items were sold to Chinese traders for the Chinese market for culinary purposes.
17. ADR 71/3 (1825): 31, 35–36.
18. Spanish *mat* is a silver coin widely used in early-modern Southeast Asia. One Spanish *mat* usually had the value of eight Spanish *reals*.
19. ADR 71/3 (1825): 26–27.
20. Campo 2005, 33.
21. SSR A31: 13–15, April 28 (April 21), 1826. *Prahu* is a general term referring to local sailing ships in the Malay Archipelago.
22. Logan 1850, 4:147–48.
23. Logan 1850, 4:152.
24. ADR 71/3 (1825): 30–32, 49–51; this information agrees with Begbie 1834, 272.
25. Logan 1850, 144.
26. ADR 71/3 (1825): 56–60. Gambir is an astringent extract used in dying and tanning. In Southeast Asia, it is also popularly used as a material for betel chewing. In Riau Chinese settlers opened gambir plantations on Pulau Bintan in the 1730s for the purpose of export.
27. Panglima is a traditional Malay title for low- and middle-ranking officials or chiefs. Petty chiefs involved in piracy in the Malacca Strait often purported this title.
28. SSR A 28: 247, September 14 (September 6), 1826. Panglima Tarah was also reported to be an elderly man, dark, short, thin, and lame from a former injury to his left leg.

29. SSR A 25: 287–91, February 2 (January 30), 1826; SSR A26: 225–55, April 28 (March 20), 1826; and SSR A 28: 247–48, September 14 (September 6), 1826.
30. SSFR 142: 62–64, September 27 (September 21), 1827.
31. Logan 1850, 148.
32. Hussin 2007, 177–84.
33. SSR A 25: 290–91, February 2 (January 30), 1826.
34. Begbie 1834, 271.
35. Logan 1850, 404–06.
36. SSR A28: 247–48, September 14 (September 6), 1826.
37. Logan 1850, 404, 406.
38. SSR A26: 259, 261–62, April 28 (April 21), 1826, and SSR A28: 361–62, December 18 (December 14), 1826.
39. SSR A28: 248–49, September 14 (September 6), 1826.
40. SSR A42: 111–12, February 18 (February 9), 1828.
41. SSR A39: 84–87, September 20 (September 7), 1827, and SSR A 39: 88, September 20 (September 7), 1827, and SSFR 142: 641–42, September 27 (September 21), 1827.
42. SSR A31: 309–10, December 7 (December 4), 1826, and SSR A39: 88–89, September 20 (September 7), 1827. *Colak* is a utensil to scoop something granular as well as a unit to measure it. Apart from Kurou, a similar kidnapping business was organized in Turang and Batu Mou, both in Perak (SSR A18: 460–63, June 23 [June 17], 1825, and SSR A25: 52–53, January 12 (January 9), 1826.
43. SSR A26: 261–62, April 28 (April 21), 1826.
44. SSR A26: 259, April 28 (April 21), 1826, and SSR A31: 15, April 28 (April 21), 1826.
45. SSR A57: 5–5A, November 3 (November 2), 1828.
46. SSR A28: 458–60, October 5 (September 1), 1826.
47. SSR A28: 460–62, October 5 (September 4), 1826.
48. SSR A28: 484–86, October 5 (September 16), 1826.
49. Hussin 2007: 80–97, 118–20.
50. SSR A25: 52–53, January 12, 1826, and SSR A39: 87-90 87–90, September 20, 1827.
51. ADR 71/3 (1825): 36–39, and Campo 2003, 202–03.
52. Logan 1850, 144.
53. Anonymous 1833, and Logan 1850, 149.
54. Logan 1850, 149.
55. Logan 1850, 157.
56. Logan 1850, 405.
57. SSR R1: 77, May 1833 (the date is not clear in the source), and Logan 1850, 159–60, 400. According to Turnbull (1972, 191), Singapore merchants were willing to put up with anything, even with piracy, rather than pay taxes, a situation that continued until 1867. For the civil opposition against the increase in custom duties in the early 1830s, see Tarling 1963, 70–73.
58. SSR R3: 157–59, April 26, 1833, and SSR R3: 167–68, May 25, 1833. On the admiralty jurisdiction among the British authorities, see Tarling 1963, 32, 99–101.
59. It is not clear how the British authorities raised the money to cover the expenses. Tarling (1963, 73) stated that the Calcutta government now inclined toward spending money for anti-piracy operations, and that the new Governor-General, Lord Auckland, strongly supported the suppression of piracy.

170 *Notes to pp. 138–146*

60. See Logan 1850, 405–10, Tarling 1963, 73, 76–77, 84–90, and Turnbull 1972, 246–47.
61. Logan 1850, 408–09.
62. SSR R4: 194, June 4, 1837.
63. SSR R4: 220–21, July 1837 (the date is not clear in the source).
64. Logan 1850, 625–26.
65. SSR R4: 199, June 4, 1837.
66. Gibson-Hill (1956, 80–81) also discusses the increase in the number of followers of the Temenggong by receiving refugees from neighboring islands in the 1820s.
67. Trocki 1979, 61–71.
68. SSR R4: 164–65, April 5, 1837.
69. SSR R4: 195–96, June 4, 1837.
70. SR R4: 195, June 4, 1837.
71. Bonham, June 20, 1836, quoted in Tarling 1979, 77–80.
72. Trocki 1979, 78, 81. Gutta-percha is the latex-like sap of diverse varieties of Blanco Palauim. From the time of its discovery in the 1840s, its most important use has been in the coating of transoceanic telegraph cables.
73. Logan 1849, 1850, 1851, and Tagliacozzo 2005.
74. Campo (2003, 208) points out this tendency on the Bugis in Dutch colonial records.

Chapter 11: Smuggling in the South China Sea

1. For references to place names mentioned in this chapter, see Map 1.1 (p. 4).
2. See, for example, the *Catalogue of the Latest and Most Approved Charts, Pilots, and Navigation Books Sold or Purchased* by James Imray and Son, 1868.
3. Chiang 1978, 136, 139.
4. ARA, 1888, MR #461.
5. La Chapelle 1885, 689–90.
6. See Bogaars 1955, 104, 117.
7. Coates 1911, 58, and Kubicek 1994, 86 passim.
8. Parkinson 1937, 351; see also de Haan 1922, 1/498 for scandals involving Chinese payoffs to an incumbent Governor General.
9. Coates 1911, 81.
10. Viraphol 1977, 124; see also Hao 1986.
11. Crawfurd 1828, 160–61.
12. Warren 1981, 8.
13. Reid 1993, 2, and Wong 1960, 114.
14. Viraphol 1977, 127.
15. See ANRI, Maandrapport der Residentie Banka 1879 (Banka #105).
16. See "Mr. Everett's Journal at Papar, 1879–80, December 5, 1879, Volume 73," in PRO/CO/874/Boxes 67–77, Resident's Diaries.
17. For Batavia, see "Jualan Chandu Gelap Dalam Betawi," *Utusan Malayu*, February 2, 1909, p. 2; for Singapore, see *Bintang Timur*, January 4, 1895, p. 2.
18. See the deliberations, discussions, and legislation of the Bertillon system as outlined in ARA, 1892, MR #1144; 1896, MR #743; 1898, MR #379.
19. See the "Secret Societies Amendment Proclamation of 1913," as declared by the Governor of British North Borneo on 8/9/1913, in CO/874/Box 803 "Secret Societies."

20. Officer of the Committee of the Privy Council for Trade to Herman Merivale, Esq., June 17, 1850, in CO 144/6; Extracts From the Minutes of the Legislative Council of Labuan, January 3, 1853, in CO 144/11; Gov Labuan to CO, January 9, 1872, #2, in CO 144/36; CO Jacket (Mr. Fairfield, and Mr. Wingfield), May 21, 1896, in CO 144/70; Gov Labuan to BNB HQ, London, November 13, 1896, in CO 144/70.
21. See Enactment #6 of 1915, Malay States; also *Bintang Timor*, December 6, 1894, p. 2.
22. *Straits Settlements Blue Books*, 1873, Spirit Imports and Exports, Singapore, 329, 379–80.
23. ANRI, Politiek Verslag Residentie West Borneo 1872 (#2/10); ARA, Extract Uit het Register der Besluiten, GGNEI, January 2, 1881, #7, in 1881, MR #18.
24. ARA, First Government Secretary to Director of Finances, November 6, 1889, #2585, in 1889, MR #773; also First Government Secretary to Resident Timor, March 8, 1892, #600, in 1892, MR #217; ARA, Dutch Consul, Manila to MvBZ, April 5, 1897, #32; MvBZ to MvK, May 24, 1897, #5768, both in (MvBZ/A Dossiers/223/A.111/"Verbod Invoer Wapens en Alcohol"); ARA, Dutch Consul, London to MvBZ, January 28, 1893, #37, and GGNEI to MvK, November 27, 1892, #2268/14, both in (MvBZ/A Dossiers/223/A.111/"Still Zuidzee").
25. The best three monographs on the history of opium in nineteenth century Southeast Asia are Trocki 1990 and 1999, and Rush 1990; also see Warren 1981, and Tagliacozzo 2000.
26. ARA, Chief Inspector of the Opium Regie to Gov Gen NEI, October 30, 1903, #3017/R in Verbaal, January 13, 1904, #34.
27. To discourage opium abuse, governments raised prices as part of the moral argument for them to take over the trade.
28. See CO/882 Eastern, 9, #114 gives some of these stipulations for the Malay Peninsula. The government formulated different laws depending on whether they involved coastal or inland areas while racially, they allowed only male Chinese over the age of 21 to smoke opium on licensed premises. This document gives a good overview of the scope and complexity of narcotics legislation.
29. See, for example, Jennings 1997, and Trocki 1999.
30. Schell stressed that these fractured outlines have been visible for some time now, though decades or even centuries may elapse before some kind of pressure or event comes along to split these divisions at the seams. Interview notes, Berkeley, California, May 1992.
31. Hansen 2000, 221–24, and Esherick 1987.
32. Polo 2001, and Hirth and Rockhill 1911.
33. Welsh 1993.
34. See discussion in Winichakul 1994. For a theoretical discussion on the nature (and evolution) of borders, see Prescott 1987.
35. "Bersaing Di Langit Terbuka BIMP-EAGA," *Suara Pembaruan*, November 25, 1977, p. 16; and "Mindanao Bakal Unggul Di Timur ASEAN," *Suara Pembaruan*, January 25, 1997, p. 17.
36. "Pos Pelintas Batas RI-Filipina Ditambah," *Kompas*, December 10, 1997, p. 8; "Tenaga Willing to Supply Power to Sumatra via Bridge Link," *Straits Times*, June 29, 1997; "Malaysia Undecided Where Bridge to Indonesia Will Begin," *Straits Times*, June 26, 1997. For boundary agreements across the land border in Borneo, see *Laporan Delegasi Republik Indonesia* 1981.
37. "Other ASEAN States Urged to Follow Singapore-KL Joint Approach to Crime," *Straits Times*, June 10, 1997; "Vietnam, Cambodia Police Sign Police Accord," *Weekly Review of*

the Cambodia Daily, March 19, 1997, p. 8; "Lao Police Delegation Back From Interpol Meeting in Beijing," *Vientiane Times*, September 20–23, 1997, p. 4.

38. Indonesia also has taken to mapping the culture of border peoples in this manner; see Suwarsono 1997; "Eye on Ships," *Straits Times*, June 7, 1997; "Seminar on New Lao Mapping and Survey Network Held in Vientiane," *Vientiane Times*, November 5–7, 1997, p. 4; "Border Market to be Opened," *Jakarta Post*, November 10, 1997, p. 2; for the other example, mentioned above, see "AFP Waging High-Tech War vs. Abus," *Philippine Daily Inquirer*, April 9, 2001, p. 2.
39. "Struggle or Smuggle," *Far Eastern Economic Review*, February 22, 1997, p. 26 passim.
40. These interviews were conducted with Bugis sailors on Jakarta's Sunda Kelapa docks in August and September of 1998; I cannot give the names of crew members (or their ships) for obvious reasons. These sailors, in fact, spoke of the maritime police as the true "outlaws" in Indonesian waters — agents who can shake down passing ships with near impunity. Interviews were also conducted with Indonesian laborers (in a variety of occupations) in Singapore.
41. "Believe it or Not," *Far Eastern Economic Review*, October 27, 1997, p. 23.
42. Bailey and Truong 2001, Figure 1.
43. See especially the very detailed expose in McCoy 1991, 193–261.
44. "Indonesia Sudah Lama Jadi Pemasaran Narkotika," *Angkatan Bersenjata*, November 4, 1997, p. 12; "Philippine Police Seize Huge Volume of Drugs This Year," *Vientiane Times*, October 29–31, 1997, p. 6.
45. "Drugs Blacklist," *Phnom Penh Post*, March 16–29, 2001, p. 2; "PM Warns of Takeover by Drug Merchants," *Weekly Review of the Cambodia Daily*, April 24, 1997, p. 12; "Medellin on the Mekong," *Far Eastern Economic Review*, September 7, 1995, pp. 29–30; "Medellin on the Mekong," *Far Eastern Economic Review*, November 23, 1997, pp. 24–26.
46. "Dadah Musush Utama Masyarakat," *Pelita Brunei*, July 2, 1997, p. 1.
47. "Pakistanis Tried for Trafficking Heroin," *Jakarta Post*, December 1, 1997, p. 3; "Drug Bust," *Straits Times*, June 26, 1997; "4 Chinese Nabbed in Drug Swoop," *Philippine Daily Inquirer*, November 10, 1997, p. 24; "3 Die in Drug Bust," *Philippine Daily Inquirer*, November 19, 1997, p. 20; "Drug Dealers Find 'Open' Market in Philippines," *Straits Times*, June 21, 1997.
48. For these larger, Asia-wide patterns, see Brook and Wakabayashi 2000, and Meyer and Parssinen 1998.
49. Kritz and Keely 1981, xiii–xiv.
50. "Foreign Maids Fight Modern Day Slavery," *Philippine News*, April 4, 2001, p. 2; "Labour Migration in Southeast Asia: Analysis, Cooperation Needed," *TRENDS* (Journal of the Institute of Southeast Asia Studies, Singapore), September 27, 1997; "AIDS Time Bomb Ticks Away Among Asia's Migrant Labor," *Viet Nam News*, November 2, 1997, p. 12.
51. "Illegal Workers Dumped Far From Shore," *Straits Times*, November 18, 1997; "Colour-Coded Tags for 1.2 Million Foreign Workers," *New Straits Times* (Malaysia), November 27, 1997, p 4; "Foreign Workers May be Sent to Key Sectors," *New Straits Times* (Malaysia), December 8, 1997, p. 14.
52. See Warren 1993.
53. For the Dutch Indies/Indonesian case, see for example Hull, Sulistyaningsih, and Jones 1997, 1–17; Ming 1983; and Stoler 1986.

54. Several excellent studies of the dynamics of prostitution in Southeast Asia have been published recently; see especially Law 2000; Lim 1998; Skrobanek 1997; and Truong 1990.
55. "Ten Foreign Women Held in Anti-Vice Operation," *New Straits Times*, November 13, 2000, p. 8; "Arrests in Singapore," *Manila Bulletin*, November 12, 1997, p. 12; "Crackdown on Rings That Bring in Foreign Call Girls," *Straits Times*, July 14, 1997; "First Students, Then Call Girls," *Straits Times*, July 22, 1997.
56. "Banyak Wanita di Bawah Umur Melacur," *Angkatan Bersenjata*, July 25, 1997, p. 7; "Fishermen Involved in Prostitution," *Jakarta Post*, November 29, 1997, p. 2; "Banyak Tempat Hiburan Jadi Tempat Prostitutsi," *Angkatan Bersenjata*, November 12, 1997, p. 6. For a view not from the "periphery," but rather from the center, see Allison Murray, 1991.
57. "Alleged Call Girls Detained," *Borneo Bulletin*, November 12, 1997, p. 1; "Pimps Jailed, Call Girls Fined," *Borneo Bulletin*, November 13, 1997, p. 3.

Glossary

Akamagaseki 赤間関
ama 海民
Andojō 安堵状
aojia 澳甲
Aotou 澳頭
Ashikaga 足利
atakebune 安宅船

Baishahu 白沙湖
baojia 保甲
baoshui 報水
bokujū 僕從
Bungo-no-kuni 豐後國
Bunshi Genshō 文之玄昌

Cai Qian 蔡牽
Cai Yuanliang 蔡元良
Changzhou 長洲
Chaozhou 潮州
Chikugo 築後
Chen Deyue 陳德樂
Chen Dong 陳東
Chen Guangsheng 陳光生
Chen Minglong 陳明隆
Chen Shangyi 陳尚義
Chen Yasan 陳亞三
Chenghai 澄海
Choseon wangjo sillok 朝鮮王朝實錄
Chouhai tubian 籌海圖編

Dadan 大擔
daizui houdai 戴罪候代
daizui ligong 戴罪立功
Damao 大茅
Dan 蛋
Danshui 淡水
Danzai 疍仔
Dapeng Wan 大鵬灣
Daya Wan 大亞灣
Dayushan 大嶼山
Deng Liao 鄧獠
Deng Zhong 鄧鐘
Dianbai 電白
Dinghai 定海
Dongguan 東莞
Donghai 東海
Donghai Ba 東海八
dou 斗

Fangjishan 放雞山
fanyi 番夷
fu zongbing 副總兵

Gao Qizhuo 高其倬
Gaozhou 高州
Gechijō 下知狀
Giang Binh (Jiangping) 江平
Goto 五島
Guandi 關帝

guanku 管庫
guanshao 管哨
guanxi 關係
Guishan 歸善

haejeok 海賊
Haicheng 海澄
haifeng 海俸
haijin 海禁
Haikang 海康
Hainan 海南
Hakata 博多
Hangzhou 杭州
He Song 何送
He Yaba 何亞八
Hengqin 橫琴
Higo 肥後
Hirado 平戶
Hizen 肥前
Hong Dizhen 洪迪珍
Hosokawa 細川
Huang Yasi 黃亞四
huiguan 會館
Huizhou (Anhui) 徽州
Huizhou (Guangdong) 惠州
hwangtang seon 荒唐船

Iki 壱岐
Imagawa Ryôshun 今川了俊
Itsukushima 厳島
Izumi 和泉

Jiangmen 江門
jiansheng 監生
Jiazi 甲子
jie fu ji pin 劫富濟貧
jin 斤
Jin Zilao 金子老
jinghai 靖海
Jinmen 金門
Jinshan 盡山
jizei 積賊

kaizoku/haejeok 海賊
kako 水夫

Kamagari 蒲刈
Kaminoseki 上関
Kannon 観音
kasho 過所
keigo 警固
keigomai 警固米
Kii 紀伊
Konishi Yukinaga 小西行長
Kōno Michinao 河野通直
kou 寇
Kutsuna 忽那
Kyoto 京都

Leizhou 雷州
li 里
Li Chongyu 李崇玉
Li Guangtou 李光頭
Li Mao 李茂
Li Rong 李榮
Li You 李佑
liang 兩
liaoli junshi 料理軍師
Lin Ban 林伴
Lin Daoqian 林道乾
Lin Feng 林鳳
Lin Jian 林剪
Lin Shuangwen 林雙文
Lin Wu 林五
Lin Xiyuan 林希元
Lin Yafa 林亞發
Lingyin Temple 靈隱寺
Liu Yaohui 劉堯誨
Lu Tang 盧鏜
Lufeng 陸豐
Luhuan 路環
Luo Yasan 羅亞三
luohan 羅漢
lüying 綠營

Magong 馬公
Matsura Takanobu 松浦隆信
Meiling 梅嶺
Minamoto 源
Ming Shi 明史
Ming shilu 明實錄

Glossary

Miyoshi 三好
monmaku 紋幕
Mōri 毛利
Mōri Motonari 毛利元就
Muromachi Bakufu 室町幕府

Nagasaki 長崎
Nan'ao 南澳
Ningbo 寧波
Noshima Murakami 能島村上
Noshima Murakami Motoyoshi 能島村上元吉
Noshima Murakami Takashige 能島村上隆重
Noshima Murakami Takeyoshi 能島村上武吉

Oda Nobunaga 織田信長
Osumi 大偶
Ōtomo 大友
Ōtomo Sōrin 大友宗麟
Ōuchi 大内
Ōuchi Yoshitaka 大内義隆

Penghu 澎湖
pinghai 平海

Qi Jiguang 戚繼光
Qianshan 前山
Qinglan 清瀾
Quanzhou 泉州
Qin Shizhen 秦世禎
Qiongzhou 瓊州

Reisen 礼錢
Renga 連歌
Ritsuryō 律令
Rōjū 郎從
Ryukyu 琉球

Sadamegaki 定書
Sakai 堺
San Po Temple 三婆廟
Sanhewo 三和窩
Sanzoku 山賊
Sappo 札浦
Satsuma 薩摩
Seto Inland Sea 瀬戸内海

Shaoxing 紹興
Shenquan 神泉
shi 石
Shimonoseki 下関
Shingoro 辛五郎
Shirai 白井
Shiwaku 塩飽
Shū 衆
Shuangyu 雙嶼
shuiju 稅局
shukōryō 酒香料
siren haishang maoyi jituan 私人海上貿易集團
Sōgi 宗祇
Song Huigyong 宋希璟
Sue Harukata 陶晴賢
Suigun 水軍

Tagaya 多賀谷
Tanegashima 種子島
Teppōki 鉄炮記
Tokugawa 徳川
Tong'an 同安
tongzhi 同知
Tosa nikki 土佐日記
Toyotomi Hideyoshi 豊臣秀吉
Tsushima 對馬
Tsusyu 津州

waegu 倭寇
wakō 倭寇
Wang Wanggao 王望高
Wang Wufeng 汪五峰
Wang Yingyuan 王應元
Wang Zhi 汪直（王直）
Wangxia 望廈
Wei Yigong 魏一恭
Weizhou 潿洲
wen 文
wokou 倭寇
Wuchuan 吳川
Wushi Da 烏石大
Wushi Er 烏石二
Wushi San 烏石三
Wuyu 浯嶼
Wuzhouyu 浯洲嶼

Glossary

Xiamen 廈門
xiancheng 縣丞
Xiangshan 香山
Xiao Ji 蕭基
Xicao Bay 西草灣
Xie He 謝和
Xin'an 新安
Xinhui 新會
Xiongzhou 硇洲
xishu caibo 檄輸財帛
Xu Chaoguang 許朝光
Xu Dong 許棟
Xu Er 許二
Xu Hai 徐海
Xu Nan 許楠
Xu Song 許松
Xu Weixue 徐惟學
Xu Zi 許梓

Ye Ming 葉明
Ye Zongman 葉宗滿
Yu Dayou 俞大猷
yuan 圓
Yuegang 月港
Yugeshima 弓削島
Yushan 漁山

zei 賊
zeizhong 賊眾
Zeng Yasi 曾亞四
Zhang Bao 張保
Zhang Jinglong 張景龍
Zhang Lianke 張連科
Zhang Wei 張維
Zhang Xingke 張興可
Zhanglin 樟林
Zhangshan 漳山
Zhangzhou 漳州
Zhaoan 詔安
Zhelin 柘林
Zheng Afan 鄭阿繁
Zheng Chenggong 鄭成功
Zheng Laodong 鄭老董
Zheng Lianchang 鄭連昌
Zheng Shungong 鄭舜功

Zheng Qi 鄭七
Zheng Yi 鄭一
Zheng Yi Sao 鄭一嫂
Zheng Zhilong 鄭芝龍
Zheng Zongxing 鄭宗興
Zhiliao 芷了
Zhou Feixiong 周飛熊
Zhou Yu 周玉
Zhu Fen 朱濆
Zhu Wan 朱紈
Zhu Yifeng 朱一馮
Zhuo Jia Cun 卓家村
zongbing 總兵
Zoumaxi 走馬溪

Bibliography

ADR. Arsip Daerah Riau. Arsip Nasional Republik Indonesia. Jakarta.
AGI. Archivo General de Indias, Filipinas. Seville, Spain.
Algadri, Hamid. 1994. *Dutch Policy against Islam and Indonesians of Arab Descent in Indonesia.* Jakarta: LP3ES.
Ali Haji Ibn Ahmad, Raja. 1982. *The Precious Gift (Tuhfat al-Nafis).* Translated by Barbara Watson Andaya and Virginia Matheson. Kuala Lumpur: Oxford University Press.
Amino Yoshihiko, ed. 1996. "Iyo no kuni Futagamijima wo megutte: Futagami-shi to 'Futagami monjo.'" In *Nihon chūsei shiryōgaku no kadai*, Part 3, 250–82. Tokyo: Kōbundō.
———. 1986. *Igyō no ōken.* Tokyo: Heibonsha.
———. 1984. *Nihon chūsei no hinōgyōmin to tennō.* Tokyo: Iwanami Shoten.
Andaya, Barbara Watson, and Leonard Y. Andaya. 1982. *A History of Malaysia.* London: Macmillan.
Andaya, Leonard. 1995. "The Bugis-Makassar Diasporas," *Journal of the Malaysian Branch of the Royal Asiatic Society* 68: 119–38.
Anderson, J. L. 1997. "Piracy in the Eastern Seas, 1750–1830: Some Economic Implications." In *Pirates and Privateers: New Perspectives on the War on Trade in the Eighteenth and Nineteenth Centuries*, edited by David J. Starkey, E. S. van Eyck van Heslinga, and J. A. de Moor, 87–105. Exeter: University of Exeter Press.
———. 1995. "Piracy and World History: An Economic Perspective on Maritime Predation," *Journal of World History* 6.2: 175–199.
Anonymous. 1825. "Malay Piracy," *The Asiatic Journal and Monthly Miscellany* 19 (March): 243–45.
Anonymous. 1833. "Singapore," *The Asiatic Journal and Monthly Miscellany*, new ser. 11 (August): Register, p. 230.
ANRI. Arsip Nasional Republik Indonesia. Jakarta.
Antony, Robert J. 2007. *Pirates in the Age of Sail.* New York: W. W. Norton.
———. 2003. *Like Froth Floating on the Sea: The World of Pirates and Seafarers in Late Imperial South China.* Berkeley: University of California, Institute of East Asian Studies.
———. 2002. "Subcounty Officials, the State, and Local Communities in Guangdong Province, 1644–1860." In *Dragons, Tigers, and Dogs: Qing Crisis Management and the Boundaries of State Power in Late Imperial China*, edited by Robert J. Antony and Jane Kate Leonard, 27–59. Ithaca, NY: Cornell University, East Asia Series.

180 Bibliography

ARA. Algemeen Rijksarchief. The Hague, Netherlands.
ARSI. Archivum Romanum Societatis Iesu. Japonica-Sinica.
Arimizu Hiroshi. 1994. *Sobre uma nova tese referente a la introducião da espingarda no Japão. Bulletin of Universities and Institutes.* In *Bulletin of Osaka University of Foreign Studies* 11: 145–153.
Arano Yasunori. 1988. *Kinsei Nihon to Higashi Ajia.* Tokyo: Tokyo Daigaku Shuppan-kai.
Bailey, Warren, and Lan Truong. 2001. "Opium and Empire: Some Evidence from Colonial-Era Asian Stock and Commodity Markets," *Journal of Southeast Asian Studies* 32 (June): 173–93.
Bairin Shuryū. 1996. "Bairin Shuryū Suō gekō nikki." In *Yamaguchi-ken shi Shiryō-hen: Kodai chūsei* 1: 467–73. Yamaguchi: Yamaguchi Prefecture.
Bakhtin, M. M. 1981. "Discourse in the Novel." In *The Dialogic Imagination*, edited by Michael Holquist, translated by Caryl Emerson and Michael Holquist, 259–422. Austin: University of Texas Press.
Baojiashu jiyao. 1838 [1896]. Shanghai. Unknown publisher.
Barnard, Timothy P. 2007. "Celates, Rayat-Laut, Pirates: The Orang Laut and Their Decline in History," *Journal of the Malaysian Branch of the Royal Asiatic Society* 80, Pt. 2, No. 293: 33–50.
Bassett, D. K. 1980. *British Attitudes to Indigenous States in South-East Asia in the Nineteenth Century.* Hull: University of Hull Centre for South-East Asian Studies.
Batten, Bruce L. 2003. *To the Ends of Japan: Premodern Frontiers, Boundaries, and Interactions.* Honolulu: University of Hawai'i Press.
Begbie, Peter James. 1834 [1967]. *The Malayan Peninsula.* Kuala Lumpur: Oxford University Press.
Bentley, Jerry H. 1999. "Sea and Ocean Basins as Frameworks of Historical Analysis," *The Geographical Review* 89 (April): 215–24.
Biblioteca Angelica. Manuscript Collection. Rome, Italy.
Blair, Emma Helen, and James Alexandra Robertson. 1903–09. *The Philippine Islands, 1493–1898.* 55 vols. Cleveland: A. H. Clark.
Blussé, Leonard. 1999. "Chinese Century: The Eighteenth Century in the China Sea Region," *Archipel*, no. 58: 107–29.
———. 1990. "Minnan-jen or Cosmopolitan? The Rise of Cheng Chih-lung Alias Nicolas Iquan." In *Development and Decline of Fukien Province in the Seventeenth and Eighteenth Centuries*, edited by Eduard B. Vermeer, 245–64. Leiden: E. J. Brill.
Bogaars, George. 1955. "The Effect of the Opening of the Suez Canal on the Trade and Development of Singapore," *Journal of the Malay Branch of the Royal Asiatic Society* 28: 117–266.
Bourgois, Philippe. 2002. *In Search of Respect: Selling Crack in El Barrio.* 2nd edition. Cambridge: Cambridge University Press.
Boxer, C. R. 1963. *The Great Ship from Amacon: Annals of Macao and the Old Japan Trade.* Lisboa: Centro de Estudos Históricos Ultramarinos.
Braudel, Fernand. 1972. *The Mediterranean and the Mediterranean World in the Age of Philip II.* 2 vols. Translated by Siân Reynolds. New York: Harper and Row.
Brook, Timothy. 1998. *The Confusions of Pleasure: Commerce and Culture in Ming China.* Berkeley and Los Angeles: University of California Press.
Brook, Timothy, and Bob Tadashi Wakabayashi, eds. 2000. *Opium Regimes: China, Britain, and Japan, 1839–1952.* Berkeley and Los Angeles: University of California Press.

Brunsson, Nils. 1989. *The Organization of Hyprocrisy: Talk, Decisions and Actions in Organization*. Translated by Nancy Adler. Chichester: John Wiley and Sons.
Buckley, Charles Burton. 1902 [1984]. *Anecdotal History of Old Times in Singapore: From the Foundation of the Settlement under the Honourable the East India Company on February 6th, 1819 to the Transfer to the Colonial Office as Part of the Colonial Possessions of the Crown on April 1st, 1867*. Singapore: Oxford University Press.
Buke Mandaiki.1644. Photographed unpublished manuscript. Yamaguchi Manuscript Library, Yamaguchi City, Japan.
Buoye, Thomas M. 2000. *Manslaughter, Markets, and Moral Economy: Violent Disputes over Property Rights in Eighteenth-Century China*. Cambridge: Cambridge University Press.
Calanca, Paola. 2008. *Piraterie et contrebande au Fujian du XVème au début du XIXème siècle*. Paris: Éditions des Indes Savantes.
———. 2007. "Fujian shuishi jiangling: yizhi 'jingying zhi shi'?" In *Faguo hanxue* (Beijing), edited by Paola Calanca, Fabienne Jagou, and Li Guoqiang, 12: 86–101.
Campo, Joseph N. F. M. à. 2005. "Zeeroof: Bestuurlijke beeldvorming en beleid." In *Zeeroof en Zeerofbestrijding in de Indische Archipel (19de eeuw)*, edited by G. Teitler, A.M.C. van Dissel, and J. N. F. M. à Campo. Amsterdam: De Bataafsche Leeuw.
———. 2003. "Discourse without Discussion: Representation of Piracy in Colonial Indonesia, 1816–25," *Journal of Southeast Asian Studies* 34: 199–214.
Cao Lütai.1959. *Jinghai jilüe*. Taipei: Taiwan Yinhang, Taiwan Wenxian congkan, no. 33.
Cao Shuji. 2000–02. "Qing shiji." In *Zhongguo renkou shi*, edited by Ge Jianxiong. Shanghai: Fudan Daxue chubanshe.
Carioti, Patrizia. 1995. *Zheng Chenggong*. Naples: Istituto Universitario Orientale, Dipartimento di Studi Asiatici. Series Minor 45.
———. 1992. "Le attività marittime del Fujian, 1567–1628," *Ming Qing yanjiu*, 61–79.
Cartas que os Padres e Irmaos de la Companhia de Jesus, que andão nos regnos de Japão escreverão - des annos 1549–1566. Impressos por mandado do Senhor Do Ioao Soares Bispos de Coimbra. Coimbra: Em casa de Antonio de Mariz, 1570.
Catalogue of the Latest and Most Approved Charts, Pilots, and Navigation Books Sold or Purchased by James Imray and Son. 1868. London: James Imray and Son.
Chaozhou fuzhi. 1893. 42 *juan*. Chaozhou: Zhulan shuwu.
Chen Renxi. 1630 [1965]. *Huang Ming shifa lu*. 92 *juan*. Taibei: Taiwan xuesheng shuju.
Chiang Hai Ding. 1978. *A History of Straits Settlements Foreign Trade, 1870–1915*. Memoirs of the National Museum, no. 6. Singapore: National Museum.
Chin, James K. Forthcoming. "Merchants, Envoys, Brokers and Pirates: Hokkien Connections in Maritime Asia." In *Offshore Asia*, edited by Anthony Reid and Momoki Shiro. Singapore: National University of Singapore Press.
Chinese Repository. Macau and Canton, 1832–51.
Chongzhen Changbian. 1964. Taibei: Guangwen shuju.
CO. Colonial Office. Public Record Office, Great Britain.
Coates, W. H. 1911 [1969]. *"The Old Country Trade" of the East Indies*. London: Cornmarket Press.
Conlan, Thomas. 2003. *State of War*. Ann Arbor: Center for Japanese Studies, University of Michigan.
Cordell, John. 1989. "Introduction: Sea Tenure." In *A Sea of Small Boats*, edited by John Cordell, 1–32. Cambridge, MA: Cultural Survival.

Bibliography

Cornets de Groot, J. P.1847–48. "Notices historiques sur les pirateries commises dans l'Archipel indien-Oriental, et sur les mesures prises pour les réprimer, par le Gouvernement Néerlandais, pendant les trente dernières années." Part 3, 1836–1840. In *Le Moniteur des indes-orientales et occidentales, Recueil de mémoires et de notices scientifiques et industriels, de nouvelles et de faits importants concernant les possessions néerlandaises d'Asie et d' Amérique*. La Haye: Belinfante Frères.

Cortesão, Armando, ed. 1944 [1978]. *A Suma Oriental de Tomé Pires*. Coimbra: Universidade.

Crawfurd, John. 1856 [1971]. *A Descriptive Dictionary of the Indian Islands and Adjacent Countries*. Kuala Lumpur: Oxford University Press.

———. 1828 [1967]. *Journal of an Embassy from the Governor-General of India to the Courts of Siam and Cochin-China*. Kuala Lumpur: Oxford University Press.

Daiganji monjo. 1978. *Hiroshima-ken shi: Kodai chūsei shiryō-hen*. Vol. 3. Hiroshima: Hiroshima Prefecture.

Dalton, Clive. 1972. *Malay Pirate*. Leicester: Brockhampton Press.

Deng Zhong. 1592 [1995]. *Chouhai chongbian*. In *Sikuquanshu cunmu congshu*, shibu, Book 227. Ji'nan: Qiru shushe.

Dening, Greg. 1980. *Islands and Beaches: Discourse on a Silent Land, Marquesas, 1774–1880*. Honolulu: University of Hawai'i Press.

DGXZ. *Dongguan xianzhi*. 103 *juan*. 1921. Unknown place of publication and publisher.

DNISK. "Dai Nihon ishin shiryō kōhon." Archives of Tokyo Daigaku Shiryō Hensanjo. Tokyo, Japan.

DQHDSL. 1899 [1908]. *Da Qing huidian shili*. 19 vols. Shanghai: Shangwu yinshuguan.

Dutton, Michael R. 1992. *Policing and Punishment in China: From Patriarchy to "the People."* Cambridge: Cambridge University Press.

EKS. *Ehime kenshi shiryōhen kodai chūsei*. 1983. Edited by Ehime Kenshi Hensan Iinkai, Matsuyama, Ehime Prefecture.

Elisonas, Jurgis. 1991. "The Inseparable Trinity: Japan's Relations with China and Korea." In *Cambridge History of Japan*. Vol. 4, *Early Modern Japan*, edited by John Whitney Hall, 235–300. Cambridge: Cambridge University Press.

Ennin. 1955. *Diary: The Record of a Pilgrimage to China in Search of the Law*. Edited and Translated by Edwin O. Reischauer. New York: Ronald Press.

Esherick, Joseph W. 1987. *The Origins of the Boxer Uprising*. Berkeley and Los Angeles: University of California Press.

Fan Zhongyi and Tong Xigang. 2004. *Mingdai wokou shilue*. Beijing: Zhonghua shuju.

Farris, William Wayne. 2006. *Japan's Medieval Population: Famine, Fertility, and Warfare in a Transformative Age*. Honolulu: University of Hawai'i Press.

———. 1985. *Population, Disease, and Land in Early Japan, 645–900*. Cambridge, MA: Harvard University Press.

Fujian shengli. 4 vols. 1873 [1964]. Taibei: Datong shuju.

Fujiki Hisashi. 1995. *Zōhyōtachi no senjō*. Tokyo: Asahi Shinbunsha.

Funing fuzhi. 1762 [1967]. Taibei: Chengwen chubanshe.

Galvão, António. 1987. *Tratado dos Descobrimentos*. 4th edition. Porto: Livraria Civilização.

GDHF. *Guangdong haifang huilan*. Guangzhou. Unknown date and publisher.

Gibson-Hill, C. A. 1956. *Singapore, Old Strait and New Harbour, 1300–1870*. Singapore: Government Printing Office.

Giraud, Yves, ed. 1990. *Voyages et aventures du Capitaine Ripon aux Grandes Indes*. Thonon-les-bains: L'Albaron.

Goodrich, L. Carrington, and Fang Chaoying, eds. 1976. *Dictionary of Ming Biography, 1368–1644*. 2 vols. New York: Columbia University Press.
Goodwin, Janet R. 2007. *Selling Songs and Smiles*. Honolulu: University of Hawai'i Press.
Gould, Eliga H. 2007. "Lines of Plunder or Crucible of Modernity?: The Legal Geography of the English Speaking Atlantic, 1660–1825." In *Seascapes: Maritime Histories, Littoral Cultures, and Transoceanic Exchanges*, edited by Jerry H. Bentley, Renate Bridenthal, and Kären Wigen, 105–20. Honolulu: University of Hawai'i Press.
Gu Yanwu. 1680 [1996]. *Tianxia junguo libingshu*. In *Siku quanshu cunmu congshu: shibu*, Books 171–172. Tainan: Zhuanyan wenhua shiye youxian gongsi.
Guangdong tongzhi. 334 *juan*. Guangzhou, 1864. Unknown publisher.
GZD. Gongzhongdang. Unpublished Qing dynasty archives, National Palace Museum, Taibei.
GZDQL. *Gongzhongdang Qianlong chao zouzhe*. 1986. Taibei: Gugong bowuyuan.
GZDYZ. *Gongzhong dang Yongzheng chao zouzhe*. 1977–1980. Taibei: Gugong bowuyuan.
Haan, F. de.1922. *Oud Batavia: gedenkboek uitgegeven naar aanleiding van het driehonderdjarig bestaan der stad in 1919*. Batavia: Kolff.
Hagi-han batsuetsuroku. 1967. Edited by Nagata Masazumi. 5 vols. Yamaguchi: Yamaguchi-ken Monjokan.
Haicheng xianzhi. 24 *juan*. 1762. Unknown place of publication and publisher.
Hall, D. G. E. 1968. *A History of South-East Asia*. 3rd ed. London: Macmillan.
Hall, John Whitney. 1966. *Government and Local Power in Japan, 500–1700: A Study Based on Bizen Province*. Princeton: Princeton University Press.
Hansen, Valerie. 2000. *The Open Empire: A History of China to 1600*. New York: W.W. Norton.
Hao, Yen-Ping. 1986. *The Commercial Revolution in Nineteenth-Century China: The Rise of Sino-Western Capitalism*. Berkeley and Los Angeles: University of California Press.
Hashimoto Yū. 1998. "Muromachi, sengoku-ki no shogun kenryoku to gaikōken," *Rekishi shigaku*, no. 708 (March): 1–18.
Hashizume Shigeru. 2000. "Sanuki kaizoku-shū no sonzai," *Setonaikai chiikishi kenkyū* 8: 197–215.
Hayashiya Tatsusaburō, ed. 1981. *Hyōgo Kitazeki irifune nōchō*. Tokyo: Chūō Kōron Bijutsu Shuppan.
He Weijie. 2007. "Miaoyu, zuqun shenfen yu shequ fazhan de shehui huayu: cong beiming wenwu he yingbian chonggou Qingdai de Danzai," *Aomen lishi yanjiu* 6: 63–74.
Hellyer, Robert I. 2005. "The Missing Pirate and the Pervasive Smuggler: Regional Agency in Coastal Defense, Trade, and Foreign Relations in Nineteenth-Century Japan," *International History Review* 37 (March): 1–24.
Henty, G. A. 1905 [2004]. *Among Malay Pirates: A Tale of Adventure and Peril*. Sandy, UT: Quiet Vision Publishing.
Hino Seisaburō. 1968. *Bakumatsu ni okeru Tsushima to Eiro*. Tokyo: Tokyo Daigaku Shuppankai.
Hirth, Friedrich, and W.W. Rockhill, trans. and ann. 1911 [1966]. *Chau Ju Kua: His Work on the Chinese and Arab Trade in the 12th and 13th Centuries*. New York: Paragon Book Reprint Co.
Ho Chuimei. 1994. "The Ceramic Trade in Asia, 1602–1682." In *Japanese Industrialization and the Asian Economy*, edited by A. J. Lathan and Heita Kawakatsu, 35–70. London: Routledge.
Hotate Michihisa. 1981. "Chūsei zenki no gyogyō to shōensei: kakai ryōyū to gyomin wo megutte," *Rekishi hyōron*, no. 376: 15–43.

Houtman, Frederick de. 1970. *Le "Spraeck ende Woord-boek" de Frederick de Houtman: Première méthode de malais parlé (fin du XVIe siècle)*. Edited by Denys Lombard. Paris: École Française. d'Extrême-Orient.
Hsieh, Winston. 1972. "Triads, Salt Smugglers, and Local Uprisings: Observations on the Social and Economic Background of the Waichow Revolution in 1911." In *Popular Movements and Secret Societies in China 1840–1950*, edited by Jean Chesneaux, 145–64. Stanford: Stanford University Press.
Hua Li. 1988. "Qingdai baojia zhidu jianlun," *Qingshi yanjiuji* 6: 87–121.
Huang Guosheng. 2000. *Yapian zhanzheng qian de dongnan sisheng haiguan*. Fuzhou: Fujian renmin chubanshe.
Huang Qichen. 1986. "Qingdai qianqi haiwai maiyi de fazhan," *Lishi yanjiu* 4: 151–70.
Huang Qinghua. 2006. *Zhongpu guanxishi*. 3 vols. Hefei: Huangshan shushe.
Hull, Terence, Endang Sulistyaningsih, and Gavin Jones, eds. 1997. *Pelacuran di Indonesia: Sejarah dan Perkembangannya*. Jakarta: Pusat Sinar Harapan.
Hussin, Nordin. 2007. *Trade and Society in the Straits of Melaka: Dutch Melaka and English Penang, 1780–1830*. Copenhagen: NIAS Press, and Singapore: NUS Press.
Igawa, Kenji. 2007. "Wakō-teki kenmin shisetsu." In *Daikōkai jidai no Higashi Ajia*. Tokyo: Yoshikawa Kōbunkan.
Iioka Naoko. Forthcoming. "Wei Zhiyan and the Subversion of the '*Sakoku*.'" In *Offshore Asia*, edited by Anthony Reid and Momoki Shiro. Singapore: National University of Singapore Press.
Imagawa Ryōshun. 1994. *Michiyukiburi*. In *Chūsei nikki kikōshū*, edited by Nagasaki Ken, 392–426. Shinpen Nihon kotenbungaku zenshū. Vol. 48. Tokyo: Shōgakkan.
Izuhara-chō Shi Henshū Iinkai, ed. 1998. *Izuhara-chō shi*. Vol. 1. Nagasaki: Izuhara-chō.
Jacobs, Hubert, ed. 1974. *Documenta Malucensia*. Vol. 1 (1542–1577). Rome: Institutum Historicum Societatis Iesu.
Jennings, John M. 1997. *The Opium Empire: Japanese Imperialism and Drug Trafficking in Asia, 1895–1945*. Westport: Praeger.
Jūroku-jūshichi seiki Iezusukai Nihon hōkokushū. 1994. Third Series, 7 vols. Translated by Matsuda Kiichi, et al. Tokyo: Dōbōsha Shuppan.
Kage Toshio. 2006. *Sengoku daimyo no gaikō to toshi ryūtsū: Bungo Ōtomo-shi to Higashi Ajia sekai*. Shibunkaku Shigaku Sōsho. Kyoto: Shibunkaku.
Kalland, Arne. 1995. *Fishing Villages in Tokugawa Japan*. Richmond, Surrey: Curzon Press.
Kanaya Masato. 1998. *Kaizokutachi no chūsei*. Tokyo: Yoshikawa Kōbunkan.
Kariyama Mototoshi. 1989. "Sengoku daimyo Mōri-shi ryōnai no ukimai ni tsuite," *Kōgakkan ronsō* 22: 50–57.
Katsumata Shizuo. 1996. *Sengoku jidairon*. Tokyo: Iwanami Shoten.
———. 1981. "The Development of Sengoku Law." In *Japan before Tokugawa*, edited by John Whitney Hall, Nagahara Keiji, and Kozo Yamamura, 101–24. Princeton: Princeton University Press.
Katsuta Hiroko. 1967. "Shindai kaikō no ran," *Shiron* 19: 27–49.
Kawai Masaharu. 1981. "Tagaya-shi no rekishi." In *Tagaya suigun to Maruya jōseki*, edited by Maruya Jōseki Chōsadan, 3–13. Hiroshima: Shimokamagari-chō.
———. 1977. "Shogun and Shugo: The Provincial Aspects of Muromachi Politics." In *Japan in the Muromachi Age*, edited by John Whitney Hall and Toyoda Takeshi, 65–86. Berkeley and Los Angeles: University of California Press.

Keirstead, Thomas. 1992. *The Geography of Power in Medieval Japan*. Princeton: Princeton University Press.
Ki no Tsurayuki. 1957. *Tosa nikki*. In *Tosa nikki, Kagerō nikki, Izumi Shikibu nikki, Sarashina nikki*, edited by Suzuki Tomotarō, et al, 5–82. Shinkoten bungaku taikei, vol. 20. Tokyo: Iwanami Shoten.
Kim, Key-Hiuk. 1980. *The Last Phase of the East Asian World Order: Korea, Japan, and the Chinese Empire, 1860–1882*. Berkeley: University of California Press.
Kishida Hiroshi. 2001. *Daimyō ryōkoku no keizai kōzō*. Tokyo: Iwanami Shoten.
Kishida Hiroshi, Hiroshi Hasegawa, and Hiroshima Daigaku. 1995. *Okayama-Ken chiiki no sengoku jidaishi kenkyū*. Tokushū-gō. Vol. 2. Hiroshima: Hiroshima Daigaku Bungakubu.
Kniphorst, J. H. P. E. 1876–81. "Vervolg der Historisch Schets van den Zeeroof in den Oost-Indischen Archipel," *Tijdschrift voor het Zeewezen* n.s. 6: 159–318, 353–452; 7: 1–64, 135–210, 237–96; 9: 1–146; 173–227; 10: 1–64, 89–204, 235–358, 11: 1–95.
Kobata, Atsushi, and Mitsugo Matsuda. 1969. *Ryukyuan Relations with Korea and South Sea Countries: An Annotated Translation of Documents in the Rekidai Hoan*. Kyoto: Atsushi Kobata.
Kobayashi Hiroshi. 1978. "Domain Laws (*Bunkokuhō*) of the Sengoku Period," *Acta Asiatica* no. 35 (November): 30–44.
Krasner, Stephen D. 2001. "Organized Hypocrisy in Nineteenth-Century East Asia," *International Relations of the Asia-Pacific* 1 (August): 173–97.
Kritz, Mary M., and Charles B. Keely. 1981. "Introduction." In *Global Trends in Migration: Theory and Research on International Migration Movements*, edited by Mary M. Kritz, Charles B. Keely, and Silvano M. Tomasi. Staten Island: Center for Migration Studies.
Kubicek, Robert V. 1994. "The Role of Shallow-Draft Steamboats in the Expansion of the British Empire, 1820–1914," *International Journal of Maritime History* 6: 85–106.
Kumano Nachi Taisha monjo. 1974. Vol. 3, *Mera Monjo*. Tokyo: Zokugunshoruijū Kanseikai.
Kunitomo, *Nanbo bunshu*. 18th-century ed. Unknown place of publication and publisher.
KXZPZZ. *Kangxi chao hanwen zhupi zouzhe huibian*. 8 vols. 1984. Beijing: Dang'an chubanshe.
La Chapelle, H. M. 1885. "Bijdrage tot de Kennis van het Stoomvaartverkeer in den Indischen Archipel," *De Economist* 2 (September): 675–702.
Lapian, Adrian. 1974. "The Sealords of Berau and Mindanao: Two Responses to the Colonial Challenge," *Masyarakat Indonesia* 1: 143–54.
Laporan Delegasi Republik Indonesia Mengenai Pertemuan Panitia Teknis Bersama Perbatasan Indonesia-Malaysia Yang Ke-12 Tentang Survey dan Penegasan Bersama Perbatasan Darat Antara Indonesia and Malaysia. Jakarta: Taud ABRI, 1981.
Law, Lisa. 2000. *Sex Work in Southeast Asia: The Place of Desire in a Time of AIDS*. New York: Routledge.
Leirissa, Richard Z. 1994. "Changing Maritime Trade in the Seram Sea." In *State and Trade in the Indonesian Archipelago*, edited by G. J. Schutte. Leiden: KITLV Press.
Lewis, Dianne. 1995. *Jan Compagnie in the Straits of Malacca, 1641–1795*. Athens: Ohio University, Center for International Studies.
Lewis, James B. 2003. *Frontier Contact between Chosŏn Korea and Tokugawa Japan*. London: Routledge Curzon.
LFZZ. Lufu zouzhe. First Historical Archives, Beijing.
Lianjiang xianzhi. 1927 [1967]. Taibei: Chengwen chubanshe.

Lim, Lin Leam. 1998. *The Sex Sector: The Economic and Social Bases of Prostitution in Southeast Asia*. Geneva: International Labour Office.

Lin Renchuan. 1987. *Mingmo Qingchu siren haishang maoyi*. Shanghai: Huadong Shifan Daxue chubanshe.

Lin Xiyuan. 1555 [1997]. *Lin Ciya xiansheng wenji*. Tainan: Zhuanyan wenhua shiye youxian gongsi.

Logan, J. R. 1849–51. "The Piracy and Slave Trade of the Indian Archipelago," *Journal of the Indian Archipelago and Eastern Asia* 3: 251–60, 581–88, 629–36; 4: 45–52, 144–62, 400–410, 617–28, 734–46; 5: 374–82.

López Nadal, Gonçal. 2001. "Corsairing as a Commercial System: The Edges of Legitimate Trade." In *Bandits at Sea: A Pirates Reader*, edited by C. R. Pennell, 125–36. New York: New York University Press.

McCoy, Alfred W. 1991. *The Politics of Heroin: CIA Complicity in the Global Drug Trade*. New York: Lawrence Hill Books.

Majul, Cesar Adib 1973. *Muslims in the Philippines*. 2nd ed. Quezon City: University of the Philippines Press.

Manzai. 1928 [1958]. *Manzai jugō nikki*. 2 vols. Tokyo: Zokugunshoruijū Kanseikai.

Matoba, Setsuko. 2007. *Jipangu to Nihon*. Tokyo: Yoshikawa Kōbunkan.

Matsubara Hironobu. 1999. *Fujiwara no Sumitomo*. Tokyo: Yoshikawa Kōbunkan.

Matsuda Kiichi. 1982. *Nanbanjin no Nihon hakken*. Tokyo: Chuo Kōronsha.

———. 1967. *Kinsei shoki Nihon kankei Nanban shiryō no kenkyū*. Tokyo: Kazama Shobō.

Matsuda, Matt K. 2006. "The Pacific," *American Historical Review* 111 (June): 758–80.

Matsuura Akira. 2003. *Chūgoku no kaishō to kaizoku*. Tokyo: Yamakawa Shuppansha.

———. 1983. "Shindai ni okeru engan bōeki ni tsuite—hansen to shōhin ryūtsū." In *Minshin jidai no seiji to shakai*, edited by Ono Kazuko, 595–650. Kyoto: Kyoto Daigaku Jinbun Kagaku Kenkyūjo.

MDTX. 1981. *Ming dang ti xinggao*. In Fang Yujin, ed., *Lishi dang'an*, no. 4.

Meyer, Kathryn, and Terry Parssinen 1998. *Webs of Smoke: Smugglers, Warlords, Spies, and the History of the International Drug Trade*. Lanham, MD: Rowman and Littlefield.

Mills, J.V.G., ed. 1970. *Ying-yai Sheng-lan, "The Overall Survey of the Ocean's Shores."* Chinese text edited by Feng Cheng Chun. London: Hakluyt Society, 2nd series.

Mineaiki. 1989. In *Hyōgo-ken shi shiryōhen: Chūsei*, 4: 36–68. Kōbe: Hyōgo Prefecture.

Ming, Hanneke. 1983. "Barracks-Concubinage in the Indies, 1887–1920," *Indonesia* 35: 65–94.

Ming shilu leizuan, Fujian-Taiwan juan. 1993. Edited by Xue Guozhong, Wei Hong, Li Guoxiang, and Yang Chang. Wuhan: Wuhan chubanshe.

Mitani Hiroshi. 2006. *Escape from Impasse: The Decision to Open Japan*. Translated by David Noble. Tokyo: International House of Japan.

Mote, Frederick W., and Denis Twitchett, eds. 1988. *The Ming Dynasty, 1368–1644*. Cambridge History of China, vol. 7, part 1. Cambridge: Cambridge University Press.

MSLSZ. *Ming shilu*, Shenzong reign. 1962–66. Taibei: Academia Sinica.

MQSLWB. *Ming-Qing shiliao, wubian*. 1972. Taibei: Academia Sinica.

Murai, Shōsuke. 1997. "Teppō denrai saikō," in *Tōhō gakkai setsuritsu 50 shūnen kinen tōhōgaku ronshū*. Tokyo: Tōhō Gakkai.

———. 1993. *Chūsei Wajinden*. Tokyo: Iwanami Shoten.

———. 1988. *Ajia no naka no chūsei Nihon*. Tokyo: Azekura Shobō.

Murray, Allison J. 1991. *No Money, No Honey: A Study of Street Traders and Prostitutes in Jakarta*. Singapore: Oxford University Press.

Murray, Dian H. 2004. "Piracy and China's Maritime Transition, 1750–1850." In *Maritime China in Transition, 1750–1850*, edited by Wang Gungwu and Ng Chin-keong, 43–60. Wiesbaden: Harrassowitz Verlag.

———. 1987. *Pirates of the South China Coast, 1790–1810*. Stanford: Stanford University Press.

Nakajima, Gakushō. 2007. "Jūroku-seiki matsu no Fukken-Fuiripin-Kyushu bōeki," *Shien* no. 144: 55–92.

Needham, Joseph. 1985. "Gunpowder as the Fourth Power, East and West," First East Asian History of Science Foundation, presented at the University of Hong Kong, October 20, 1983.

Needham, Joseph, et al. 1954–. *Science and Civilisation in China*. 7 vols. to date. Cambridge: Cambridge University Press.

Newbold, T. J. 1839. *Political and Statistical Account of the British Settlements in the Straits of Malacca, etc*. 2 vols. London: John Murray.

Ng Chin-keong. 1983. *Trade and Society: The Amoy Network on the China Coast, 1683–1735*. Singapore: National University of Singapore Press.

Ng Wai-ming. 2004. "Overseas Chinese in the Japan-Southeast Asia Maritime Trade during the Tokugawa Period (1603–1868)." In *Maritime China in Transition, 1750–1850*, edited by Wang Gungwu and Ng Chin-keong, 213–26. Wiesbaden: Harrassowitz Verlag.

Ningbo fuzhi. 16th century ed. Unknown place of publication and publisher.

NYC. Nayancheng. *Nawenyigong zouyi*. 1834 [1968]. Taibei: Wenhai.

Obama-shi shi: Shoke monjo-hen. 1979. Ed. by Obama City Hall. Obama: Obama City Hall.

Okuno Takahiro, ed. 1969–70. *Oda Nobunaga monjo no kenkyū*. 2 vols. Tokyo: Yoshikawa Kōbunkan.

Organtino, Claudio Acquaviva, Giovanni Battista Peruschi, and Luigi Zanetti. 1597. *Copia Di Dve Lettere Scritte Dal P. Organtino Bresciano Della Compagnia Di Giesv Dal Meaco De Giapone Al Molto r. in Christo P.N. Il P. Clavdio Acqvaviva Preposito Generale*. Roma: Presso Luigi Zannetti.

Osa Setsuko. 2002. *Chūsei kokkyō kaiiki no Wa to Chōsen*. Tokyo: Yoshikawa Kōbunkan.

———. 1965. "Tsushima shima Sō no uji sekei no seiritsu," *Nihon rekishi* no. 208: 42–53.

Ōta Kōki. 2002. *Wakō: shōgyō, gunjishiteki kenkyū*. Yokohama: Shunpūsha.

Ouyang Zongshu. 1998. *Haishang renji: haiyang yuye jingji yu yumin shehui*. Nanchang: Jiangxi gaoxiao chubanshe.

Parkinson, C. Northgate. 1937. *Trade in the Eastern Seas (1793–1813)*. Cambridge: Cambridge University Press.

Pastells, Pablo. 1926. *Catálogo de los Documentos Relativos a las Islas Filipinas* Existentes en el Archivo de Indias de Sevilla. Vol. 2. Barcelona: Compañia General de Tabacos de Filipinas.

Polo, Marco. 2001. *The Travels of Marco Polo*. Edited by Manuel Komroff. Translated by William Marsden. New York: Modern Library.

Porter, Jonathan. 1996. *Macau the Imaginary City: Culture and Society, 1557 to the Present*. Boulder, CO: Westview Press.

Prescott, J. R. V. 1987. *Political Frontiers and Boundaries*. London: Allen and Unwin.

Ptak, Roderich. 1998. "Sino-Japanese Maritime Trade, circa 1550: Merchants, Ports and Networks." In *China and the Asian Seas: Trade, Travel and Visions of the Other (1400–1750)*, edited by Roderich Ptak, 281–311. Aldershot: Ashgate/Variorum.

Putnam, George Granville. 1924. *Salem Vessels and their Voyages: A History of the Pepper Trade with the Island of Sumatra*. Salem: Essex Institute.

Qing shi gao. 1927 [1976–77]. Comp. by Zhao Erxun, et al. Beijing: Zhonghua shuju.
QSLSR. *Qing shilu, Shengzu Ren Huangdi shilu*. 1985. Beijing: Zhonghua shuju.
QSLSZ. *Qing shilu, Shizu Zhang Huangdi shilu*. 1985. Beijing: Zhonghua shuju.
Raffles, Thomas Stamford. 1817. *The History of Java*. 2 vols. London: Black, Parbury, and Allen.
Reid, Anthony. 1997. "A New Phase of Commercial Expansion in Southeast Asia, 1760–1850." In *The Last Stand of Asian Autonomies: Responses to Modernity in the Diverse States of Southeast Asia and Korea, 1750–1900*, edited by Anthony Reid, 57–81. Basingstoke: Macmillan.
———. 1996. "Flows and Seepages in the Long-term Chinese Interaction with Southeast Asia." In *Sojourners and Settlers: Histories of Southeast Asia and the Chinese*, edited by Anthony Reid, 15–49. Honolulu: University of Hawai'i Press.
———. 1993. "The Unthreatening Alternative: Chinese Shipping in Southeast Asia, 1567–1842," *Review of Indonesian and Malaysian Affairs* 27: 1–24.
———. 1969. *The Contest for North Sumatra: Atjeh, the Netherlands, and Britain, 1858–1898*. Kuala Lumpur: University of Malaya Press, and New York: Oxford University Press.
Reid, Anthony and Zheng Yangwen, eds. 2009. *Negotiating Asymmetry: China's Place in Asia*. Singapore: National University of Singapore Press.
Reimon, 1562. *Cartas dal Regno de Chicugo*. Manuscript, Biblioteca de Ajuda, Lisbon, Portugal.
Resink, G. J. 1968. "The Eastern Archipelago under Joseph Conrad's Western Eyes." In *Indonesia's History between the Myths: Essays in Legal History and Historical Theory*, edited by G. J. Resink. The Hague: W. van Hoeve.
Risso, Patricia. 2001. "Cross-Cultural Perceptions of Piracy: Maritime Violence in the Western Indian Ocean and Persian Gulf during a Long Eighteenth Century," *Journal of World History* 12.2: 293–319.
Retana, W. E., ed. 1910. *Sucesos de las Islas Filipinas*. Madrid: Librería General de Victoriano Suárez.
Ruijūsandaikyaku Kōninkakushō. 1973. Edited by Kuroita Katsumi. *Shintei zōhō kokushitaikei*, vol. 25. Tokyo: Yoshikawa Kōbunkan.
Rush, James R. 1990. *Opium to Java: Revenue Farming and Chinese Enterprise in Colonial Indonesia, 1860–1910*. Ithaca, NY: Cornell University Press.
Sakurai Eiji. 1996. *Nihon Chūsei no keizai kōzo*. Tokyo: Iwanami Shoten.
———. 1994. "Sanzoku, kaizoku to seki no kigen." In *"Shokunin" to "Geinō"*, edited by Amino Yoshihiko, 113–48. Tokyo: Yoshikawa Kōbunkan.
Sanagi Nobuo. 1972. *Setonaikai ni okeru Shiwaku kaizokushi*. Takamatsu: Miyawaki Shoten. Originally published by Kyōzai Kenkyūsha, 1934.
Schneider, Friedrich, and Dominik H. Enste. 2002. *The Shadow Economy: An International Survey*. Cambridge: Cambridge University Press.
Schurhammer, Georg, ed. 1996. *Epistolae S. Francisci Xaverii aliaque Eius Scripta*. Vol. 2, *Missions Orientales*. Rome: Institutum Historicum Societatis Iesu.
SCSX. *Shichao shengxun* (Jiaqing reign). 1965. Taibei: Wenhai chubanshe.
Shen Yourong. 1628 [1959]. *Minhai zengyan*. Taibei: Taiwan Yinhang.
Shapinsky, Peter D. 2007. "With the Sea as their Domain: Pirates and Maritime Lordship in Medieval Japan." In *Seascapes: Maritime Histories, Littoral Cultures, and Transoceanic Exchanges*, edited by Jerry H. Bentley, Renate Bridenthal, and Kären Wigen, 221–38. Honolulu: University of Hawai'i Press.

Shimizu, Yūko. 2005. "Nihon fukyō kyoten Fuiripin no seiritsu to *sakoku*," in *Kirisutokyō Shigaku*, 59: 85–108.
Shinjō Tsunezō. 1995. *Chūsei suiunshi no kenkyū*. Tokyo: Hanawa Shobō.
Skrobanek, Siriporn, Nattaya Boonpakdi, and Chutima Janthakeero. 1997. *The Traffic in Women: Human Realities of the International Sex Trade*. New York: Zed Books.
So Kwan-wai. 1975. *Japanese Piracy in Ming China during the Sixteenth Century*. East Lansing: Michigan State University Press.
Sōgi. 1990. *Tsukushi no michi no ki*. In *Shin Nihon koten bungaku taikei*, edited by Kawazoe Shōji, 405–32. Chūsei nikki kikōshū, vol. 51. Tokyo: Iwanami Shoten.
Song Hŭigyŏng. 1987. *Nosongdang Ilbon haegnok (Rōshōdō Nihon kōroku: Chōsen shisetsu no mita chūsei Nihon)*. Edited by Murai Shōsuke. Tokyo: Iwanami Shoten.
SSFR. Straits Settlements Factory Records. National University of Singapore Library, Singapore.
SSMI. 2005. *Sengoku Suigun to Murakami Ichizoku: Nihon Saikyō no Setouchi Suigun o Hikiita Kaizoku Taishō "Murakami Takeyoshi" to Umi no Samuraitachi*. Bessatsu Rekishi-Dokuhon. Vol. 17. Tōkyō: Shin Jinbutsu Ōraisha.
SSRA. Penang, Malacca and Singapore Consultations, 1806–1830, Straits Settlements Records. National University of Singapore Library, Singapore.
SSRR. Governor's letters to Bengal, 1831–1867, Straits Settlements Records. National University of Singapore Library, Singapore.
Starkey, David J. 2007. "Privateering." In *The Oxford Encyclopedia of Maritime History*, edited by John Hattendorf. New York: Oxford University Press.
Staunton, George. 1856. *The History of the Great and Mighty Kingdom of China and the Situation thereof*. 2 vols. Translated by T. Parke. London: Hakluyt Society.
Steinberg, Philip E. 2001. *The Social Construction of the Ocean*. Cambridge: Cambridge University Press.
Stoler, Ann Laura. 1986. *Capitalism and Confrontation in Sumatra's Plantation Belt, 1870–1979*. New Haven: Yale University Press.
Straits Settlements Blue Books. 1873. Singapore. Unknown publisher.
Sugiyama Shinya. 1984 "Thomas B. Glover: A British Merchant in Japan, 1861–70," *Business History* 26: 115–38.
Sutherland, Heather. 2003. "Southeast Asian History and the Mediterranean Analogy," *Journal of Southeast Asian Studies* 34 (February): 1–20.
Suwarsono. 1997. *Daerah Perbatasan Kalimantan Barat: Suatu Observasi Terhadap Karekteristik Sosial Budaya Dua Daurah Lintas Batas*. Jakarta: Pusat Penilitian dan Pengembangan Kemasyarakatan dan Kebudayaan [LIPI].
Suzuki Atsuko. 2000. *Nihon chūsei shakai no ryūtsū kōzō*. Tokyo: Azekura shobō.
Suzuki Chūsei. 1975. "Re-chō koko no shin to no kankei." In *Betonamu Chūgoku kankei shi*, edited by Yamamoto Tatsurō, 405–92.Tokyo.
———. 1967. "Kenryū Annan ensei kō," *Tōyō Gakuhō* 50.2: 1–23, and 50.3: 79–106.
Tagliacozzo, Eric. 2005. *Secret Trades, Porous Borders: Smuggling and States along a Southeast Asian Frontier, 1865–1915*. New Haven: Yale University Press.
———. 2000. "Kettle on a Slow Boil: Batavia's Threat Perceptions in the Indies' Outer Islands, 1870–1910," *Journal of Southeast Asian Studies* 31 (March): 70–100.
Tanaka Akira, ed. 1991. *Kaikoku*. Nihon kindai shisō taikei, vol. 1. Tokyo: Iwanami Shoten.
Tanaka Takeo. 1997. *Higashi Ajia tsūkōken to kokusai ninshiki*. Tokyo: Yoshikawa Kōbunkan.

———. 1986. *Wakō: Umi no Rekishi*. Kyōiku Rekishi Shinsho. Tokyo: Kyōikusha.

Tarling, Nicholas. 1963. *Piracy and Politics in the Malay World: A Study of British Imperialism in Nineteenth-Century South-East Asia*. Melbourne: F. W. Cheshire.

Tashiro Kazui. 2001. "Bakumatsu-ki Nitchō shibōeki to Wakan bōeki shōnin, yunyū yotsuhin me no torihiki o chūshin ni." In *Kaikoku*, edited by Inoue Katsuo. Tokyo: Yoshikawa Kōbunkan.

———. 1981. *Kinsei Nitchō tsūkō bōeki-shi no kenkyū*. Tokyo: Sobunsha.

———. 1976. "Tsushima *han's* Korean Trade, 1684–1710," *Acta Asiatica* 30 (February): 85–105.

Teitler, Ger. 2002. "Piracy in Southeast Asia: A Historical Comparison," *MAST* 1: 67–83.

Teixeira, Manuel. 1994. "A Porcelana no Comércio Luso-Chinês." In *Dongxifang wenhua jiaoliu: guoji xueshu yantaohui lunwenxuan*, edited by Wu Zhiliang, 207–15. Macau: Macau Foundation.

Thomas, J. J. 1992. *Informal Economic Activity*. New York and London: Harvester Wheatsheaf.

Thomson, Janice E. 1994. *Mercenaries, Pirates, and Sovereigns: State-Building and Extraterritorial Violence in Early Modern Europe*. Princeton: Princeton University Press.

Toby, Ronald P. 1991. *State and Diplomacy in Early Modern Japan: Asia in the Development of the Tokugawa Bakufu*. Stanford: Stanford University Press. Originally published by Princeton University Press, 1984.

Tomaru, Fukuju. 1942. *Wakō kenkyū*. Tokyo: Chūō kōronsha.

Tonomura, Hitomi. 1992. *Community and Commerce in Late Medieval Japan*. Stanford: Stanford University Press.

Toyoda Takeshi, and Sugiyama Hiroshi. 1977. "The Growth of Commerce and the Trades." In *Japan in the Muromachi Age*, edited by John Whitney Hall and Toyoda Takeshi, 129–44. Berkeley and Los Angeles: University of California Press.

Toyooka Yasufumi. 2006. "Shindai chūki no kaizoku mondai to tai Annan seisaku," *Shigaku zasshi* 115: 44–67.

Trocki, Carl A. 1999. *Opium, Empire, and the Global Political Economy: A Study of the Asian Opium Trade, 1750–1950*. New York: Routledge.

———. 1990. *Opium and Empire: Chinese Society in Singapore, 1800–1910*. Ithaca, NY: Cornell University Press.

———. 1979. *Prince of Pirates: The Temenggongs and the Development of Johor and Singapore, 1784–1885*. Singapore: Singapore University Press.

Truong, Thanh-Dam. 1990. *Sex, Money, and Morality: Prostitution and Tourism in Southeast Asia*. London: Zed Books.

Tsuruta Kei. 2006. *Tsushima kara mita Nitchō kankei*. Tokyo: Yamakawa Shuppansha.

Turnbull, C. M. 1972. *The Straits Settlements, 1826–67: Indian Presidency to Crown Colony* Singapore: Oxford University Press.

Turner, John. 1814. *Captivity and Sufferings of John Turner, First Officer of the Ship John Jay of Bombay, among the Ladrones or Pirates, in the Coast of China, Showing the Manners and Customs of the Natives –Their Mode of Warfare, Treatment of Prisoners, and Discipline, with the Difference between the Pirate and the Chinese, in the Year 1807*. New York: Published by G. and R. Waite.

Twang Peck Yang. 1998. *The Chinese Business Élite in Indonesia and the Transition to Independence*. Kuala Lumpur: Oxford University Press.

Udagawa Takehisa. 2002. *Sengoku suigun no kōbō*. Tokyo: Heibonsha.

———. 1984. "Ōuchi-shi keigoshū no shōchō to Mōri-shi no suigun hensei." In *Mōri-shi no kenkyū*, edited by Fujiki Hisashi, 438–61. Tokyo: Yoshikawa Kōbunkan
———. 1981. *Setouchi suigun*. Tokyo: Kyōikusha.
Udagawa Takehisa, Morimoto E., Yamauchi Y.,Nakamura E., Fukugawa I., Okada M. 2005. *Sengoku Suigun to Murakami Ichizoku: Nihon Saikyō no Setouchi Suigun o Hikiita Kaizoku Taishō "Murakami Takeyoshi" to Umi no Samuraitachi*. Tokyo: Shin Jinbutsu Ōraisha.
Umi no michi. 1995. Edited by Board of Education, Kagoshima Prefecture. Kagoshima: Tokudaya Shoten.
Usami Takayuki. 1999. *Nihon chūsei no ryūtsū to shōgyō*. Tokyo: Yoshikawa Kōbunkan.
Van Dyke, Paul A. 2005. *The Canton Trade: Life and Enterprise on the China Coast, 1700–1845*. Hong Kong: Hong Kong University Press.
Van Vliet, Jeremias. 1636 [1910]. "Description of the Kingdom of Siam." Translated by L.F. van Ravenswaay. *Journal of the Siam Society* 7.
Varela, Consuelo, ed. 1983. *El Viaje de don Ruy López de Villalobos a las Islas del Poniente 1542–1548*. Milano: Cisalpino-Goliardica.
Viraphol, Sarasin. 1977. *Tribute and Profit: Sino-Siamese Trade, 1652–1853*. Cambridge, MA: Harvard University Press.
Vos, Reinout. 1993. *Gentle Janus, Merchant Prince: The VOC and the Tightrope of Diplomacy in the Malay World, 1740–1800*. Translated by Beverly Jackson. Leiden: KITLV Press.
Wakeman, Frederic, Jr. 1972. "The Secret Societies of Kwangtung, 1800–1856." In *Popular Movements and Secret Societies in China, 1840–1950*, edited by Jean Chesneaux, 29–48. Stanford: Stanford University Press.
Wang Muming. 2000. "Ping puren pingtuo suozhuan zhi youji," *Shijie lishi* 4: 50–57.
Wang Tai Peng. 1994. *The Origins of Chinese Kongsi*. Petaling Jaya: Pelanduk Publications.
Ward, Kerry. 2007. "'Tavern of the Seas'?: The Cape of Good Hope as an Overseas Crossroads during the Seventeenth and Eighteenth Centuries." In *Seascapes: Maritime Histories, Littoral Cultures, and Transoceanic Exchanges*, edited by Jerry H. Bentley, Renate Bridenthal, and Kären Wigen, 127–52. Honolulu: University of Hawai'i Press.
Warren, James Francis. 2003. "A Tale of Two Centuries: The Globalisation of Maritime Raiding and Piracy in Southeast Asia at the End of the Eighteenth and Twentieth Centuries," Asia Research Institute Working Paper Series, no. 2. NUS, Singapore.
———. 2002. *Iranun and Balangingi: Globalization, Maritime Raiding, and the Birth of Ethnicity*. Singapore: National University of Singapore Press.
———. 1993. *Ah Ku and Karayuki-san: Prostitution in Singapore, 1880–1940*. Singapore: Oxford University Press.
———. 1981. *The Sulu Zone, 1768–1898: The Dynamics of External Trade, Slavery, and Ethnicity in the Transformation of a Southeast Asian Maritime State*. Singapore: Singapore University Press.
WCXZ. *Wuchuan xianzhi*. 1888. Unknown place of publication and publisher.
Welsh, Frank. 1993. *A Borrowed Place: The History of Hong Kong*. New York: Kodansha.
White, Richard. 1995. "'Are You an Environmentalist or Do You Work for a Living?': Work and Nature." In *Uncommon Ground: Rethinking the Human Place in Nature*, edited by William Cronon, 171–85. New York: W. W. Norton.
Wicki, Joseph, ed. 1948. *Documenta Indica*. Vol. 1, *1540–1549*. Rome: Institutum Historicum Societatis Iesu.

Wigen, Kären. 2007. "Introduction." In *Seascapes: Maritime Histories, Littoral Cultures, and Transoceanic Exchanges*, edited by Jerry H. Bentley, Renate Bridenthal and Kären Wigen, 1–18. Honolulu: University of Hawai'i Press.
Wilkinson, R. J. 1959. *A Malay-English Dictionary*, Romanized. 2 vols. London: Macmillan.
Williams, Colin. 2006. *The Hidden Enterprise Culture: Entrepreneurship in the Underground Economy*. Cheltenham: Edward Elgar Publishing.
Wills, John E., Jr. 1979. "Maritime China from Wang Chih to Shih Lang: Themes in Peripheral History." In *From Ming to Ch'ing: Conquest, Region, and Continuity in Seventeenth-Century China*, edited by Jonathan D. Spence and John Wills, Jr., 211–19. New Haven: Yale University Press, 1979.
Winichakul, Thongchai. 1994. *Siam Mapped: A History of the Geo-Body of a Nation*. Honolulu: University of Hawai'i Press.
Winn, Jane Kaufman. 1994. "Not by Rule of Law: Mediating State-Society Relations in Taiwan through the Underground Economy." In *The Other Taiwan: 1945 to the Present*, edited by Murray A. Rubinstein, 185–214. Armonk, NY: M. E. Sharpe.
Wong, Lin Ken. 1960. "The Trade of Singapore, 1819–1869," *Journal of the Malayan Branch of the Royal Asiatic Society* 30.4: 1–315.
Xie Jie, 1595. *Qiantai wozhuan*. Xuanlantang congshu ed. Shanghai.
XKTB. Xingke tiben. First Historical Archives, Beijing. (Citations are from the *dao'an* category.)
XSXZ. *Xinxiu Xiangshan xianzhi*. 1827. Unknown place of publication and publisher.
Xu Fuyuan and Chen Zilong, eds. 1640 [1964]. *Huangming jingshi wenbian*. Beijing: Zhonghua shuju.
Xu Ke. 2008. "The Rise and the Fall of Contemporary Maritime Piracy in Southeast Asia," International Symposium on Piracy and Maritime Security in the South China Sea, Sanya, China, March 15–17, 2008.
Yamauchi Yuzuru. 2005. *Setouchi no kaizoku: Murakami Takeyoshi no tatakai*. Tokyo: Kōdansha.
———. 2004. *Chūsei Setonaikai no tabibitotachi*. Rekishi Bunka Raiburarī, vol. 169. Tōkyō: Yoshikawa Kōbunkan.
———. 1997. *Kaizoku to umijiro*. Tokyo: Heibonsha.
Yanai Kenji, ed. 1967–73. *Tsūkō ichiran zokushū*. 5 vols. Osaka: Seibundō Shuppan.
Ye Xianen, ed. 1989. *Guangdong hangyun shi, gudai bufen*. Beijing: Renmin jiaotong chubanshe.
Yin Guangren and Zhang Rulin, comps. 1751 [1992]. *Aomen jilue jiaozhu*. Annotated by Zhao Chunchen. Macau: Aomen wenhua sishu.
Yu Dayou. 1565 [1996]. *Zhengqitang ji*. Jinan: Qilu shushe.
Yuan Yonglun. 1830 [2007]. *Jinghai fenji*, in *Tianye yu wenxian: Huanan yanjiu ziliao zhongxin tongxun* 46 (January 15).
Yuedong shengli. 1846. Guangzhou. Unknown publisher.
Zhang Weihua. 1982. *Mingshi ouzhou siguozhuan zhushi*. Shanghai: Guji chubanshe.
Zhang Weixiang and Xue Changqing. 2006. *Guangdong gudai haigang*. Guangzhou: Guangdong renmin chubanshe.
Zhang Xie. 1618 [1981]. *Dongxiyang kao*. Beijing: Zhonghua shuju.
Zhangzhou fuzhi. 17th cent. ed. [2000]. Nanjing: Jiangsu guji chubanshe.
Zheng Guangnan. 1999. *Zhongguo haidao shi*. Shanghai: Huadong ligong daxue chubanshe.

Zheng Liansheng. 1995. *Min-Nichi kankeishi no kenkyū*. Tokyo: Yūzankaku shuppan.
Zheng Shungong. 1566 [1939]. *Riben yijian*. Unknown place of publication and publisher.
Zheng Ruozeng. 1562 [2007]. *Chouhai tubian*. Beijing: Zhonghua shuju.
Zheng Weiming. 1987. "Aomen fujin daoyu Danzai, Luhuan lishi chutan." M.A. thesis, University of East Asia, Macau.
Zheng Zhenduo, comp. 1947. *Xuanlantang congshu xuji*. Nanjing: Guoli zhongyang tushuguan.
Zhou Jinglian. 1936. *Zhongpu waijiao shi*. Shanghai: Shangwu yinshuguan.
Zhu Kejian. *An Min zouyi*. Fuzhou. Unknown date and publisher.
Zhu Wan. 1590 [1997]. *Piyu zaji*. Jinan: Qilu shushe.
ZPZZ. Zhupi zouzhe. First Historical Archives, Beijing. (Citations from the *junwu fangwu* and *nongmin yundong* categories.)

Index

Abe Masahiro, 124
Aceh, 22, 24–25
Afonso de Melo Coutinho, Martim, 44
ama, see sea peoples
Amenomori Hōshū, 121
Amoy, 5, 104, 145
    clandestine trade and, 10, 12–13
An Lu Shan Rebellion, 148
aojia (anchorage groups), 94, 95–96, 98
Aotou, 105, 112
Arano Yasunori, 115
Armenians, 9, 147, 152
Army of the Green Standard, 95
ASEAN, 152
Ashikage Shogunate, 31
atakabune, 68, 69
Audiencia, 83, 163 n. 49

Baishahu (unsanctioned port), 105, 110
Balangingi, *see* sea peoples
Bangka, 146
Bangkok, 5
bans, *see* sea bans
baojia, 94, 95, 98
Basilan, 77
Batam, 154
Batavia, 5, 7, 144
bazaars (Macau), 107–108
Belawa, Prince Aru, 133
Bentley, Jerry, 3
Bias Bay, 103, 112

BIMP-EAGA development triangle, 149–150
black markets, 2, 13, 106, 113
Blussé, Leonard, 7
Boggs, Eli, 9
Bonham, Sir Samuel George, 139, 140
Borneo, 5, 73, 76, 77, 134, 137, 147
Boxer Uprising, 148
Braudel, Fernand, 5, 14
Brooke, James, 22
Brunei, 74, 77, 152, 154
Bugis, *see* sea peoples
Buke Mandaiki, 67, 68
Bungo, 51, 60, 64, 66, 70

Cai Qian, 101
Cai Yuanliang, 92
Canton, 5, 44, 50, 54, 91, 101–104 *passim*,
    107–108, 114
    clandestine trade and, 108, 111, 145
Cape of Good Hope, 107
Carletti, Francesco, 83
Carneiro, Bishop Belchior, 65
Carrion, Juan Pablo de, 82–83
Cebu, 74, 75
Celebes, 75, 77
Changzhou, *see* Cheung Chau
Chaozhou, 5, 52, 103, 104, 110–114 *passim*
Chen Dele, 81
Chen Dong, 51
Chen Zui, 17
Chenghai (port), 80, 104, 108

Index

Cheung Chau Island, 103
China Century, 7
China market, *see* trading networks
Chouhai Tubian, 60, 78–79
clandestine trade, *see* smuggling *and* shadow economy
Coates, W. H., 145
Cochrane, Admiral Sir Thomas, 22
Coedès, Georges, 155 n. 2
Coloane Island, 103
colonialism, 15–16, 127, 141
commercialization, 29, 60, 70, 85, 159 n. 2
corruption, 88, 151
Crawfurd, John, 18, 145

D'Almeida, Luys, 66, 68, 70
Da Nang, 107
Dadan, 46
Damao, 46, 47, 50
Dan (Tanka), *see* sea peoples
Danshiu (Taiwan), 80, 92
Danshui (Guangdong), 110, 112
Danzai, *see* Taipa
Dapeng Wan, *see* Mirs Bay
Daya Wan, *see* Bias Bay
Dayak, *see* sea peoples
Dayushan, *see* Lantao
decolonization, 151
Deng Liao, 44, 49
Deng Zhong, 44
Dinghai, 47
Donghai Ba, 101, 110
Donghai Island, 103, 109
Du Zhonglü, 18
Dutch Colonial Packet Service, 144
Dutch East India Company, 121
Dutch War of 1784 (Riau), 10, 129

East China Sea, 3
Edo, 122
Edo period, *see* Tokugawa Shogunate
Empress of Heaven (Tian Hou) Temples, 103, 105, 107
English East India Company, 131
Ezo, 116

Fangjishan Island, 103
Feringhees, 44, 55
Fidalgo, Pero, 76
Fillmore, President Millard, 124
firearms, as contraband, 146
Fróis, Luís, 37, 70, 77
Fujian, 8, 10, 44, 46, 48–56 *passim*, 62, 85*ff*, 100–101, 107–108, 145–148 *passim*

Galang, 132–134 *passim*
Galvão, António, 76, 77
Giang Binh (unsanctioned port), 9, 105, 106–108 *passim*, 112
Goa, 77, 107
Golden Triangle, 152
Goto, 60
Gould, Eliga, 8
Greater China Seas, 5, 7, 9, 12–13, 14, 40, 57, 59, 74, 82, 84, 98
  defined, 2–3, 3–5
Guangdong, 46, 50–56 *passim*, 78, 80, 85*ff*, 100*ff*, 145, 148
Guangzhou, *see* Canton
gunpowder, 12, 63–66 *passim*, 70–71, 135

Hainan, 107, 110, 145
Hakata, 50, 62, 116
Han dynasty, 91
Han River, 104, 108, 111
Hayes, Bully, 9
He Song, 111
He Yaba, 50
Hengqin Island, 112
hidden economy, *see* shadow economy
high imperialism, 5, 20–25
Hirado, 50, 69, 70, 78
Hizen, 51, 60
Hoi An (port), 107
Hokkaido, *see* Ezo
Hokkiens, 44–55 *passim*, 159 n. 3
Hong Dizhen, 52
Hong Kong, 21, 103, 148–149 *passim*, 152
Hu Zongxian, 65
Huang Yasi, 110
Huizhou (Anhui), 48, 50, 51, 60

Huizhou (Guangdong), 103, 112
Humong, Panglima, 133
Husain, Sultan, 19, 131, 132, 136, 137
Hyuga, 64

Ibrahim, Temenggong Daing, 139–140
Illanun, *see* Iranun *under* sea peoples
Imagawa Ryōshun, 34
Indonesia, 26, 150
informal economy, *see* shadow economy
Inland Sea (Japan), *see* Seto Inland Sea
International Maritime Organization, 23
International Telegraphic Union, 22
Iranun, *see* sea peoples
Itsukushima, 10, 37, 38
Itsukushima, Battle of (1555), 68

Ja'afar, Raja, 130, 131, 135, 138
Jakarta, 24, 25, 151
Japan House, 119–120, 123
Java, 5, 21, 56, 132, 133, 137, 146
Jesuits, 37, 66–69 *passim*, 71, 76, 77
Jiangmen (port), 104
Jiangping, *see* Giang Binh
Jiazi (port), 104, 112
Jin Zilao, 47
Johor, 23, 129, 130, 140

kaizoku, 27*ff*, 60, 157 n. 3
Kamagari, 34, 35
Kamakura Shogunate, 66
Kamo Manuel Akimasa, 70
Kangxi Emperor, 91, 94
Keppel, Captain Henry, 22
Kibe, 64
Kita, 64
Kobayakawa Takakage, 68
Konishi Yukinaga, 83
Kōno Michinao, 38
Korea, 5, 10, 12, 13, 118*ff*
Kotera Yasumasa, 66
Koxinga, *see* Zheng Chenggong
krisses, 133
Kurou, 134, 135–136
Kyoto, 28, 31, 69

Ladrones (islands), 102, 103, 165 n. 9
Lantao Island, 103, 108
Lark's Bay, 112
Legazpi, Lopez de, 77, 79–80, 83
Leirissa, Richard, 9
Leizhou Peninsula, 103, 111
Lewis, James B., 120
Li Chongyu, 112
Li Guangtou, 47, 50, 79
Li Mao, 81
Li Rong, 91
Li You, 80
Li Yunlian, 110
Limahon, *see* Lin Feng
Limbang, Panglima, 133
Lin Ban, 108
Lin Daoqian, 80
Lin Feng, 12, 73, 77–82 *passim*
Lin Jian, 50, 55
Lin Shuangwen Rebellion (Taiwan), 100
Lin Wu, 108
Lin Xiyuan, 55, 160 n. 40
Lin Yafa, 112
Lingga, 127*ff*
Lingyin Temple, 51
Liu Yaohui, 80
Liyumen, 103
Logan, J. L., 140
London Treaty (1824), 21, 131, 136
López Nadal, Gonçal, 108
Loyola, Ignatius, 76
Luhuan, *see* Coloane
Luo Yasan, 112
Luzon, 74, 76*ff*

Macau, 50, 54, 65, 82, 91, 103–108 *passim*, 114, 152, 163 n. 42, 165 n. 25
  clandestine trade and, 87, 107–108, 111, 112
Magellan, Ferdinand, 74, 76
Magong (unsanctioned port), 105
Mahmud, Sultan, 129–130
Maki Hyogonosuke, 66
Malacca Strait, 3, 9, 14, 19–25 *passim*, 128–140 *passim*, 150
Malacca, 5, 47, 49, 74–82 *passim*, 134

Index

Malays, labeled as pirates, 8, 16, 25, 129, 131, 140
Maldonado, Juan Pacheco, 83
Manchus, *see* Qing dynasty
Manila, 5, 7, 24, 49, 73, 80, 84, 87
Mascarenhas, Jorge, 44
Matsuda, Matt, 3
Matsuura Takanobu, 62–63, 66–67, 83
Meiji Restoration, 115, 125–126
Meiling Island, 46
Mendoza, Juan Gonzalez de, 80, 81
mercenarianism, *see* sea lords
Mexico, 20, 73, 75, 76
Mindanao, 74–77 *passim*
Ming dynasty, 7, 12, 16–17, 43, 50, 52, 57, 64
Ming-Qing transition, 12, 85, 89, 94
Mirs Bay, 103, 112
Moluccas, 74–82 *passim*, 137
monsoons, 47, 104, 145
Morga, António de, 74, 75, 76, 77, 82
Mōri Motonari, 38
Mōri, 39, 65, 68–69
Mota, António de, 54
Mozambique, 134
Muda, Engku, 130
Muntinghe, Herman W., 131, 137
Murai Shōsuke, 29
Murakami Takeyoshi, 71
Murray, Dian, 109
Muslims, 9, 24, 152
mutual responsibility system (China), *see baojia* and *aojia*

Nagasaki, 5, 17, 83, 116, 119, 121
Nagato, 60
Nan'ao Island, 46, 51, 87, 110
Nanjing, 47, 89
natural disasters, 87, 100, 163 n. 7, 165 n. 5
Ningbo, 46, 53, 54
Noshima Murakami Takeyoshi, 37
Noshima Murakami, 28*ff*

Oda Nobunaga, 69
Ōmura Sumitada, 66–67
Opium War, 101
opium, 9, 112, 133, 136–137 *passim*, 145–148 *passim*, 151–152, 171 n. 28

Orang Laut, *see* sea peoples
organized hypocrisy, 11, 15–16
Osaka, 68, 122
Ōtomo Sōrin, 38
Ōtomo Yoshishige, 65–67 *passim*, 71
Ōtomo, 39, 64
Ouchi Yoshinaga, 65, 71
Ōuchi Yoshitaka, 38

Padi, Panglima, 135
Pahang, 49–50, 56, 132
Palembang, 17
Park So Sen, 64
Parsees, 9
Patani, 17, 47, 49–50, 80
Pearl River, 44, 102, 103, 111
Peixote, António, 54
Penang, 133, 136, 137
Penghu Island, 87
Peres de Andrade, Fernão, 44
Perry, Commodore Matthew, 124
piracy
 causes of, 129
 commercialization and, 9, 11
 defined, 2, 7, 14, 15, 16, 17, 18–19, 27, 115, 127, 129
 economic consequences of, 9
 large-scale, 97
 local support and, 10
 maritime suzerainty/hegemony and, 37, 114
 networks, 111–113, 140–141
 petty/small-scale, 91, 93, 97
 sanctioned, 8, 12, 19, 20
 suppression of, 16, 20–25, 138–139
 survival strategy, 87, 94
 trade and, 17, 29, 43*ff*, 82–83, 108, 109–111, 113, 135
 underreporting of, 93
pirates
 bases/strongholds, 10, 81, 92, 102–104, 106, 112, 114, 134, 135
 contrasted with smugglers, 2, 116
 criminality and, 2, 93
 defined, 7, 8
 extortion and, 88–89, 113
 heroes as, 2, 8

identity and, 2, 28, 30–34, 40
loot and, 109
maritime security guards and, 60, 62, 67
occasional, 62, 91, 93, 97, 131–132
pacts, 110–111
popular support and, 87–88, 92
professional, 62, 135
protection rackets and, 28, 32, 34–37, 38–40 *passim*, 97, 109, 111, 114
ransoms paid to, 109–110, 136
slave raiding and, 22, 39, 134, 140, *see also* slave trade
social backgrounds of, 9, 13, 91, 93
toll barriers and, 28, 32, 34–37, 68
violence and, 2, 11, 14, 16, 19, 27–29, 32, 36, 39, 64, 94, 116, 118, 129, 141
Pires, Tomé, 74, 76
Philippines, 5, 8, 12, 24, 73*ff*, 87, 89, 150, 151
Act of Incorporation by Spanish Monarchy (1851), 24
Port Royal (Jamaica), 107
ports, 5, 7, 10, 16, 19, 38, 50
development of new, 9, 12, 13, 46–49 *passim*, 69–70, 101, 113
sanctioned, 102, 104, 107
unsanctioned, 10, 102, 104, 105–107 *passim*, 109
Portuguese traders/explorers, 44, 46, 52–56 *passim*, 59, 64–67 *passim*, 74–77 *passim*; see also *Feringhees*
prahus, 132, 133, 135, 136, 138, 144, 168 n. 21
privateers, 20, 30
protection racket, *see* pirates
Pusan, 119, 123

Qi Jiguang, 80
Qianshan, 107
Qing dynasty, 7, 10, 12, 16–17, 85, 89
Quanzhou (port), 10, 54, 80

Rachman, Sultan Abdul, 12, 131
Rachman, Temenggong Abdul, 131
Raffles, Thomas Stamford, 19, 21, 131
Rahman, Engku Abdul, 130

Reimão, Pedro, 66
Riau, 9, 10, 23, 127*ff*, 151
Ritsuryō Codes (Japan), 30, 32
Ryukyu, 12, 18, 43, 44, 63, 116, 121, 124

Saigon, 5, 25, 107
Sakurai Eiji, 60
San Po Temple, 103
Sanhewo (unsanctioned port), 105, 108
Sarawak, 22
Satsuma, 8, 50, 51, 54, 64, 116, 124
Schell, Orville, 148
sea bans (China), 7, 9, 12, 17–18 *passim*, 44–52 *passim*, 60, 65, 73, 86–98 *passim*, 101
sea lanes, *see* shipping routes
sea lords, 10, 12, 27*ff*, 60, 119
autonomy of, 38, 40
feudal vassalage and, 29
mercenarism, 29, 37–40 *passim*
sea peoples, 5, 16, 19, 31, 158 n. 22
ama, 5, 31, 158 n. 20
Balangingi, 5, 8, 24
Bugis, 5, 9, 14, 22, 129, 131, 140, 168 n. 7
Dan (Tanka), 5, 95
Dayak, 22
Iranun, 5, 8, 19, 22, 129, 131, 168 n. 8
Orang Laut, 5, 19, 23, 129, 131, 132, 138, 140, 168 n. 9
secret societies, *see* Triads
security, coastal, 86–87, 91, 94–97 *passim*
Selewatang, 132
Senado da Camara, 107
Serram, Francisco, 76
Seto Inland Sea, 3, 10, 11, 12, 28*ff*, 60*ff*, 115
shadow economy, 9, 13, 43, 56–57 *passim*, 99–100, 106–113 *passim*
Shanghai, 145
Shaoxing, 53
Shenzhen, 148
Shi Chenglian, 112
Shimonoseki, Straits of, 38, 39
Shingoro, 51, 63
shipping routes, 5, 11–12, 31, 34, 62, 64, 71, 73*ff*, 87, 103, 118
Shirai, 12, 28, 33, 67–71 *passim*

Shiwaku, 37, 38
Shuangyu, 9, 12, 44, 46*ff*, 62–63, 78–79, 84, 160 n. 22
Si Kooi, 137
Siam, *see* Thailand
Singapore, 5, 7, 22, 25, 115, 127*ff*, 144, 146, 150
Sino-French War, 106
Sioco, 80
slave trade, 22, 133; *see also* slave raiding *under* pirates
smugglers
    contrasted with pirates, 2, 116
    country traders as, 144–145
    firearms, use of 47
    identity and, 2
    social backgrounds of, 9, 47
    violence and, 2
smuggling
    commercialization and, 9, 43, 55
    defined, 2
    economic consequences of, 9, 12
    human trafficking and, 153–154
    illicit trade as, 44*ff*, 147
    local support of, 10
    prostitution and, 153–154
    sanctioned, 2, 8
    suppression of, 47
Sō, 118*ff*
Sō Yoshiyori, 124–125
Society of Jesus, *see* Jesuits
Somalia, 26
Song dynasty, 64, 95
Song Hŭigyŏng, 34
sovereign equality, 15
Spanish traders/explorers, 74–77 *passim*
steamships, 10, 22, 138, 144
Sudin, Panglima, 135, 136
Sue Harukata, 38
Suez Canal, 144
Sukezaemon, 62–63, 161 n. 8
Sulu, 24, 145
Sulu Sea, 3, 149
Suma Oriental, 74
Sumatra, 5, 24, 133, 137
Sunda Strait, 3

Tagaya, 28, 33, 35, 37, 40
Taipa Island, 103, 107
Taiwan, 8, 13, 78, 80, 85–91 *passim*, 101, 104, 107, 148
Tanaka Takeo, 62, 69
Tanegashima, 54, 63
Tang dynasty, 103, 148
Tarah, Panglima, 133
Tay Son Rebellion (Vietnam), 18, 20, 100, 106, 112
Teppōki, 54, 78
Ternate, 77
Thailand, 5, 51, 56, 78, 108
Thomson, Janice, 11, 29–30 *passim*
Toby, Ronald, 121
Tokugawa Shogunate, 7, 8, 10, 40, 115–121 *passim*
toll barriers, *see* pirates
Tosa Diary, 31, 33
Toyotomi Hideyoshi, 37, 40, 70, 71, 83, 119
trade routes, *see* shipping routes
trading networks, 5, 7, 14, 33, 35, 56, 78, 81, 111
    China market and, 9, 14, 137
Treaty of Kanghwa (1876), 126
Triads, 99, 100, 111, 112–113, 146, 152
tribute system/missions, 16, 17, 48, 60, 64, 71, 73, 74, 78
Trocki, Carl, 19, 140
Tsushima Island, 10, 13, 51, 115*ff*
Tsushima Strait, 3
Twang Pek Yang, 25

Udagawa Takehiso, 68
Udin, Pangulu, 136
United Nations Charter (1945), 15
United Nations Law of the Sea, 16

Van Angelbeek, Christiaan, 131, 132, 137
Van Dyke, Paul, 111
Van Leur, Jacob, 155 n. 2
Van Ranzow, Lodewijk Carel, 133, 136, 137
Vieira, Francisco, 79
Vietnam, 5, 18, 20, 73, 100–101, 106, 108, 150
Villalobos, Ruy López de, 74, 75, 76

Vintoquián, *see* Lin Daoqian
Viraphol, Sarasin, 145

waegu, see *wakō*
wakō, 7, 12, 17, 18, 29, 49, 60, 73, 77–84 *passim*, 95, 97, 156 n. 6, 157 n. 3, 162 n. 14
Wang Wanggao, 80
Wang Wufeng, *see* Wang Zhi
Wang Yingyuan, 89
Wang Zhi, 33, 37, 48–52 *passim*, 54, 60, 62–65 *passim*, 69, 70, 78–79, 160 n. 18
Wangxia, 107
Warren, James, 24, 25
Wei Zhiyuan, 17
Weizhou Island, 103
White Lotus Rebellion, 100
Wilkinson, R. J., 19
Wills, John, 51
wokou, see *wakō*
Wushi Er, 101, 110, 111, 112
Wuyu Island, 52
Wuzhouyu Island, 46

Xavier, Francis, 76, 79
Xiamen, *see* Amoy
Xiao Ji, 95
Xie He, 50, 52
Xiongzhou Island, 103, 109
Xu brothers, 47–50 *passim*
Xu Chaoguang, 52
Xu Dong, 49–53 *passim*, 79, 160 n. 22
Xu Hai, 51
Xu Hong, 51
Xu Nan, 49
Xu Song, 49
Xu Weixue, 50, 51
Xu Zi, 49

Yantian, 110
Ye Ming, 51
Ye Zongman, 50, 78
Yu Dayou, 46
Yuegang (port), 10, 52

Zeimoto, Francisco, 54
Zeng Yasi, 110
Zhang Bao, 33, 37, 101, 103, 108, 111
Zhang Jinglong, 92
Zhang Lianke, 111
Zhang Wei, 52
Zhanglin (port), 104–105, 108
Zhangshan (unsanctioned port), 105, 109
Zhangzhou (port), 44, 52, 54
Zhejiang, 44, 46, 48–49, 50, 56, 62, 79, 92, 95, 101, 107, 145
Zhelin (port), 108
Zheng Afan, 110
Zheng Chenggong, 8, 10, 18, 33, 37, 89–91 *passim*
Zheng He, 17
Zheng Jinxin, 92
Zheng Laodong, 108
Zheng Lianchang, 103
Zheng Liangsheng, 79
Zheng Qi, 111
Zheng Ruozeng, 8, 60, 62
Zheng Shungong, 44, 49
Zheng Yi Sao, 101, 111
Zheng Yi, 101, 103, 110, 111
Zheng Zhilong, 8, 10, 18, 87–89 *passim*, 95
Zheng Zongxing, 50
Zhiliao (port), 104
Zhou Feixiong, 108
Zhou Yu, 91
Zhu Fen, 101, 108, 112
Zhu Wan, 46, 79, 160 n. 22
Zhu Yifeng, 88
Zhuhai, 148
Zhuo Jia Cun (village), 105, 107–108
Zoumaxi Island, 46